# Psychology of Language

# PSYCHOLOGY OF LANGUAGE

# Psychology of Language

**David S. Palermo**
The Pennsylvania State University

**Lyle E. Bourne, Jr.,** Consulting Editor
University of Colorado at Boulder

Scott, Foresman and Company  Glenview, Illinois
Dallas, TX  Oakland, NJ  Palo Alto, CA  Tucker, GA  London, England

Dedicated to Scott, Craig, Lynn, and Lisa

Library of Congress Cataloging in Publication Data

Palermo, David Stuart, 1929–
   The psychology of language.

   Includes bibliographies and index.
   1. Psycholinguistics.   2. Children—Language.
I. Bourne, Lyle Eugene, 1932–      II. Title.
PZ37.P36      401.'9      77–17312
ISBN 0–673–07715–2

12345678910-MPC-858483828180797877

## Acknowledgments for Figures
   1-2. From Maclay, Howard, "Overview," in D. D. Steinberg and L. A. Jakobovits (Eds.), *Semantics*. Copyright © 1971 Cambridge University Press. Reprinted by permission of the author and the publisher.
   2-3. Reprinted with permission of Macmillan Publishing Co., Inc., from SPEECH PHYSIOLOGY AND ACOUSTIC PHONETICS by Philip Lieberman. Copyright © 1977 by Philip Lieberman.
   3-4. From Liberman, A. M., Cooper, F. S., Shankweiler, D. P., and Studdert-Kennedy, M., "Perception of the Speech Code," in *Psychological Review*, 1967, Vol. 74. Copyright © 1967 by the American Psychological Association. Reprinted by permission.
   5-1. From Osgood, Charles E., "Meaning Cannot Be an $r_m$?" in *Journal of Verbal Learning and Verbal Behavior*, 1966, Vol. 5. Reprinted by permission of Academic Press, Inc., and the author.
   5-2. From Bransford, J., and Johnson, M., "Contextual Prerequisites for Understanding," in *Journal of Verbal Learning and Verbal Behavior*, 1972, Vol. 11. Reprinted by permission of Academic Press, Inc., and the author.
   5-4. From Clifton, C., and Odom, P., "Similarity Relations Among Certain English Sentence Constructions," in *Psychological Monographs*, 1966, Vol. 80, No. 5. Copyright © 1966 by the American Psychological Association. Reprinted by permission.
   6-1. From Brown, R., Cazden, C., and Bellugi, U. "The Child's Grammar from I to III," in J. P. Hill (Ed.), *Minnesota Symposium on Child Psychology*, Vol. 2. Copyright © 1969 by the University of Minnesota Press.

# Preface

In the past twenty years there has been an ever increasing interest in the psychology of language. Research ideas have blossomed, and important new theories have made psycholinguistics one of the most exciting areas within the field of psychology. The focus of this book is on the formulation, testing, discarding, and reformulation of theories about how humans acquire and use language. *Psychology of Language* is written as an introduction to the field for the undergraduate or beginning graduate student. It is appropriate as the main text for courses in psycholinguistics, and can also be used for courses in cognitive psychology, human learning, experimental psychology, and educational psychology.

The Introduction describes the processes of "scientific revolution" and, within the philosophical framework suggested by Thomas Kuhn, recounts how psychology has developed. Chapter 1 discusses the nature of language as a system, providing an understanding of issues concerning the structure of language. Chapter 2 focuses on the biological characteristics which make it possible for humans to use language. Chapters 3, 4, and 5 discuss research concerned with the three components of language: sound, syntax, and semantics. Chapters 6 and 7 focus on how the child acquires those components of language and becomes able to communicate.

A great deal of research is covered in this volume. In a sense, it is a historical documentation of recent developments in psycholinguistics. I have tried to show why particular theoretical ideas developed, to describe the research programs those theories engendered, and to explain the reasons for one theoretical approach being discarded for another. Finally, I have pointed to researchable problems so that interested students may become actively involved.

The current interest in psycholinguistics results from the impact of Noam Chomsky's theoretical papers in linguistics and the work of psychologists like George Miller, Eric Lenneberg, and Roger Brown, and later, Dan Slobin, David McNeill, Jerry Foder, and Tom Bever.

At first, many of these persons were primarily influenced by the thinking of linguists. Gradually, however, linguistics became less important as psychologists considered the broader cognitive capacities of the human mind. Linguistic theory was too narrow to encompass cognitive psychology; psychologists had to develop their own theories and to generate new research programs to test and expand their ideas.

Through the study of psycholinguistics, we are beginning to see more of the ways in which the human mind works. I hope that this book communicates to the reader some of the excitement of working in this challenging field. If it succeeds in this, it will have been worth the writing.

I would like to express my gratitude to the many persons who have directly and indirectly contributed to this volume through their discussions with me and their comments on various chapters as they were written and revised. Many former graduate students have been helpful. I particularly want to mention Dennis Molfese, Susan Belmore, Steven Wilcox, and Donna Hummel. My colleagues Simon Belasco, Robert Brubaker, Charles Cofer, James Martin, and Walter Weimer have been generous in commenting on various chapters. I am grateful to all of them, but the blame for any errors in the content remains with me. Finally, I should like to thank Professor Richard A. Champion, who made it possible for me to work full time on this book at the University of Sydney.

David S. Palermo

# Contents

# INTRODUCTION

Psychology is in a turmoil! Perhaps all psychologists are not touched by this turmoil, but certainly those psychologists now working on problems relating to human beings that are connected in any way with the cognitive aspects of human behavior and specifically problems of language are affected. And what is all the fuss about? The answer turns out to be related to your interpretation of the history and philosophy of science, and to the current developments in psychology.

In order to see the big picture into which we shall try to fit the details later in this book, let's begin with a brief look at the background of the psychology of language. This may enable us to better understand not only why there is turmoil but, more importantly, why psychologists are asking the kinds of questions about language they are asking today. Perhaps we will understand better the arguments in the psychological literature, the current research, and the theories within which these arguments and research are cast. We will start with a brief look at one conception of the nature of the scientific endeavor followed by a look at how psychology, as one of the sciences, fits into that conception, and finally, we will look specifically at the psychology of language. Obviously, we will do little more in this introduction than scan the issues and build the framework before going on to the subject matter at hand. If you become interested in the psychology of language, and I hope you will, there are many directions in which you could explore further, and, in succeeding chapters, I will try to point some of them out to you.

In 1962, T. S. Kuhn, a physicist turned philosopher, published the first edition of a fascinating little book called *The Structure of Scientific Revolutions*. (A second edition included a postscript in which Kuhn responded to some of his critics and clarified his position [Kuhn, 1970].) Kuhn attempted to analyze how the sciences advance through

1

the efforts of researchers working within their various disciplines. He focused most of his attention on the physical sciences, with which he was most familiar, but a number of psychologists have found the book particularly apropos of the historical development of psychology to the present time.

Kuhn argued that periodically within the individual disciplines of science there are *revolutions*. Scientific revolutions occur when *normal science* is disrupted by the process of discarding one *paradigm* for another. That is, the traditionally conceived endeavors of the scientist are diverted, in part, to concerns over the nature of the discipline per se and how the efforts within the discipline should be expended.

A paradigm, in Kuhn's terminology, refers to a consensually agreed-upon *modus operandi* or set of rules which, at any particular time in the history of a discipline, are generally accepted for the working of the science. These rules pertain to the nature of the theory that guides the research, the types of problems considered worthy of investigation, the research methods that are appropriate for investigating those problems, and even, on occasion, the instrumentation which is required. These rules focus attention on particular problems within the field. They do not necessarily apply to all the problems which might be investigated by workers in a given discipline but, rather, define the researchable problems in the field. This relegates other problems to metaphysics, thereby regarding them as not scientific; to other disciplines; or to sets of problems which, while possibly researchable in the future, are too complicated or problematical for the present. In essence, the rules define the field. They are a set of assumptions about the nature of the science which are generally inferred by example from the scientific journals and books and are not generally challenged except at times of crisis and/or paradigm clashes. One paradigm is always incommensurate with another in the same sense that the rules of baseball are incommensurate with the rules of football—they are never in the same ball park, so to speak. A full-fledged science, however, must have such rules and not until a paradigm has been adopted is a discipline of science considered to have reached maturity.

Once the scientists within a discipline have accepted a paradigm, they may use it to proceed with what Kuhn called normal science. Research efforts to actualize the promises of the paradigm consist of designing and conducting experiments which will determine significant facts. The facts, in turn, are matched with theory. The theory, finally, is articulated in more detail. Thus, normal science consists of determining the laws, quantifying the laws, and determining the relevant constants. The theory is tied to data, made more specific with the resolution of ambiguities, and then extended to new areas of data not initially encompassed. These enterprises are highly cumulative in the sense in which many people conceive of science as a search for more and more empirical information about a circumscribed area. The search is confined, however, to what is relevant to the theory. Normal science is a search to solve puzzles but most of the answers are known in advance since the theory specifies the outcome. The search is not directed to producing major novelties, but, rather, to supporting existing theoretical ideas. Experiments that result in *anomalies*—unexpected or unusual findings which do not support the theory—are generally considered to be inadequately designed and researchers direct their efforts to discover what went wrong and to the subsequent design of experiments which *do* demonstrate support for the theory.

There come times in every scientific discipline, however, when anomalous results are either so dramatically unexpected or accumulate to the point that some scientists in the discipline are unable to work further within that paradigm or framework. At such times, extraordinary investigations occur which may result in a scientific revolution—the adoption of a new paradigm. Crises that usually precede such revolutions seem to result from two types of situations. In one instance, a particularly dramatic anomaly is observed and, instead of the result being ignored, it is followed up by extensive exploration and the eventual adjustment of the paradigm so that the anomalous discovery, as well as a broader range of related problems, is now expected, that is, theoretically predictable. In the second case, no major discovery is involved but a new theory is advanced as a result of persistent failure of normal scientific efforts in a number of areas. In the first case, extensive empirical research is done following a discovery and a new theory is advanced to account for the initially anomalous result. In the second case, the theory may be advanced to integrate and account for a number of anomalous results which may previously have caused the proliferation of a number of smaller, unrelated theories. In the latter case, the breadth of the impact of the paradigm shift on the discipline may be much greater.

In either case, the revolution is usually preceded by a time of crisis distinguished by the recognition that something is wrong with the paradigm within which the discipline has been operating. Experiments which should produce particular predictable results too often fail. The continual failure becomes recognized by a few researchers as not just another puzzle to be solved by experimental and theoretical adjustments but instead as caused by the inadequacy of the current paradigm to solve the problems being attacked. As a result of this recognition, some of the scientists involved begin to reconsider and reevaluate the paradigm itself and cast about for fresh approaches to their problems. There is now a blurring and loosening of the paradigm rules. Research is directed not just to demonstrating the theory, as in times of normal science, but to testing the paradigm itself, that is, to testing the assumptions which are an inherent part of the paradigm.

These times of crisis inevitably lead to resistance to changing the paradigm. The resistance takes the form of defending the old paradigm and trying to patch it up so that it will take account of the anomalous results. Heated debates may develop about values relating to the best research methods, the most significant problems to investigate, and the way the discipline should be conceptualized with respect to its scope and philosophical foundations.

Since more than one interpretation may be placed on any one set of data, and since the arguments at times of crisis are about the value of the paradigms, or which paradigm is best, it is not merely logic and data which lead to the success of one point of view over another. The success of a revolution also depends on the elegance of presentation of the alternatives. The exponents of an alternative paradigm win converts on the basis of how convincingly they can present the case for viewing their science within the framework of a new paradigm. Their arguments show how the new paradigm can account for the problems which caused the crisis; how it accounts for problems not even considered by the old one; the promise of the new paradigm for yet other problems; the quantitative precision of the new paradigm; and the aesthetic characteristics of the new paradigm.

Direct confrontations of new and old paradigms in the form of debates between their respective adherents succeed in winning converts insofar as the arguments are elegant, articulate, and emotionally stirring, because the debaters do not argue on the same premises, with the same language, nor with the same view of the world in mind. Clearly, the adherents of the new paradigm must confront the adherents of the old with some data and logical arguments, particularly with respect to the problems relevant to the crisis, but since adherence to a paradigm involves a particular way of looking at the world, the proponents of each paradigm talk at cross-purposes in different languages so that the arguments of one often appear irrelevant to those of the other. A good deal of effort is required in such debates to translate from one language to the other, without assurance that either side always understands the other. But since it is recognized that the old paradigm has problems and the new paradigm has not been fully developed, some scientists must convert to the new on the basis of minimal data and maximal aesthetic considerations so that eventually they may provide additional data-based arguments to convince more of those still working within the old paradigm. The revolution succeeds insofar as scientists within the field with questions about the old paradigm are concerned enough to consider alternatives; teachers convince their students to accept the new paradigm; and adherents of the old paradigm die off so that resistance subsides.

Once a revolution has succeeded and the new paradigm has achieved the status of consensual acceptance, the discipline settles down to normal science once again. There is again an accepted, though new, language for discussing problems, new problems to investigate, new methods for solving the problems, and new books to use in training students within the field. This reorientation to the discipline generally leads to some discontinuity between the normal science which preceded the shift and that which follows it. The cumulative nature of normal science is disrupted although there is always some overlap between what went before and what is subsequently relevant. In particular, at least some portion of the problems which caused the revolution must be satisfactorily handled by the new paradigm despite the fact that these problems will be conceptualized in quite different ways. At the same time, portions of what may have seemed important problems prior to the shift will be of little interest to those working within the new paradigm. Thus, after a paradigm shift, normal science sets about articulating and extending the new paradigm, that is, fulfilling the promises of the new set of rules by doing research, the results of which are once again known in advance as a function of the new theory.

Before delving into the relation of psychology to the highly condensed and rather abstract discussion of the preceding few pages, let's look at a couple of neutral and unrelated examples which may help to clarify some points. First, consider the Necker cube in Figure I–1. As you are probably aware, there are two ways of viewing this cube: you can see it with the front face turned to the left or with the front face tilted upward and turned to the right. It is exactly the same line drawing but it may be seen in two different perspectives, and, if you see one, you cannot see the other at the same time. It is as if you have two different conceptual or perceptual theories of the drawing. Now imagine for a moment that you can only see the cube one way and I can only see it the other way. With that limitation in mind, imagine a conversation in which we attempt to discuss the properties of the object before us. Although the object is exactly the same for both of us, we would certainly say quite different things about it as a function of our different views of it. There would be some overlap in our statements, but for the most part our descriptions, inferences, and predictions about that object would differ and often conflict.

The point of this exercise is to illustrate in the simplest and barest essentials what Kuhn means when he suggests that scientists operating within different paradigms see the world differently, have trouble communicating with each other, approach research problems differently, and so on. If I were suddenly able to view the cube within

**Figure I-1**

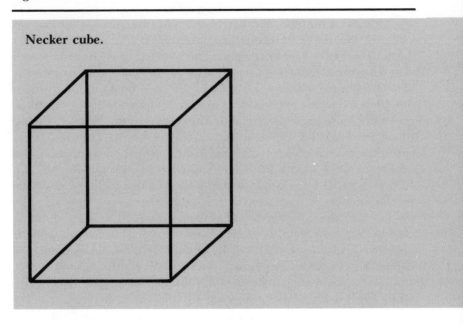

**Necker cube.**

your framework, I would have been converted to a new paradigm and, if most scientists in the discipline were also to shift, we would have a scientific revolution. Once we all see the object the same way, there is no problem and we can proceed with our own interests relative to the cube with the same basic underlying orientation and assumptions.

Now consider an example elaborated by Kuhn which is directly related to a scientific discipline. You probably know that oxygen was "discovered" at least twice in the eighteenth century, once by the British clergyman and chemist, Joseph Priestley, and also by the French chemist, Antoine Lavoisier. The reason for putting the word "discovered" in quotation marks above is to call attention to the fact that while both men did much the same experiments with red oxide of mercury and both recognized that a gas was produced in the heating process, they did not *see* the same thing. Priestley saw in his research what he first called nitrous oxide and later identified as common air minus its usual amount of phlogiston (a hypothetical substance then believed to be a component of fire). Lavoisier, on the other hand, saw the gas as purer, more respirable air and later concluded that it was one of the two main constituents of the atmosphere. The point is that Priestley viewed the gas within the framework of the phlogiston theory while Lavoisier used the results of his experiments to support a new oxygen theory of combustion which subsequently led to the reformulation of chemistry. That is, it led to a scientific revolution in chemistry. The two men looked at the same data but they looked through different paradigms and, as a result, they saw (discovered) different phenomena. Priestley, incidentally, never was able to shed his phlogiston glasses and see what Lavoisier saw with the spectacles of the new paradigm he helped to create. At this point, I think we can look to the history of psychology for the occurrence of similar phenomena.[1]

The scientists who are generally identified as the first psychologists, the British Associationists, did not have a scientific paradigm, and I think few historians would argue that psychology was a science in the traditional sense at that stage in its development. It certainly does not appear that the shift from the "arm-chair" psychology of the British Associationists in the late nineteenth century to the structuralist experimental psychology of the German tradition which followed would be considered a revolution in the sense in which Kuhn uses the term. It is, perhaps, more appropriately viewed as the emergence of psychology as a science.[2]

It does seem, however, that one might argue that psychology during the period of the late nineteenth and early twentieth centuries had a paradigm. In fact, Wilhelm Wundt and his followers made the paradigm clear in their writings about the science of psychology and its relation to the paradigms of the other sciences. Wundt argued that ". . . the *natural sciences* . . . concern themselves with the *objects* of experience, thought of as independent of the subject" (Wundt, 1907, p. 3), and defined the science of psychology as an examination of "the whole content of experience in its relations to the subject and also in regard to the attributes which this content derives directly from the subject" (p. 3). Psychology, thus, was considered to study "immediate experience" while the natural sciences studied "mediate experience."

The apprehension of the content of experience was studied

[1] Kuhn does not deal with psychology in his discussions and has implied that the social sciences have not yet achieved the maturity of a paradigmatic science while he has suggested in at least one place that, "This century appears to be characterized by the emergence of a first consensus in parts of a few of the social sciences" (Kuhn, 1963, p. 347). In the discussion to follow, I will try to sketch a case to support the contention that at least some areas of experimental psychology have had two paradigms already with the expected scientific revolution between them. You may find more extended versions of this analysis elsewhere (Palermo, 1971; Weimer & Palermo, 1973).

[2] The reconstruction of history, is however, problematic (Weimer, 1974a) and the perspective which follows will need much more extensive historical documentation. Weimer (1974a, 1974b) has indicated the methodological problems involved in such an endeavor and provided the beginnings of some of the necessary documentation.

through the method of pure *introspection*. "Pure" meant that scientific, as opposed to common, everyday introspection, required training to ensure impartiality, attention, freshness, and a favorable disposition (Titchener, 1902) as well as a good short-term memory. Thus, introspection was important as the paradigmatic method used in research at that time in psychology. Furthermore, "To distinguish it from the observation of physical science, which is inspection, a looking-at, psychological observation has been termed introspection, a looking within" (Titchener, 1910, p. 20). While the analysis of immediate experience into elements by Wundt and his students was opposed by "act psychology" at the time, both agreed on the method as indicated by Brentano's statement that ". . . psychic phenomena are the exclusive objects of inner perception" (Brentano, 1874).

Thus, the paradigm of normal science at that time established psychology as a science distinct from other sciences, identified the substantive area for research, and specified a method by which acceptable scientific data were to be collected. Note that the definition and, particularly, the method also implied other assumptions within the paradigm. Since introspection was a verbal report about the mental elements and/or processes (acts) of the mind, psychology pertained only to the study of humans as lower animals obviously could not give such reports. Furthermore, introspection required training defined in such a way that there was little likelihood that human children could be studied with confidence. In essence, psychology, therefore, was considered to be the study of the elements of consciousness: the sensations, feelings, emotions, volitions, and ideas of the human adult. The glue holding the elements of this mentalistic psychology together was associationism—a concept common to the position of the British philosophers who preceded the structuralists and to the behaviorists who succeeded them. While this characterization of the paradigm of the structuralists does not take into account the fact that other methods of research were used even in Wundt's own laboratory (Marshall, 1970), it is certainly not unjustified by Wundt's writings and may be interpreted as a part of what led to the first scientific revolution in psychology. Across the ocean from Wundt's laboratory came the revolutionary behaviorist cry from John B. Watson.

"Psychology as the behaviorist views it is a purely objective experimental branch of natural science. Its theoretical goal is the prediction and control of behavior. Introspection forms no essential part of its methods, nor is the scientific value of its data dependent upon the readiness with which they lend themselves to interpretation in terms of consciousness. The behaviorist in his efforts to get a unitary scheme of animal response, recognizes no dividing line between man and brute. The behavior of man, with all of its refinement and complexity, forms only a part of the behaviorist's total scheme of investigation" (Watson, 1913, p. 158). This statement marks the official launching of behaviorism as the new paradigm for the major portion of American experimental psychology.

But we move too quickly ahead in the story for, as Kuhn has noted, revolution is frequently preceded by a crisis and that seems to be the case for the behaviorist revolution. While much of American psychology had developed within a functionalist tradition separate from structuralism, the behaviorist revolution was a reaction, at least in part, to three major aspects of the structuralist paradigm: (1) the unreliability of the introspective method; (2) the interest in animal behavior and the resultant necessity to anthropomorphize about animal consciousness in order to maintain the old paradigm; and (3) the interest in extending psychological principles to practical application.

In the first case, it became painfully evident that the requirement of impartiality in the trained introspecting subject could not be maintained. Each laboratory found in the introspective reports of their subjects the kinds of data which supported the theoretical conception of the contents of consciousness of the scientist in that laboratory. This, of course, is not out of line with the typical efforts of normal science but the fact that experiments in one laboratory could not be replicated in others made the procedure suspect. While Watson criticized the method severely, he did not wish to rule out the study of verbal behavior, or even introspective reports, a position of which he has often been accused. Verbalizations are behaviors in the same sense as any others and, therefore, subject to study. The paradigm difference is that in the former case the verbal report was the method and in the latter case it was part of the behavior to be studied.

The second important factor in the crisis relates to the study of animal behavior. Since Darwin's theory of evolution argued for the continuity of the species, there seemed every reason to suppose that animals might also evidence aspects of consciousness or mind. Romanes, one of the early comparative psychologists operating within the structuralist paradigm, began with the premise that psychology is the study of the mind, regardless of whether of humans or lower animals. Since animals cannot introspect, ". . . we can only *infer* the existence and the nature of thoughts and feelings from the activities of the organisms which appear to exhibit them. . . . Starting from what I know subjectively of the operations of my own individual mind, and the activities which in my own organism they prompt, I proceed by analogy to infer from the observable activities of other organisms what are the mental operations that underlie them" (Romanes, 1882, p. 12). Gradually, however, psychologists studying animal behavior seemed to become aware that they were moving away from inferences about mental states or processes of consciousness and toward the description of animal responses in relation to the experimentally presented stimuli. Their experiments dealt with associative processes of memory, discrimination learning, and perception. It seemed unnecessary to bring in consciousness to describe or account for the results. In Watson's picturesque language, "One can assume either the presence or absence of consciousness anywhere in the phylogenetic scale without affecting the problems of behavior by one jot or one tittle; and without influencing in any way the mode of experimental attack upon them" (Watson; 1913, p. 161). Thus, animal psychologists embraced behaviorism because it allowed them to proceed unencumbered by the concept of consciousness. In the same way, psychologists interested in child behavior were able to attack the problems at hand under the behaviorist umbrella.

Finally, in the pragmatic American fashion, psychologists in the United States were interested in things practical. The impetus for this aspect of behaviorism came from the functionalist school of psychology initiated by James and carried on by Angell in psychology and by Dewey in education. Thus, functionalism preceded behaviorism in loosening the ties with the old paradigm but it was more of an effort to patch up the old paradigm than to break away from it. Introspection was not rejected but was supplemented; and although the analysis of the elements of consciousness and their combination was not rejected, the emphasis shifted to the analysis of how and why conscious processes operate as they do. The functionalists found the paradigm of the structuralists stultifying in the sense that in neither theory nor practice could it make any contributions to education or mental health which were concerns of many American psychologists. Functionalism failed to produce the revolution, however, because it had no strong evangelic spokesman to make its case nor even anyone who would take the courageous step of cutting the silver cord to structuralism. It was left to Angell's student Watson to step to the front and boldly state, ". . . I, as an experimental student, feel that something is wrong with our premises and the types of problems which develop from them" (Watson, 1913, p. 163).[3]

We should note that the crisis also produced a group of scientists who advanced Gestalt psychology as another candidate for the future paradigm for psychology. Due in large part to Watson's persuasive presentation, however, this rival to behaviorism failed to achieve the allegiance of the majority of scientists within the discipline and behaviorism became the paradigm for most experimental psychologists.

---

[3] Bergmann (1956) has argued that functionalism was not merely a last form of Wundt's structural psychology prior to the behaviorism conceived by Watson. Rather, he suggests that Watson was the greatest of the functionalists and made the most significant methodological contribution to functionalism. Thus, although Bergmann's paper preceded Kuhn's introduction of this terminology by six years, the paradigm shift in his view was from structuralism to functionalism.

True to Kuhn's analysis of the other sciences, psychologists of the old paradigm resisted the new. Despite the opposition, behaviorism did become the new paradigm and rose to its zenith in the 1940s and 1950s when the psychological journals were filled with experimental work fulfilling the promises Watson had foretold. The research efforts of Tolman, Guthrie, Hull, and their students marked the period of normal science within the behaviorist paradigm. Data were collected at fever pitch. Different theoretical points of view led to controversy, but all psychologists accepted the behaviorist paradigm and thought little of questioning the premises.

These psychologists were all working on problems of learning which were considered the central core of psychology. Pavlovian classical conditioning, seized upon early by Watson as an important methodological and analytical tool, was taken as the simplest and most basic form of learning. Instrumental or operant conditioning was also extensively studied as a slightly more complicated first cousin of classical conditioning. Occasionally research ventured into the problems of trial-and-error learning but this was considered by many to be a bit too complicated. Thus, the associationistic mechanism of structuralism was carried over into behaviorism and incorporated into the learning theories which grew out of the research on conditioning.

The study of the basic conditioning unit of learning led to a second tenet of behaviorism, also a carry-over from structuralism, which was that you must build from the simple elements to the more complex forms. The argument runs as follows: behavior is learned; the simplest form of learning is conditioning; all other complex forms of learning derive from conditioning; once we know the basic laws pertaining to simple conditioning, we will be able to study more and more complex forms of behavior which will involve the laws of conditioning related by various composition rules; the composition laws will be determined once the simple laws are known. In essence, complex behavior was agreed to be paradigmatically possible but too problematical for that stage in the development of the discipline.

Compatible with the latter premise were the assumptions about working with animals. The behavior of animals was considered of interest in its own right but of more importance in the long run was the argument that lower animals were simpler organisms and the research strategy was to build from the simple to the complex. Animals provided the means to build from understanding organisms lower on the phylogenetic scale to animals in a higher position with a promissory note to the eventual understanding of human behavior in all its complexity. Humans were also used in experiments and large numbers of classical conditioning studies were conducted with people as well as was extensive research dealing with verbal behavior. The latter area of research, while always a bit out of the mainstream in terms of the construction of learning theories, was acceptable because the kinds of tasks used were also regarded and analyzed as forms of conditioning.

This continuum of complexity from lower animals through man spoke to yet another premise. Behaviorism was anti-emergent, that is, the behavior of human organisms was considered basically no different from that of the chimpanzee, the dog, or the rat—it differed in complexity but not in terms of the basic underlying mechanisms. There was, therefore, no difficulty in relating the behavior of rats to that of humans as long as the need to take into account more variables with human behavior was made clear.

Since learning was the heart of the subject matter of psychology and since most behavior was assumed to be learned, another aspect of behaviorism was its anti-nativistic premises. No behaviorist would argue that genetic characteristics played no part in behavior, but the basic assumption was that one need be little concerned about heredity because of its unimportance as compared to the environment. Primary attentions, therefore, should be directed toward the effects of environmental factors on the determination of behavior. Watson probably took the most extreme position on this point when he said, ". . . the cry of the behaviorist is, 'Give me the baby and my world to bring it up in and I'll make it crawl and walk; I'll make it a thief, a gunman, or a dope fiend.' The possibility of shaping in any direction is almost endless" (Watson, 1928, pp. 31–32).

Thus, the behaviorists found genetics of minor importance and left that area to the geneticists. Much the same attitude was directed toward physiology. While the behaviorists were interested in comparative psychology because it provided the opportunity to study principles of behavior in a less complicated form, they were not basically interested in the physiological differences among animals nor in physiological behavior as such within any species. Psychologists devoted most of their research attention to overt behavior and its environmental determinants. They took the position that while physiological correlates of behavior certainly could be established, that was the task of the physiologists and whatever correlates were found were of little more interest for the laws of behavior than correlations of any other kind. As Spence put it, "We should be able to work out the laws governing behavioral changes without having to stop and consider . . . physiological matters" (Spence, 1951, p. 725).

The psychology of behaviorism was the study of stimuli and responses. The laws of behavior showed the relationships between variations in stimulus input and response output. Theoretical efforts were limited for the most part to the postulation of intervening variables between stimuli and responses but these were tightly tied to and defined in terms of the stimulus (S) and response (R) measures.

Since S-R psychology was a reaction to structuralism and its method of introspection, any "looking within" was rejected as smacking of introspection. The new empiricism of behaviorism needed to concern itself only with objective, externally defined, observable relationships measured by the same techniques used by all the other sciences. The concept of motivation provided for an active organism but the particular actions were determined by the stimuli present and the past learning of the organism. So characterized, behaviorism implied that the organism is a passive receiver of stimuli which produce, in a mechanical fashion, particular responses determined by its past history. It was assumed that the contents of the "black box" and the influence those contents might have on the incoming stimulus or outgoing response need not be considered.

The behaviorist paradigm produced considerable research which at least partially fulfilled Watson's claims. The theory of learning was elaborated from the simple Pavlovian conditioning model from which it began to related problems such as transposition (e.g., Spence, 1937), and then, more broadly, to new areas such as social behavior (e.g., Miller & Dollard, 1941), and personality (Dollard & Miller, 1950). In the midst of this success, however, the inevitable anomalies arose. Experimental results with unpredicted and disturbing results began to be reported and many individuals became disenchanted with the behaviorist paradigm as it became increasingly difficult to adjust the theory to account for the various results. It appears that behaviorism has run into difficulties such that what Kuhn has called a crisis has arisen. For some time now, psychologists in many areas in the discipline have been questioning the paradigm of behaviorism. While the questioning has come from many sources and for many reasons, we shall not go into them all because our focus is on the psychology of language, or, as it has been known in the past few years, *psycholinguistics.*

The study of language and language acquisition which has led to the new subspecialty of psycholinguistics has, perhaps, presented the most open and direct attack on the paradigm of behaviorism. Furthermore, it is here that a new paradigm which may replace behaviorism seems to be emerging. Since behaviorism is still very much alive, and since the emerging paradigm has not swept the entire field of psychology—and is not likely to do so for some time yet, even if it should eventually become the paradigm—we cannot know the breadth of this shift in orientation as far as all psychology is concerned. It does appear that many scientists who are currently working in the general area of cognitive behavior and psycholinguistics have begun to look at the world of their discipline differently. That is, they have already adopted a new paradigm. In Chapter 1, we shall try to elucidate some of the reasons for this shift and the general nature of the new paradigm. Within the framework of each succeeding chapter, however, we will continuously be confronted with research and theory which come from both the old and some form of the new paradigm.

# REFERENCES

Bergmann, G. The contribution of John B. Watson. *Psychological Review,* 1956, *63,* 265–76.

Brentano, F. *Psychologie vom empirischem standpunkte* (translated by E. G. Boring). In R. J. Herrnstein & E. G. Boring (Eds.), *A source book in the history of psychology.* Cambridge, Massachusetts: Harvard University Press, 1965. P. 605.

Dollard, J., & Miller, N. E. *Personality and psychotherapy.* New York: McGraw-Hill, 1950.

Hull, C. L. *Principles of behavior.* New York: Appleton-Century-Crofts, 1943.

Kuhn, T. S. *The structure of scientific revolutions* (2nd ed.). Chicago: University of Chicago Press, 1970.

Kuhn, T. S. The essential tension: Tradition and innovation in scientific research. In C. W. Taylor & F. Barron (Eds.), *Scientific creativity: Its recognition and development.* New York: Wiley, 1963. Pp. 341–54.

Marshall, J. C. E. A. Esper: Mentalism and objectivism—the sources of Leonard Bloomfield's psychology of language. *Semiotica,* 1970, *2,* 277–93. (Review.)

Miller, N. E., & Dollard, J. *Social learning and imitation.* New Haven: Yale University Press, 1941.

Palermo, D. S. Is a scientific revolution taking place in psychology? *Science Studies,* 1971, *1,* 135–55.

Romanes, G. J. *Animal intelligence.* London: Kegan, Paul, Trench, & Company, 1882.

Spence, K. W. The differential response in animals to stimuli varying within a single dimension. *Psychological Review,* 1937, *44,* 430–44.

Spence, K. W. Theoretical interpretations of learning. In S. S. Stevens (Ed.), *Handbook of experimental psychology.* New York: Wiley, 1951. Pp. 690–729.

Titchener, E. B. *An outline of psychology.* New York: Macmillan, 1902.

Titchener, E. B. *A textbook of psychology.* New York: Macmillan, 1910.

Titchener, E. B. *Systematic psychology: Prolegomena.* New York: Macmillan, 1929.

Watson, J. B. Psychology as the behaviorist views it. *Psychological Review,* 1913, *20,* 158–77.

Watson, J. B. *The ways of behaviorism.* New York: Harper & Brothers, 1928.

Weimer, W. B. The history of psychology and its retrieval from historiography: I: The problematic nature of history. *Science Studies,* 1974a, *4,* 235–58.

Weimer, W. B. The history of psychology and its retrieval from historiography: II: Some lessons for the methodology of scientific research. *Science Studies,* 1974b, *4,* 367–96.

Weimer, W. B., & Palermo, D. S. Paradigms and normal science in psychology. *Science Studies,* 1973, *3,* 211–44.

Wundt, W. *Outline of psychology* (7th ed.) . (C. H. Judd, trans., 3rd ed.) Leipzig: Wilhelm Englemann, 1907.

# The Linguistics
# in
# Psycholinguistics

## CHAPTER 1

Psycholinguistics, as the word implies, involves a combination of some aspects of psychology (with which we will be most concerned in this book) and some aspects of linguistics. In this chapter, we will focus on the historical development of the goals and techniques of the science of linguistics in order to see how its effect on psychology has been so marked that it has become incorporated into the name of this part of the discipline. Since we shall see by the end of the chapter that there is an intimate relation between the historical developments in linguistics and the development of the present-day disillusionment with behaviorism by the psychologists working in this area, it is, perhaps, best to set the scene by describing the behavioristic account of language. In this way, some of the succeeding material may be seen in better perspective.

## BEHAVIORIST ANALYSES OF LANGUAGE

A number of psychologists have attempted to account for the acquisition and use of language within the behavioristic framework. Some have attempted to do so primarily in terms of simple conditioning principles (e.g., Mowrer, 1960; Skinner, 1957) and others, including the present author, by elaborating the principles of conditioning with mediation models (e.g., Jenkins & Palermo, 1964; Osgood, 1953, 1963; Palermo, 1971 [1]) or a related theoretical concept of contextual generalization (Braine, 1963). We shall use Staats' (1971) theoretical

---

[1] Although this paper was published in 1971, it was written in 1965 and, as will be seen in this book as well as in other publications (e.g., Palermo, 1970), the author has changed his theoretical position to one more compatible with the new paradigm discussed later in this chapter.

presentation as an exemplar of this position, however, for it is one of the most recent efforts to deal with language and most clearly presents the behavioristic learning model.

Staats argues that a broad application of the principles of classical and instrumental or operant conditioning can be applied to account for all aspects of language. When Staats uses the term *language,* he is referring to speech and meaning which, as we shall see, is a different use of the word than that of others in the field whom we will discuss later. Previous attempts by learning-oriented behaviorists to explain language were not entirely successful, according to Staats, because they did not use adequate learning theories or the complete set of conditioning principles available, and/or they were concerned with only limited aspects of the problem. It is necessary to consider both forms of conditioning and their interactions to fully account for all the complexities of language.

Staats begins by assuming that the early vocalizations of infants are differentially reinforced such that children more and more frequently emit the sounds associated with their particular language community and drop out sounds they are capable of producing but which are irrelevant to the language they are to learn. In addition, he suggests that the vocalizations of the parents in association with positive reinforcers, such as food in the feeding situation, lead to the parental voices taking on secondary reinforcing qualities. Subsequent generalization of the reinforcement value of the parents' voices to the child's own vocalization results in those vocalizations becoming reinforcing in and of themselves. Thus, the direct reinforcement of the parents for the particular speech sounds of the language and the self-reinforcement of the infant lead to the child's gradual acquisition of sounds, then syllables, and finally, words.

At first, approximations to words are reinforced; then the speech of the child is shaped through the process of differential reinforcement as the parent begins to restrict the reinforcement to better and better approximations of particular words. Once the child is saying words, the words become response units and the child begins to match its behavior to that of others in the sense that if the parent says, "Say 'bread,' " for example, the child will be reinforced for repeating the word. The child does not, at this stage, have to build up the individual sounds into the unit "bread." The successive approximation to the words is short-circuited because words are now the units under the control of the appropriate speech sound stimuli of the parents. The verbal responses may also come under the control of environmental stimuli which are nonverbal in nature. The child is continually reinforced for labeling objects in the environment and, thus, learns to say "Mommy" in the presence of the mother, "dog" in the presence of a dog, and so on. In addition, internal stimuli, such as are associated with hunger or thirst, can come to act as stimuli for verbal responses when the verbal responses are reinforced by food or water.

In these ways, many stimuli come to control many verbal responses. Any particular verbal response occurrence is dependent on the stimulus complex present at the time and is a function of the strength of that response to that stimulus, relative to the strength of other competing responses that may be present at the time. Language is a part of the environment and, therefore, becomes both the stimulus and a response. The child acquires language responses which, in turn, act as stimuli for other language responses, and the analysis of the verbal behavior of the child becomes very complex rather early in the language acquisition process.

Once the child does acquire a repertoire of words, he or she begins to hook them up in two-word utterances as learning skills improve to the extent that grammatical speech can occur. This development is not a matter of maturation but is rather a function of training procedures introduced by the parents. For example, the child may utter a single word response which the parent expands into a sentence. The child, in turn, learns to produce longer utterances because the parent does not allow reinforcement to occur until the child imitates the expansion. Staats suggests that such expansions frequently take the form of adding a single word to other single words which the child utters. He illustrates this with the example of the child saying words such as "milk" or "meat" or "apple" which the parent expands by saying, "Milk, please," "Meat, please," and "Apple, please," and withholds reinforcement until the child gives some approximation of the parent's two-word utterance. Thus, the parental utterances become discriminative stimuli which bring about the expansion of the child's language and response chains of word-word associations of different strengths are developed for various stimulus situations. In addition, after the child has learned to respond "boy" to many physical *boy* stimuli and, say, "running" to many observed instances of *running*, seeing both a *boy* and *running* simultaneously may elicit the response, "boy running" or "running boy." Thus, the external stimuli as well as the specific training by the parents may bring about two-word utterances.

Since words have particular privileges of occurrence in sentence frames, the child learns grammatical habits which take the form of the sentence structures used by adults. The child, for example, hears such things as "See the house," "Own the car," and "Walk the dog," and learns the appropriate stimulus conditions for the occurrence of the word, that is, the words "see," "own," and "walk" are stimuli appropriate for uttering "the." In addition, the words that follow "the" are conditioned to the word "the." In a short time, the words come to be interconnected with other words in rather complex networks. Since particular words have particular grammatical privileges of occurrence in the parental speech, only certain words get conditioned to other particular words. Eventually, however, some of the two- and three-word sequences become unit responses and they can become inserted into other grammatical sequences. The length of the utterances increases as a function of an increase in the skilled vocal responses and associations between sequences of responses which the child learns. Such sequences involve the conditioning of words to their inflections, words to other words, and sequences of words to other sequences of words.

While children are learning to build up their repertoire of words and to formulate grammatical sequences, they are also learning the meaning of words. The initial contact a child has with a word is meaningless in the sense that no responses have been conditioned to that word stimulus. The originally neural stimulus comes to have meaning through responses that are classically conditioned to it. Thus, a word such as "no" comes to stand for the actual aversive stimuli associated with it through the conditioning process. Initially, words need to be conditioned directly, but as the child acquires the meanings of some words, these words, in turn, can be used as unconditioned stimuli for conditioning the meanings of other words. Thus, the child builds up a repertoire of meanings, or responses, for words which vary as a function of responses that are conditioned to them.

In summary, Staats argues that language behavior, in all its complexity, is reducible to the simple principles of classical and instrumental conditioning which behavioristically oriented psychologists have found so valuable in analyzing many kinds of behaviors by animals at all phylogenetic levels in a variety of laboratory tasks. He argues that language can be explained only within a general learning framework that provides an analysis of the stimuli and responses and establishes causal relations between the two. Whitehurst and Vasta (1975) have offered a more recent account within the same theoretical framework.

The theoretical position outlined here is perhaps the most straightforward behaviorist account of language and its acquisition but it differs little in principle from that of the other theoretical efforts made by psychologists within this framework. The addition of mediation to the model, for example, merely adds other stimulus-response connections to the chains which are established through conditioning procedures. The mediating links are assumed to be conditioned in the same way, and the major difference is only in the fact that mediating stimulus-response connections are usually covert and, therefore, less easily observed. Thus, we note from this outline that the learning model emphasizes conditioning and the building from the simplest conditioned responses to more and more complex behaviors. Sentences are acquired as linear sequences of longer and longer stimulus-response chains. Sentences are produced in a left-to-right sequence conceived as a series of probabilistic events in which each stimulus word in the sequence has a specifiable probability of eliciting the next word response which, in turn, acts as a stimulus for the succeeding word response. The probability of a word eliciting the next word is based on the past learning history of the speaker. Generalization from one learning situation to another is based on the overlap of identical stimulus elements in the learning and generalization situations. Maturation is specifically denied as a significant variable. Physiological and genetic characteristics of the organism are ignored and the direct relationship between principles established with lower animals and those affecting humans are taken for granted. There is little concern with the nature of language per se and no consideration is given to the structure of the mind and how that may influence the way the organism behaves. Finally, the emphasis is placed entirely on the empirical relationships between the observable stimulus and the observable response.

## LINGUISTIC ANALYSES OF LANGUAGE— BLOOMFIELDIAN LINGUISTICS

Turning our attention now to linguistics, it is of some interest to find that Leonard Bloomfield, who is considered the father of the "American school" of structural linguistics, was a strong advocate of behaviorism. The field of linguistics was markedly influenced by Bloomfield from the time of the appearance of his first book, *Introduction to the Study of Language* (1914). His revised and extended version of that book, entitled simply *Language* (1933), was such a thorough and provocative coverage of the field that it was considered the bible of American linguistics for many years thereafter. In essence, Bloomfield established the paradigm for linguistics by delineating the field, the important problems to be investigated, and the methods for approaching those problems. He was particularly concerned with establishing linguistics as an autonomous and scientific field.

His concern about autonomy apparently was directed, in part, toward psychology from which he wished linguistics to remain separate. In his 1914 book, Bloomfield had tried to relate linguistics to psychology but the psychology to which he related it was that of Wundt. Unfortunately for Bloomfield, he had pinned his linguistics to a psychology which had just been rejected by Watson (1913) the year before. Between the time of his first book and his second, however, Bloomfield himself was converted from the psychology of Wundt to that of Watson. He was evidently influenced in making this shift by A. P. Weiss, one of the most exacting behaviorists in psychology. Weiss

(1929) felt that all psychology could be reduced to what he called biophysical and biosocial terms which made it possible to dispense with mental elements, the primary concern of the earlier German psychology. He reduced mind to biological and socially observable events and Bloomfield extended this general notion to linguistics by adopting the same antimentalistic position. Bloomfield felt that *mechanism* was the necessary form of scientific discourse and he interpreted this to mean that the facts were to be observed and reported without any additional assumptions about other factors playing a part. He assumed that the proper way to approach the problems of linguistics was to gather a sample of speech, or a group of authentic utterances (corpus), and then derive the rules of the grammar for the language from the corpus itself based on the distributional characteristics of its units.

In adopting the behavioristic, empiricist orientation for his science, Bloomfield was reacting to the dualistic conceptions of language such as the "inner form" and "outer form" of von Humboldt and the "langue-parole" distinction of de Saussure which played an important part in the traditional linguistics of Europe. The latter distinctions were directed toward clarifying the difference between the system of language (inner form or *langue*) known to the speaker and the actual speech behavior (outer form or *parole*) of the speaker. Bloomfield felt that the concepts of inner form and langue were mentalistic excess baggage and the focus should be on speech behavior in the form of attested utterances, that is, grammatically correct sentences by native speakers of a language. The Watsonian reaction of psychology to the study of consciousness and the introspective method seemed just the right solution to Bloomfield for eliminating mentalism from his science and he led linguistics down the same path. Bloomfield felt that the descriptive, fact-collecting approach to the field which he advocated was scientifically exact and unprejudiced by theory. He assumed that inductive generalizations about language would emerge from the descriptive data when enough descriptive information was known. It should be clear, however, that while Bloomfield adopted the behavioristic approach for his science, he rejected any affiliation with the changeable science of psychology and maintained that linguistics would stand on its own as a science. He focused on the scientific characteristics psychology had adopted which he felt linguistics should strive to meet.

The linguistics of Bloomfield made inductive generalizations about particular languages based on data obtained in an objective manner without historical or theoretical biases. Bloomfield would agree heartily with Staats' description of the acquisition of syntax and, in particular, the acquisition of the meaning of words. The latter, Bloomfield felt, was important but essentially the subject matter of another science; as he put it, ". . . we define the meaning of linguistic form, wherever we can, in terms of another science" (Bloomfield, 1933, p. 140). He was strongly antimentalistic, antiphilosophical, and anti-psychological. He felt that language universals might be of interest, but only when adequate data about many languages became available could such generalities be expected to emerge.

## PROBLEMATIC ASPECTS OF BLOOMFIELDIAN LINGUISTICS

The American school approach of Bloomfield led to an accumulation of many valuable descriptive statements about many languages. The general approach ran into difficulties, however, because it failed to produce inductions of broad generality within the limits of the paradigm. In addition, it could not handle many of the interesting problems of language, some of which Bloomfield assumed could be resolved. For example, Fries (1952), operating within the American school tradition, assumed that it would be possible to define grammatical classes objectively by showing that one class of words, say nouns, fit into a slot in a standard sentence frame while other classes fit into different slots in other sentence frames. This substitution-in-frames technique failed however, because it turns out that you have to know in advance something about the grammatical structure of the sentence frame in order to know whether a particular constituent will fit into it. For example, the slot in the frame "_____ was good," which may be used to define a noun (with an article), can be filled by "The concert" and by "He was bad or he" but these two parts of sentences are clearly not comparable although both form perfectly grammatical sentences. Fries seemed aware that it was necessary to have some additional knowledge, or intuition, about the language to use his system, but, if that is the case, then the objective nonmentalistic approach advocated by Bloomfield is not being adhered to and thus may not be a viable approach.

Now consider the problem posed by a sentence of the sort:

(1) The man who greases the cars wishes to eat the lemons.

Analysis of this sentence on the basis of a left-to-right so-called Markov chain model assumes that each word occurs as some probabilistic function of the word to its left. "Man" follows "the" with some probability, "who" follows "man" with some probability, and so on. The difficulty, however, arises when we get to the word "wishes" which follows "cars" in this sentence. It is clear that the word "wishes" is not at all related to "cars" but, in terms of both content and number agreement, is related to the word "man" which is five words before it. Since the length and number of embeddings in sentences is unlimited, and dependencies of this sort always occur across such embeddings, it is difficult to see how a left-to-right surface structural analysis may be utilized for describing sentences. In fact, Chomsky has shown that such an account is logically impossible (Chomsky, 1957).

Another problem that poses difficulties for this approach to linguistics arises in connection with ambiguous sentences. Consider the sentence:

(2) You can't imagine how good oysters taste.

There are several possible meanings, including the meanings that oysters taste good to someone, good oysters as opposed to bad oysters have a particular taste, and oysters themselves have a good sense of taste. The words in the sentence have different grammatical functions, depending on which reading is given to the sentence. One more example may make the point clear:

(3) They were fascinating girls.

This sentence is ambiguous and difficult to handle because the slot filled by the word "fascinating" may be used to define a verb or an adjective, depending on the meaning of the sentence. Only by recognizing this fact can the sentence be *disambiguated* and the two different structures of the sentence identified and related to the meanings.

While not wanting to give up the behavioristic and mechanistic orientation to the field, some linguists tried to avoid the difficulties of the substitution-in-frames analysis of sentences by postulating a hierarchical analysis of the relations of the parts within sentences. This approach becomes more abstract because it goes beyond the surface structure level but it does solve some of the problems which the analysis of sentences as a series of slots arranged from left to right cannot. The hierarchical analyis, usually referred to as phrase structure or constituent structure analysis, was an attempt to show that there are two structures to sentence (3) discussed above and that one structure relates "fascinating" more closely to "were" in one interpretation and to "girls" in the other interpretation. This type of analysis shows that a sentence is composed of phrases or constituents and that those constituents in turn are composed of constituents. The constituents are related to each other in a hierarchical manner which may be represented by tree diagrams or by the use of brackets. Furthermore, the constituents at each level of analysis may be labeled and formalized by a series of *rewrite rules,* so called because the constituent represented by a symbol on the left side of the rule statement is rewritten as the constituent or constituents represented by the symbol or symbols on the right side of the statement.

Consider again the two interpretations of sentence (3) and we will illustrate the distinctions between the two interpretations in terms of sets of rewrite rules, the use of bracketing and tree diagrams. Note that these are three different ways of representing the same things.

| | |
|---|---|
| S → NP + VP | S → NP + VP |
| NP → $\begin{Bmatrix} \text{Pro} \\ \text{N} \end{Bmatrix}$ | NP → (Adj) + $\begin{Bmatrix} \text{Pro} \\ \text{N} \end{Bmatrix}$ |
| VP → N + NP | VP → V + NP |
| V → Aux + MV | Pro → they |
| Pro → they | N → girls |
| N → girls | V → were |
| Aux → were | Adj → fascinating |
| MV → fascinating | |

((They) ((were fascinating) (girls)))     ((They) ((were) (fascinating girls)))

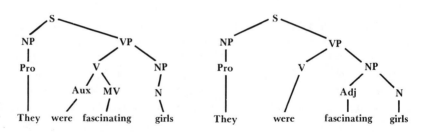

The linguistic symbols are to be read in the following manner: S = sentence, NP = noun phrase, VP = verb phrase, Pro = Pronoun, N = noun, V = verb, Aux = auxiliary verb, MV = main verb, Adj = Adjective; the parentheses in the rewrite rules indicate that what is within the parentheses is optional; the brackets mean that one and only one of the symbols must be chosen and the arrow means "to be rewritten as."

Now notice that in the bracketed representation above we have not labeled the brackets, but in listing the rules and in constructing the tree diagrams we have used labels which imply a particular grammar specifying the relationships among the constituents. In the first case, the phrase structure is given in a neutral and essentially atheoretical form. Technically speaking, labeled bracketing and labeled tree structures are referred to as *phrase markers*. The phrase markers specify the relationships among the parts of the sentence. Any sentence may be formally analyzed in this manner with a series of rules which take the general form A → x + y, read as A is rewritten as x and y, where x and y are elements or constituents which make up A. In the case above, the constituents from which a sentence (S) is constructed are a noun phrase (NP) and a verb phrase (VP) and these, in turn, are made up of constituents. The constituents which may not be broken down further in this type of sentence analysis are the words. A phrase structure analysis of a sentence, therefore, begins with a sentence symbol on the left and proceeds through the levels of the sentence structure to the terminal symbols on the right side which may not be further analyzed. The final level is referred to as the *terminal string* and the entire labeled analysis is called the phrase marker.

Finally, we should note that phrase structure grammars that allow us to assign two different structures to sentences such as (3) will not allow us to handle sentences with embeddings. Sentences such as (1), for example, in which one sentence is embedded in another, require a more powerful set of rules. Phrase structure grammars with rules of the form A → x A y seem to be needed. This type of rule allows the use of a nonterminal symbol on the left side of the rule to occur on the right side of the rule as well. Such rules are called *recursive rules* in the mathematical sense of the term recursive, that is, there is no limit to the number of times this form of the rule may be applied. The addition of recursive rules to the phrase structure rules, therefore, allows an infinite output and the potential for accounting for all the sentences in a language although, as we shall see later, it appears that this type of rule alone is not satisfactory for a complete description of language. Thus, with a recursive rule of the form S → a S b, we can account for sentence (1) by reapplying the sentence rule at some level within the phrase marker. This procedure makes it possible to describe the structure of a sentence composed of one sentence embedded within another and may, of course, be used with noun phrases, verb phrases, or other constituents in addition to the recursion of S as we have illustrated. We shall deal with this problem further a little later in this chapter.

While the introduction of the phrase structure analysis, even with recursion rules, solved some kinds of problems in the analysis of sentences, it left others still unsolved. Consider the sentence:

(4) He was killed by the bridge.

This sentence does not have two different phrase markers to differentiate the two meanings which any native speaker of the language can recognize, that is, one describing *where* he was killed and the other *how* he was killed. If one put different labels on parts of the phrase structure description, it might help in this case but even that would not solve the problem posed by a sentence such as:

(5) Bill likes Jill more than Will.

Here the ambiguity results from the lack of an overt manifestation of parts of the sentence which would disambiguate it. We need to know whether the sentence should have the meaning that Bill likes Jill more than *he likes Will* or that Bill likes Jill more than *Will likes Jill*. The phrase structure analysis provides no way of expressing this ambiguity.

There are still other problems with a phrase structure grammar. Such a grammar cannot express the relation between the following two sentences:

(6) I gave the key back.
(7) I gave back the key.

Sentences (6) and (7) are clearly related but the phrase structure analyses of the two sentences are quite different. Phrase structure grammar does not allow one to show the relation between a sentence and a paraphrase of a sentence or between two paraphrases of a sentence. Finally, there is no way for phrase structure grammars to handle the problem of the difference between the sentences:

(8) Grace is hard to please.
(9) Grace is glad to please.

While they have the same phrase structure, "Grace" is the subject of the sentence in one case and the object in the other, a point which is clear as soon as you attempt to paraphrase the two sentences. In the case of (8), the paraphrase would be, "It is hard to please Grace," while in (9), the paraphrase would be, "Grace is glad to please someone."

Adherence to the type of science Bloomfield outlined for the field of linguistics appears to be inadequate to account for aspects of language which are intuitively clear to any native speaker of the language, despite the fact that the data have pushed linguists of this persuasion to postulate abstract phrase structure types of analyses that are not directly observable in the data. Language users seem to know more about language than the behavioristic linguist, restricted by the type of acceptable scientific procedures allowed by Bloomfield's prescription, is able to capture.

## CHOMSKY'S LINGUISTICS

In 1957, Noam Chomsky wrote a little book entitled *Syntactic Structures* in which he convincingly pointed out some of the inadequacies of the Bloomfieldian approach and, more importantly, offered a solution in the form of what he called *transformational generative grammar*. The solution involved redefining the field of linguistics and the methodology to be used. It prescribed an end to the radical empiricism of behaviorism characteristic of the Bloomfieldian era and the adoption of a mentalist and rationalist approach to the science of linguistics. Although Chomsky was apparently not aware of it when he wrote his first book, the linguistics he advanced was closely related to the European linguistics Bloomfield had rejected earlier. Chomsky later wrote a book making the historical connection (Chomsky, 1966). In any case, Chomsky rebelled against the empiricist, mechanistic paradigm within which he had received his training and, because linguistics was in a crisis state at the time, his persuasive arguments precipitated a scientific revolution.

Since linguistics has been markedly changed by Chomsky's work, and since the influence of Chomsky's position has spilled over to affect most of psycholinguistics, we will take time here to try to make clear some of the most important aspects of his position. We will delve into linguistics only so far as is minimally necessary for a psychologist to work in the area of language. More detailed accounts for beginners may be found in Langacker (1973), Jacobs and Rosenbaum (1968), Liles (1971), and Lyons (1969), as well as in Chomsky's original works.

## The Sentence Unit

First, we should note that the sentence is the largest basic unit of description with which the linguist is concerned. Second, any language consists of an infinite number of these sentence units. Thus, it is impossible to list all the sentences of any language, for no matter how long the list, we could always add more to it. This point may be made obvious when it is recognized that there is, in principle, no longest sentence. For example, the sentence "The old man who saw the bum sleeping by the red fence went to the department store to buy some wash and wear shirts for his brother who lives next door to the lady with the big black car" is a long but perfectly grammatical sentence which could be made longer by adding more adjectives or relative clauses, for instance. While in principle there is no longest sentence, we ordinarily limit their length because if they become too long we might lose track of the beginning of the sentence by the time we reach the end. But we do learn to understand and produce an unlimited number of grammatical sentences in our language! Since we do not have enough time in our lives to learn an infinite number of sentences, it must be that we learn a finite set of rules for constructing sentences and not the sentences themselves. Finally, as we noted earlier, there is more to understanding a sentence than appears on the surface. Thus, it would appear that we must know something about sentences at an underlying or deep level in addition to what we know about what we actually speak or hear at the surface level. In addition, we must know how the deep structure is related to the surface structure. With these factors in mind, let's turn to Chomsky's form of linguistics.

### The Grammar of Language

The goal of linguistics, according to Chomsky (1957, 1965, 1968), is to construct a theory of language, by which he means to construct a grammar made up of a finite set of rules capable of generating the infinite set of gramatically correct sentences possible in any language and none of the possible grammatically incorrect utterances. Such rules would, for example, generate the English sentence "Horatio squandered his money," but not "Money his squandered Horatio," nor "The tree squandered his money." The set of rules forming the grammar of a particular language would describe the knowledge a native speaker has about his or her language. This knowledge is referred to as the linguistic *competence* of the language user. Put another way, the competence of a language user consists of the set of rules which allow the user to speak and understand the language by relating the meaning system to the sound system, the semantic representation to the phonological representation. In a sense, competence is a description of the language code of the idealized speaker/listener of the language—an abstraction which describes a part of the mental equipment of the language user. It is in this sense that linguistics is mentalistic, for it attempts to discover "a mental reality underlying actual behavior" (Chomsky, 1965, p. 4).

*Performance*, of course, refers to the actual behavior. Any theory of the processes governing performance, which is also an abstraction, must in some way be related to the theory of competence. Just how the theories of competence and performance may eventually be interrelated is still a matter which is not entirely clear (Fodor & Garrett, 1966; Watt, 1970; Straight, 1971). The point is, however, that a distinction is made between competence and performance, between the mental knowledge of the language and the processes of implementing that knowledge. The distinction must be made because we need an understanding both of the knowledge itself and of how that knowledge is acquired and, once acquired, how it is used. Overt language behavior of a speaker/listener thus reflects the knowledge a person has of language as it is processed to produce and understand sentences. The theories constructed to account for overt language behavior will be idealized versions of the knowledge and processes which determine that behavior. The insertion of the word "idealized" in the previous sentence merely reflects the fact that any theory of knowledge or process will hold only for idealized conditions as, for example, the law of gravity holds only in the idealized conditions of a vacuum.

The processing of language observed in overt behavior would, according to Chomsky, *directly* reflect competence only in a completely homogeneous speech-community in which all the persons know the language perfectly and are unaffected by the grammatically irrelevant factors of memory limitations, distractions, changes in attention and interest, and errors in applying the knowledge. In order to understand performance, it is necessary to understand the nature of the structure of competence or the grammar which characterizes it. Grammatical competence, however, is viewed as one segment of a more comprehensive cognitive competence. In this sense, linguistics, according to Chomsky, is a part of psychology and not independent of it as Bloomfield attempted to establish. Thus, the theory of performance must relate the perceptual, motor, and other cognitive processes to the use of the knowledge represented by linguistic competence.

The grammar of a language, in Chomsky's view (1965), consists of a tripartite system of rules pertaining to semantics or meaning, syntax or structure, and phonology or the sounds of the language. Chomsky argues that the syntactic component relates the deep structure of the semantic component to the surface structure of the phonological component. Thus, the semantic component consists of the rules pertaining to the underlying meaning to be expressed; the syntactic component consists of rules for converting the deep structure to a surface structure form which can be interpreted or converted by the phonological rules into actual sounds. There are, therefore, rules for interpreting meaning, rules for interpreting the sounds, and rules for pairing the appropriate meanings with the appropriate sounds.

**Language Universals**

The rationalist aspect of the new approach proposed by Chomsky is concerned primarily with conceiving the mind as being structured in such a way as to determine the form language will take. The form human mental processes take is determined by the nature of the organism. It is argued that there is an innate latent mental structure which is characteristically human and which becomes active as a function of sensory experience, that is, when appropriate environmental conditions are presented so the latent structures may manifest themselves.

Applying this approach specifically to language, Chomsky argues that all languages have a common or universal core. The general form and even some of the substantive features of the grammar for particular languages overlap with those of all other languages, that is, they are determined by the nature of the mental structures and processes which characterize human beings. Chomsky argues that there are substantive universal aspects of language and formal universal aspects. Neither has been well specified as yet but both have been characterized in a general way. The *substantive universals* refer to the nature of the phonological, syntactic, and semantic units of which language is composed. It has been suggested, for example, that all languages have a particular set of syntactic classes such as nouns and verbs, or subject and predicate. It has also been argued that the phonological component can be characterized with a small set of features, defined in terms of articulatory and acoustic properties, which are independent of any particular language. *Formal universals,* on the other hand, refer to the form of the rules which will appear in the grammar. Transformational rules for example, may be required to handle the syntactic component of the grammar satisfactorily.

The concept of language universals explicates further the goals of the linguist. The assumption is that all languages have some commonalities and that a theory of language should capture those commonalities in such a way that any specific language may be seen as only a variant of language in general. A linguist of Chomsky's persuasion is looking for those descriptions of language which allow insights across languages rather than merely within a language. Note, again, how this approach is in contrast to that of Bloomfield.

## Transformational Generative Grammar

Up to this point we have talked at a somewhat abstract level about the reorientation of linguistics within the paradigm Chomsky outlined. Now let's look more specifically at transformational generative grammar and just what that means. A grammar, as we have already indicated, is a set of rules which pertains to semantics, syntax, and phonology and which characterizes the knowledge a person has of his or her language. What does it mean, however, to say that the grammar is generative?

Actually, the term *generative* has been used in two ways by Chomsky as well as others in the field. First, Chomsky makes the point that a language user is creative with the language the individual knows and can make up appropriate sentences for any occasion which arises. The language used is composed of an infinitely large set of potential sentences but only a few of the set are actualized. The user, however, is capable, in principle, of generating any of the sentences from the set and at least some of them are likely to be new or novel but at the same time appropriate to the situation, whatever that situation may be. Thus, the sentence you have just read is one I have probably never created before nor one that you have ever seen before but it is presumably a grammatical and understandable creation from the infinite set of English sentences. Thus, the first meaning of generative refers to the creative aspects of the grammar, the use of a finite set of rules to create sentences appropriate to an unlimited number of situations.

The second meaning of generative refers to the mathematical explicitness or preciseness of the grammar constructed. The rules which generate the sentences are explicit enough to allow the derivation of sentences mechanically without any use of intuition by the person applying the rules. The rules generate a certain output in the form of sentences and, therefore, define as grammatical those sentences which are derived by those rules. Strings of words which are not generated are, by definition, not grammatical.

One of the novel aspects of Chomsky's approach to linguistics is his use of generative in both of these senses because the traditional grammarians prior to Bloomfield tried to create grammars which were generative in the first sense in which Chomsky uses the term but failed to concern themselves with the second of these meanings. The Bloomfieldian linguists strove for mathematical precision in the second sense of the term *generative* but failed to take into account the first of these meanings.

We can turn now to the meaning of the term *transformational* in connection with the transformational generative grammar. In some ways, transformational is a more difficult term to explain because it is a more technical term specifically related to linguistics. We can begin by noting that transformational refers to a particular type of rule used in the generation of sentences. That is, grammars are transformational if they include rules which perform transformations. Obviously then, something must be transformed. You will remember that we have referred a number of times to the idea that sentences have a deep structure and a surface structure. Transformational rules are those rules which relate or transform the deep structure of a sentence to the surface of a sentence.

For example, look closely at the sentence:

(10) The delicate girl, who smokes a pipe, grows the mushrooms.

We can, with our linguistic intuitions about the English language, analyze it in a manner similar to that of a linguist. When we consider the underlying meaning of the sentence, it becomes apparent that several assertions are being made in it and that these assertions could be broken up into separate sentences. There is a main sentence, often called the *matrix sentence,* and there are at least two embedded sentences. We might analyze it as follows:

Matrix sentence: The girl grows the mushrooms.
Embedded sentence: The girl is delicate.
Embedded sentence: The girl smokes a pipe.

This kind of analysis shows that the speaker of the sentence has combined three underlying sentences into a single surface structure sentence composed of two auxiliary sentences within the matrix sentence. By representing it within a phrase structure grammar, we could conceptualize the sentence in a tree diagram of the sort shown in Figure 1–1. This tree diagram indicates the relationships among the underlying ideas represented in the single sentence we observe in the surface structure. This is a representation of the deep or base structure of the sentence. But notice that as it is represented in the phrase marker the sentence would read, "The girl, the girl is delicate, the girl smokes a pipe, grows the mushrooms." Obviously we need some additional rules which will allow us to convert this base structure representation into the surface structure we ordinarily use. It is the transformational rules which serve this function by rearranging, deleting, and inserting elements into the phrase structure. The transformational rules are applied from the bottom to the top of the phrase marker in a cyclical fashion, that is, they would be applied to the bottommost sentence first and then reapplied at the next level up if necessary. Furthermore, when a choice of rules is possible, the transformational rules will be ordered so that some rules must be applied before others in order to properly relate the deep structure to the surface structure.

In the case of our sentence (10), we will need, for example, rules that will delete two instances of "the girl." One rule will replace "the girl" by the relative pronoun "who" while in the next sentence up other rules will delete "the girl" and move the word "delicate" into the adjective position in front of the noun at the next higher level. (Note that both these transformations are possible because the NP of the sentence immediately above, that is, the sentence which dominates it, is the same as the sentence to which the transformational rule applies.) The transformational rules thus apply to the output of the base structure given in the form of a phrase marker. These rules convert the base structure to the surface structure which is also represented as a phrase marker but with the constituents rearranged in such a way that they may be interpreted by the phonological rules. The resulting phrase marker to which the phonological rules apply is called the *final derived phrase marker*.

This is, of course, an abstract formal representation of the knowledge of the speaker and should not be conceived as indicating that the mind actually goes through all these steps in the process of producing a sentence. One must, however, know all of the relationships in order to use the language and the linguist attempts to formalize the knowl-

**Figure 1-1**

---

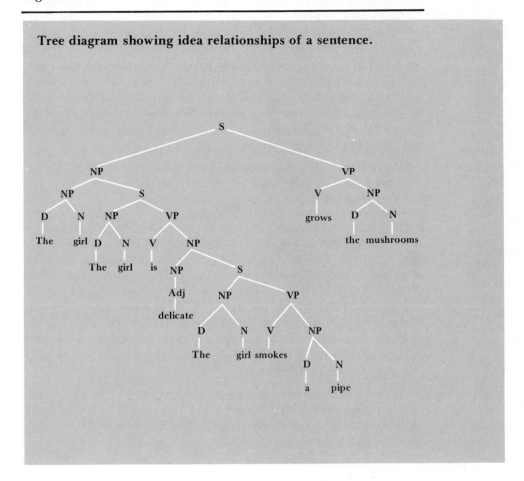

**Tree diagram showing idea relationships of a sentence.**

edge of the speaker in this manner. Thus, this is not a representation of consciousness but is rather a precise representation of what has been called tacit knowledge.

Let's consider a couple of more examples to try to further clarify the problems involved and the solutions which transformational generative grammar attempts to provide. Take the sentence:

(11) Flying planes can be dangerous.

This is a syntactically ambiguous sentence like (2), which means that it has at least two different base phrase markers which happen to result in the same surface structure. Loosely speaking, the sentence can mean either that if you fly planes you may be engaging in a dangerous activity or that planes which are flying may be dangerous objects. In the latter case, "flying planes" is related to an underlying string in which "planes" is the subject of the verb "fly" and in the other case, "planes" is related to an underlying string in which it is the object of the verb "fly." The transformational rules used to convert these two different deep structures to their surface structure form, however, result in the same surface structure. Thus, the two different underlying meanings, which all native speakers of English can easily recognize in the surface structure of this sentence, result from the operations of two different sets of transformations to two different base structures.

Now look at the two sentences:
(12) John is easy to please.
(13) John is eager to please.

Superficially, these two sentences, as in the case of (8) and (9), appear to have the same surface structural relations but if we consider their base structures we can see that they are quite different in much the same way as the ambiguous sentence (11) we just considered. In the case of (12), John is the object of the underlying string, "It is easy to please John," while in the case of (13), the underlying string is, "John is eager to please someone," where John is the subject of the sentence. As a result of the transformational rules the sentences look alike, but we know by virtue of knowing the structure of our language that they are quite different.

Finally, examine the sentences:
(14) John hit the ball.
(15) The ball was hit by John.
(16) Did John hit the ball?
(17) John didn't hit the ball.
(18) Wasn't the ball hit by John?

In this case, we have what might be called a family of sentences because they all derive from essentially the same base structure. All may be conceived as deriving from a string in the base structure which is something like the surface form of (14). In each case, different transformations have been applied: a passive transformation in the case of (15), a question transformation in the case of (16), a negative transformation in the case of (18). At the deep structure level, they are very similar and clearly related but at the surface structure level they are quite different and not obviously related. Incidentally, you might notice that in the case of sentences (16) and (17), for example, the transformational rules must add an element which will become a part of the final derived phrase marker and be realized in the surface structure. The word "did" is inserted in the surface structure of these sentences for the sole purpose of constructing a question and for carrying the negative element. If an auxiliary verb were available in the underlying string, then this "dummy" element would not be required because the auxiliary verb would serve the same purpose as in, "John should hit the ball," and "Should John hit the ball?"

In summary, the word "transformational" in transformational generative grammar refers to the rules which relate the terminal string of the base phrase marker to the final derived phrase marker which is the basis of the surface structure. While the phrase structure rules are rewrite rules of the simple form $A \rightarrow b + c$ or the recursive form $A \rightarrow b \, A \, c$, transformational rules take a structural description specified by the phrase structure rules and rearrange the structure by the addition and deletion of elements as well as the reordering of elements. These rules provide the links which show the relationship between the deep and the surface structure of sentences. Note that they are not a series of ad hoc rules made up for each sentence—they apply across all sentences with a particular base structure. Furthermore, the rules closely interlock within a closed system so that rules that account for one aspect of sentence structure are likely to affect other parts of the grammatical system and must not lead to derivations which conflict with other rules within that system.

## SEMANTICS

Up to this point, our discussion has focused primarily on syntax which, at least until recently, has drawn the most linguistic attention and stimulated the most psycholinguistic attention. But language also involves two other components: a semantic component and a phonological component. Let's look first at what the linguists have to say about the semantic component. Our discussion of semantics will lead us into some theoretical controversy because it is in this area that Chomsky's theory has undergone major revision forced by empirical results and alternative theoretical approaches. At this stage we can only present an outline of the issues which have arisen, the theoretical controversies which have appeared in the literature, and recognize that no resolution is in the offing at the moment. Linguists have had little success in developing a satisfactory semantic theory. In fact, Chomsky did not even approach the problem of semantics in his first book (Chomsky, 1957).

Semantics obviously relates to the meaning aspect of language as opposed to the structural aspects of syntax and the sound aspects of phonology. Those interested in semantics deal with the meanings of words or word forms and the meanings of the combination of word forms which make up sentences. The meaning of words seems pretty simple. Take the word *cow*, for instance, or *love*. We don't have much trouble with those words, for if someone asks what *cow* means we say something like this: "Well, a cow is a domesticated animal with four legs, about the size of a horse, from which we obtain milk." Then we might point to a cow or a picture of a cow and say, "See, that is a cow." In the case of *love,* we might say, "Love is a strange and complicated emotion which involves craving the presence of another and the desire to please that other person." Then we might add, "Do you know *Romeo and Juliet?* That, man, is love!" If you examine these crude efforts at semantic analysis, you will note that we have provided two kinds of relationships to the words in each case. We began with an attempt to define a concept or give the sense of the meaning of the words and then we gave an example of a particular instance or referent. This is an important distinction, for the linguist is primarily interested in the concept or sense of the word form and not in its referent. The reason for this distinction and the focus of interest on the concept is clearly because there is no single object which is, for example, a *cow.* Each instance of a cow is different, but in some abstract sense there is an underlying concept of *cow* which makes it possible for most of us to recognize which referents in our environment are cows and which belong to other conceptual classes. Thus, we can see that referents are only instances of the meaning of a word and it is the underlying sense which defines those referents as members of the class signified by the word.

In order to deal with meaning, it would seem necessary to have a dictionary of lexical items (words) and some rules for the combination of those lexical items. We need to know, for example, the underlying characteristics of the concepts conveyed by the words "wish" and "want" so that we can specify explicitly the nature of their near synonymity. In addition, however, we need to know the rules associated with these lexical items which make it grammatically possible to say,

(19) I wish that he would go home,

but not

* (20) I want that he would go home.[2]

Furthermore, we need to know how to specify that it is ungrammatical to say,

* (21) Chair wish (want) that he would go home.

One approach (Katz & Fodor, 1963) has been to postulate that the meaning of the concepts underlying the lexical items may be specified in terms of a set of features (semantic markers) which define the

[2] An asterisk in front of a sentence is the linguist's indication that the linguistic example is ungrammatical.

meaning of a dictionary entry uniquely, relative to all other nonsynonymous entries. These relations would hold whether the features were hierarchically arranged or merely listed (Katz, 1972). There would, of course, be a number of such semantic markers corresponding to the number of concepts or meanings associated with any particular word form. The word "bank," for example, would have one semantic marker for the concept of a place where money is kept, another semantic marker for the concept of the rising ground along the side of a river or lake, and still other markers for the many other meanings of bank. Let's illustrate further by thinking for a moment about the concept underlying the lexical item "woman." We could specify at the highest level of our semantic marker that "woman" possesses the feature of animateness (expressed as +animate) as opposed to being inanimate; at a lower level that "woman" is human (+human) as opposed to nonhuman; "woman" is adult (+adult) as opposed to child; and female (+female) as opposed to male. Now if we think about the concept underlying the lexical item "man," we find the same semantic markers, at least at the higher levels, and the basic difference comes at the lowest level we have specified, that is, "man" is marked as having the feature +male as opposed to +female. The semantic markers defining the characteristics of man and woman specify both their similarity and the critical differences between them. At the same time, the semantic markers for these two lexical items define how they are more similar to each other than either is to the concept underlying "chair," which would have quite a different semantic marker with respect to the dimensions specified above.

Assuming that we could specify the semantic markers for each lexical item in the language, we would still need, as a part of the semantic component, a set of rules to specify which syntactic combinations of lexical items in sentences are grammatical. These rules would specify that "chairs" may not "wish," for example, because lexical entries marked as inanimate may not be combined with verbs whose semantic markers are associated with the cognitive processes. Further, other rules would specify particular syntactic relationships among lexical entries so that the entries "wish" and "want" would be covered by different syntactic rules. It is little wonder that the linguists have had difficulty in solving the theoretical problems associated with this component of the grammar.

Earlier I mentioned that there is currently some controversy among the transformational generative linguists with respect to semantics. What has been described up to this point is a part of what has come to be known as the standard theory. In that theory, proposed by Chomsky in *Aspects of a Theory of Grammar* (Chomsky, 1965), the grammar consists of a base composed of a phrase marker with category terminal nodes into which are inserted lexical items following the lexical insertion rules. The semantic component of the grammar interprets the meaning of the base sentence by means of projection rules which combine the word meanings into a whole sentence. The word meanings are conceived as bundles of features (after Katz and Fodor, 1963). The base with its semantic interpretation is referred to as the deep structure to which transformational rules are applied to realize the surface structure. Thus, the meaning of the sentence is established at the base level and transformations should never affect the meaning of a sentence. The semantic aspect of the standard theory is referred to as interpretative because the complex of symbols of the base phrase marker, which represent the structural relationships among the ideas to be expressed in the sentence, are interpreted by the semantic component through the insertion of lexical entries into the base phrase marker contingent on their meeting the criteria of appropriate semantic markers and syntactic restrictions for the base phrase marker in question. Figure 1–2, taken from Maclay (1971), illustrates these relations.

At least four theoretical variants of the interpretative semantic theory have appeared in the literature since Chomsky first grappled with the problem of semantics. In the late 1960s, alternatives were offered by Lakoff (1968), McCawley (1968), and Ross (1967). Their arguments centered around the idea that it is not possible to separate the semantic and syntactic components of the grammar. According to these linguists, there is no single base phrase marker but, rather, sentence generation begins with the semantic component and subsequent interaction between lexical insertion and transformational rules leads eventually to the surface structure and the application of the phonological component. Thus, the focus of linguistic inquiry should give at least equal billing to the semantic component rather than merely relegating semantics to a role of interpreting the syntactic component. The generative semanticists, as these linguists have come to be called, have argued that the underlying structures in standard theory are too concrete. Once the presuppositions and implications of sentences are analyzed in more detail, it becomes necessary to postulate more abstract underlying structures which make the deep structures of sentences deeper and more complex. Ross (1974), for example, shows how a simple causative sentence such as "Dr. Grusel is sharpening the spurs" involves more than seven underlying sentence forms or propositions encompassed within its meaning including, for example, the presuppositions that Dr. Grusel and the spurs exist.

A second alternative approach to semantics is related to that of the generative semanticists but takes a different form. Fillmore (1968) has argued that while the centrality of syntax and deep structure categories in linguistic theory are to be assumed, a semantically justified universal syntactic theory, that is, one with semantic deep struc-

**Figure 1-2**

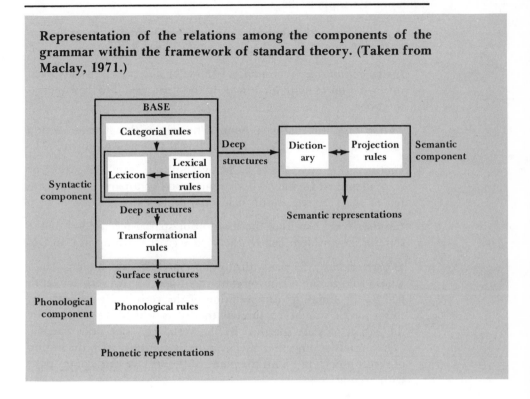

**Representation of the relations among the components of the grammar within the framework of standard theory. (Taken from Maclay, 1971.)**

tures, will have greater explanatory adequacy than a theory based on syntactic data alone. Fillmore introduces the term "case" to express the syntactic-semantic relations in deep structure. Case elements are optionally associated with verbs and take the form of propositions in deep structure. The propositions are marked for negative, tense, mood, aspect, interrogative, and with some adverbs, by a modality constituent. Thus, the basic structure of a sentence consists of a proposition which is a set of relationships devoid of tense that involve verbs and their associated nouns and on which the modality constituent operates as a whole. The proposition consists of a verb and case categories that involve the nouns. No case may appear more than once in a proposition, although recursion is possible by embedding one simple sentence into another through one of the cases. The cases themselves are assumed to be universal, innate concepts which identify concepts, category relations, or judgments people are capable of making about events in their environment. Fillmore has in mind such propositions as who did it, who it happened to, what got changed, and where it happened. For example, the initial cases Fillmore introduced were (Fillmore, 1968, pp. 24–25) :

*Agentive case:* the typically animate perceived instigator of the action identified by the verb, e.g., John opened the door.

*Instrumental case:* the inanimate force or object causally involved in the action or state identified by the verb, e.g., The key opened the door.

*Dative case:* the animate being affected by the state or action identified by the verb, e.g., John believed that he would win.

*Factitive case:* the object or being resulting from the action or state identified by the verb, or understood as a part of the meaning of the verb, e.g., John made the table shorter.

*Locative case:* identifies the location or spatial orientation of the state or action identified by the verb, e.g., It is windy in Chicago.

*Objective case:* the semantically most neutral case for any noun whose role in the action or state identified by the verb is identified by the semantic interpretation of the verb itself; conceivably, this concept should be limited to things which are affected by the action or state specified by the verb, e.g., The door opened. (The notion of objective case is not to be confused with the notion of direct object, nor with the name of the surface case synonymous with accusative.)

The arguments of the generative semanticists and Fillmore, along with the research provoked by their theoretical ideas, led Chomsky (1971) to modify the interpretive semantic component of the standard theory. While Chomsky (see also Katz, 1970) has argued that most of the theoretical ideas offered by the generative semanticists and by Fillmore are no more than notational variants of the standard theory with no differential empirical consequents, some of the research stimulated by the alternative theoretical efforts resulted in insights which led Chomsky to change the standard theory. He now offers the *extended standard theory,* in which he suggests that the interpretive component applies primarily to the deep structure but also operates at the surface structure level. Thus, extended standard theory is a move toward the position advocated by the generative semanticists while maintaining the interpretive position that differentiates syntax and semantics conceptually. It should be noted, incidentally, that sentence processing is not to be conceived as a series of steps which flow from deep structure to surface levels in real time. The theory is a model formulated to conceptualize processes which must take place at some level, but nothing in Chomsky's model implies that those processes occur either in series or parallel form, or in some combination thereof.

The fourth and most recent theoretical variant of standard theory is still being formulated and therefore is not fully developed (e.g., Jackendoff, 1975, 1976; Bresnan, 1976). In contrast to the approach of the generative semanticists, the lexical interpretive model of transformational grammar proposed by Jackendoff and Bresnan has moved in the direction of reducing the deep structure-surface structure distance. The generative semanticists have made deep structure deeper by including the presuppositions and implications of a sentence in the derivational structure. The lexical interpretive model, on the other hand, is a theoretical effort to make deep structure less deep by shifting some of the transformational rules, such as those associated with the derivational forms of words, into the lexical component of the grammar. Thus, the lexical interpretive model assumes a semantic component which consists of functional composition rules at the deep structure level and surface interpretive rules at the surface structure level, as in the extended standard theory. The lexical component, which is part of the semantic component of the base in Chomsky's version of the theory, is separated from the semantic component, and the lexicon and lexical rules are assumed to have interactive relations with the semantic component and the phonological component as well as with the deep structure itself (Bresnan, 1976).

Finally, we should note that Fodor has recently changed his position (Fodor, Fodor, & Garrett, 1975) with respect to specifying the meaning of the concepts that underlie the lexical items in terms of a hierarchically-arranged set of features (Katz & Fodor, 1963), as we described earlier. Fodor, Fodor, and Garrett have argued that the earlier theory, which used feature-defining expressions, does not have psychological validity. There is, in short, little evidence that constructions which are more complex semantically in terms of their defining expressions are more complex psychologically. Fodor et al. suggest that an approach to semantic representations in terms of meaning postulates (Carnap, 1956; Kintsch, 1974) may prove more fruitful. The effect of such a proposal is to eliminate semantic decomposition of lexical items into features in favor of a more wholistic paraphrase approach to semantic representation. While it is not clear how this approach can resolve the complicated issues of semantics, it does result in a theoretical move compatible with the efforts of Jackendoff and Bresnan to reduce the deep structure-surface structure disparity.

There is still no settled, accepted theory that satisfactorily explains semantics. Linguists and psychologists alike recognize that we cannot ignore the problem, as the earlier, behavioristic approaches did, but the way it is to be handled theoretically and explored empirically is far from resolution. We can expect greater attention to and the most controversy in this area of linguistics in the future. As we shall see in later chapters, the problematic nature of semantics has spilled over into psycholinguistics where research has been increasingly directed toward the issue of meaning.

## PHONOLOGY—THE PHONEME

We now turn our attention to phonology, the sound system of language. Most of us think of the sounds of our language in terms of the alphabet. When we see the letter "p," for example, we know that it represents a particular sound formed by closing the lips, building up a force of air behind them, and then releasing the air suddenly. But is that really the case? Consider the words in which the letter "p" occurs in this paragraph. In the words *phonology* and *alphabet,* the "p" is pronounced as if it were an "f." "Well," you say, "that's because it is followed by an 'h,' and 'ph' is pronounced as if it were an 'f.' " Leaving aside the question of why "f" is not used to represent the sound in these words (to say nothing of why the letter "p" appears at all in *psychology*), look more carefully at the "p" in *up* and the "p" in *lips,* which you may think you pronounce the same way. If you put the corner of a piece of paper in front of your mouth when you speak the "p" in *up* and the "p" in *lips,* you will find that in the former case the paper will flutter when you pronounce the "p" but in the latter case it won't. That is, you aspirate the "p" in *up* but not the "p" in *lips.* In English, whether or not you aspirate sounds makes no difference in the meaning of the word, but in some languages, such as Hindi, for example, it *is* important and aspiration or nonaspiration of a sound makes a difference as significant as whether or not you vibrate your vocal chords in English when you pronounce a "p." If you vibrate your vocal cords when you make the "p" sound, it will turn out to be a "b" and not a "p." The smallest units of speech that can be distinguished from each other are *phonemes;* the difference between "b" and "p" in the English language is a phonemic difference. The difference between an aspirated ,ind an unaspirated "p" is an allophonic difference; that is, the two "p" sounds in *up* and *lips* are *allophones* or variations of the phoneme "p" in English. However, this allophonic difference in English is a phonemic difference in Hindi.

Although the letters of the alphabet used to spell English words may represent different sounds in different words, and the same sounds may be represented by different letters in different words, the alphabet cannot be used to represent the sound system of English uniquely because the English language uses about 44 sounds and there are only 26 letters to represent them. Consequently, linguists have developed another alphabet, called the International Phonetic Alphabet, which describes the sounds of all languages and thus avoids the problem associated with using alphabets or other kinds of descriptive techniques. The common vowel sound in the words meat, meet, mete, key, people, pity, and machine, for example, are all represented as /i/ in IPA and spelled with that symbol when a phonological transcription is given. Thus, the word *pea* is represented as /pi/ when the phonemic alphabet is used to symbolize the phonemes which make up the sounds of the word. The slanted lines differentiate between conventional spellings of words and the phonemic representation of a word. Table 1–1 gives one set of symbols used by some phonologists to represent certain phonemes along with some words which exemplify the sounds

**Table 1–1** *Illustrative Phonemic Symbols with Word Examples of Sounds*

## CONSONANTS

| | | | | | |
|---|---|---|---|---|---|
| Plosives | /p/ *pea, pan* | | /t/ *tea, tan* | | /k/ *cat, kite* |
| or Stops | /b/ *bat, bill* | | /d/ *date, dog* | | /g/ *gas, golf* |
| Nasals | /m/ *man, mill* | | /n/ *now, nice* | | /ŋ/ *sing, hung* |
| Fricatives | /f/ *fat, phone* | | /v/ *vat, vice* | | /s/ *sip, soup* |
| | /z/ *zoo, xylophone* | | /š/ *shall, sugar* | | /ž/ *pleasure, seizure* |
| | /ð/ *thy, either* | | /θ/ *thigh, ether* | | |
| Liquids | /r/ *run, ring* | | /l/ *let, list* | | |
| Glides | /y/ *you, use* | | /w/ *win, wet* | | /h/ *hit, house* |
| Affricates | /č/ *chew, chum* | | /ĵ/ *judge, jury* | | |

## VOWELS

| | | |
|---|---|---|
| | /i/ *key, me* | /ʊ/ *full, could, hook* |
| | /ɪ/ *did, hit* | /u/ *fool, true, moon* |
| | /e/ *late, rave* | /a/ *father, hot* |
| | /ɛ/ *pet, neck* | /o/ *hope, soak* |
| | /æ/ *cat, fast* | /ɔ/ *ought, caught* |
| | /ʌ/ *cut, putt* | |
| Diphthongs | /au/ *house, plow* | /ai/ *mice, right* |
| | /oi/ *boy, oil* | |

## WORD EXAMPLES

| | |
|---|---|
| /kɔt/ = caught | /saicalogɛ/ = psychology |
| /klač/ = clutch | /intɛlɛjɛnt/ = intelligent |
| /siŋk/ = sink | /yunɪform/ = uniform |
| /manapolɛ/ = monopoly | |

represented by the symbols. It should be noted that since different linguists have used various modifications of IPA, the symbols may vary from one to another. However, confusion is avoided because examples that illustrate which sound each symbol designates are usually given.

## DISTINCTIVE FEATURES

Analysis of language sound systems in terms of phonemes as the basic units has a long linguistic history, but prior to World War II, a group of phonologists in Czechoslovakia known as the Prague school of linguistics, in particular Trubetzkoy and Jakobson, argued that the phonemic analysis misses many of the important relations within the sound system. These men suggested that the phoneme can be further analyzed into *distinctive features*. In fact, they would just as soon dispense with the notion of a phoneme and talk about language sounds as bundles of distinctive features.

What is a distinctive feature? Recent efforts to establish the features that are used to identify unambiguously the sounds of languages in general have included the place and manner in which sounds are articulated and the acoustic characteristics of the sounds as the defining characteristics (Jakobson & Halle, 1956; Jakobson, Fant, & Halle, 1952; Chomsky & Halle, 1968). We will attend primarily to the articulatory aspects of these features. Do you remember the distinction we made earlier between /p/ and /b/? The /p/ phoneme is just like the /b/ phoneme except that we vibrate our vocal cords when we produce the /b/ but not the /p/. The same is true of the difference between /t/ and /d/, /k/ and /g/, /s/ and /z/, /f/ and /v/, /č/ and /ǰ/, and between /θ/ and /ð/. In each of these pairs, we articulate the first sound *without* voicing and the second one *with* voicing. The distinctive feature which is the only difference between these pairs of sounds is that /p/, /t/, /k/, /s/, /f/, /č/ and /θ/ are [− voice] and /b/, /d/, /g/, /z/, /v/, /ǰ/, and /ð/ are [+ voice]. If you want to feel the difference between these sounds, place your hand on your larynx or Adams apple and you can feel the vocal cords vibrate for those sounds which have the feature [+ voice].

All the sounds we have discussed thus far are made with air forced from the lungs out through the mouth. But some sounds result from air being forced out through the nose instead. Thus, /m/, /n/, and /ŋ/, which have this characteristic, are distinguished by the feature [+ nasal] while all other sounds are [− nasal]. Note that these sounds are [+ voice] as well as [+ nasal] although the feature that distinguishes them from all the other voiced sounds is the distinctive feature [+ nasal].

Now notice that some consonants are articulated by a complete blockage of the air flow through the mouth from the lungs. Sometimes the flow is blocked by the lips, as with /p/, /b/, and /m/, sometimes with the tongue against the alveolar ridge in the mouth, as with /t/, /d/, and /n/, and sometimes with the tongue against the soft palate, as in the case of /k/, /g/, and /ŋ/. These sounds, along with /č/ and /ǰ/, which include the /t/ and /d/ sounds respectively when they are produced, have the feature [− continuant]. All other sounds in English are [+ continuant] in that the air flow continues through the vocal tract throughout articulation.

Next, consider the difference between the consonant and vowel sounds. If you go through the vowel sounds, you will notice that you produce them with an open vocal tract but when you produce the consonants there is some sort of radical obstruction, although not necessarily a complete closure of the vocal tract as in the case of [− continuant] sounds. All sounds with a radical obstruction are said to have the feature [+ consonantal] and all the other sounds are [− consonantal].

Finally, we can recognize that the position of the tongue varies considerably in the articulation of different sounds. In producing the vowel sounds, for example, we vary the height of the tongue and the place in which the variation in height occurs. The position of the tongue in articulating /e/ is considered the neutral or midposition, and any sound in which the tongue is above that height is [+ high] as in the vowels /i, ɪ, u, ʊ/ and also the consonants /y, w, k, g, ŋ, š, ž, č, ǰ/. Sounds produced with the tongue lower than the midposition of /e/ are identified as [+ low] as in /æ, a, ɔ, h/. When the sound is produced with the tongue further back in the mouth than for /e/, it is assigned the feature [+ back] as in /u, ʊ, o, ɔ, a, ʌ, w, k, g, ŋ/.

At this point, you can begin to see that this approach to the analysis of sounds identifies each sound as a complex of elements or features which is a unique combination resulting in a particular sound different from all other sounds in terms of a particular feature or features. Table 1–2 shows some of the sounds we have discussed and some of the features associated with those sounds. It is the pattern of features which identifies each sound. Table 1–2 is obviously incomplete since each sound is not uniquely defined but it does give you the idea of the system. Seven additional features would completely fill out the matrix to identify the set of attributes that are simultaneously activated in the production of all the sounds of English. Some of you may have already recognized that thirteen binary features is more than is necessary to uniquely identify 44 sounds which means that there is some redundancy in a complete table. Phonologists (e.g., Harms, 1968; Chomsky & Halle, 1968; Schane, 1973) can provide us with a set of redundancy rules for English although we will not go into them here.

**Table 1-2** *Sounds*

| Feature | p | t | k | b | d | g | m | n | ŋ | f | v | s | r | l | h | y | w | i | ɪ | e | ɛ | æ | a | u |
|---|---|---|---|---|---|---|---|---|---|---|---|---|---|---|---|---|---|---|---|---|---|---|---|---|
| Voice | − | − | − | + | + | + | + | + | + | − | + | − | + | + | − | + | + | + | + | + | + | + | + | + |
| Nasal | − | − | − | − | − | − | + | + | + | − | − | − | − | − | − | − | − | − | − | − | − | − | − | − |
| Continuant | − | − | − | − | − | − | − | − | − | + | + | + | + | + | + | + | + | + | + | + | + | + | + | + |
| Consonantal | + | + | + | + | + | + | + | + | + | + | + | + | + | + | − | − | − | − | − | − | − | − | − | − |
| High | − | − | + | − | − | + | − | − | + | − | − | − | − | − | − | + | + | + | + | − | − | − | − | + |
| Low | − | − | − | − | − | − | − | − | − | − | − | − | − | − | + | − | − | − | − | − | − | + | + | − |
| Back | − | − | + | − | − | + | − | − | + | − | − | − | − | − | − | − | + | − | − | − | − | − | + | + |

Theoretically it would take only twelve to fourteen features of the type we have been discussing to identify the sounds in any language and the particular features will overlap considerably from one language to another. Thus, there is a universal pool of features that occur in all languages from which a subset is drawn for each particular language.

The big advantage the feature system has over the phonemic system is that the similarities and differences among sounds are precisely specified. We have already noted that in the case of /p/ and /b/, two different phonemes may differ only in terms of the single voicing feature. The feature system allows us to show that /p/ and /b/ both differ from another phoneme, say /h/, more than they differ from each other and that /h/ is more similar to /p/ than to /b/ because /h/ has only two feature differences with /p/ but three feature differences with /b/. This is certainly a refinement of the phonemic system and allows much greater insight to the sound system. The features are not necessarily equally distinctive, however, so you should not assume that a pair of sounds which differ in terms of one feature will be equally different psychologically from another pair of sounds which differ on another feature.

The other advantage of the distinctive feature theory is that the combination of sounds in syllables or words is clarified. The transitions from one sound to another may be analyzed and the reasons why, for example, the sound associated with past tense inflection of verbs, spelled "ed," is sometimes pronounced /t/, sometimes /d/, and sometimes /ɪ d/, or why we modify the articulation of *photograph* when we utter *photographer*. These examples give you some idea of the intricacies of the distinctive feature approach to phonology and suggest the complexities, abstractness, and underlying structure of what we hear and produce as language. Furthermore, the historical changes in the sound systems of languages can be analyzed with more detailed understanding within this theoretical system. The shifts in English pronunciation from Chaucer's time to Elizabethan times to the present, for example, can be more precisely understood within this framework (e.g., Halle & Keyser, 1971).

We have said nothing as yet of the acoustic correlates of the various sounds but will consider this in some detail in Chapter 4. Finally, our discussion has been limited primarily to the inherent features of sounds but has not touched on the prosodic features that are superimposed on the inherent features and refer to the tone (voice-pitch), force (voice-loudness) and quality (subjective duration) which can only be specified in terms of sequences of sounds. Prosodic analyses deal with the relative stress of the syllables in words, and words in sentences. For example, you can hear that you place a greater stress on the second syllable than on the first in the word *relate,* you stress the third syllable in *evolution,* and you change the stress pattern in the word *produce* from the second syllable to the first when you use it as a noun rather than a verb. You also vary the stress patterns over sequences of words so that "John is going to the store" means quite a different thing than "John is going to the store?" In the first case your intonation falls at the end of the sentence while in the question form the intonation rises at the end of the sentence. You can change the message conveyed in the four-word sentence "John bought the cake" just by placing the main stress on the different words. Try saying the sentence four times to yourself, placing the major stress on a different word each time.

## SUMMARY

Well, that should be enough linguistics for the moment. We may introduce a few other points as we go along, but with this general background you should have some idea of what problems the linguist faces in the study of the syntax, semantics, and phonology of the grammar. More importantly, you should now have some idea of the nature of the complexity underlying the behavior associated with language. When we speak or listen to another person speak, we are engaging a rather complex system of rules relating meaning to a sound system mediated by syntax. If you are not impressed by the complexity of the language system alone, consider the fact that we have said nothing about the relation of the language system to the cognitive processes that underlie language. The human mind is a masterful creation, far more complex than any computer, and all neatly packaged in a rather small container.

In conclusion, it appears that in view of the complexity of this system, in which rules range over abstract semantic, syntactic, and phonological entities, the relatively simple associationist learning models which deal only with stimuli and responses and generalize only on the basis of identical elements have little chance of success. Chomsky made this point very forcefully in reviewing Skinner's book on verbal behavior (Chomsky, 1959; see also the rebuttal by MacCorquodale, 1970). The nature of the problem suggests that the environmental input, stimuli if you wish, are only instances of concepts that exist in the mind of the person perceiving them. Thus, words, for example, have conceptual meanings that define which referents are included as instances. Sentences are also instances of underlying structures which have undergone various transformations. Even the sounds that form the surface structure are instances of an underlying phonological system. The difficulty from the traditional associationist point of view is that somehow humans acquire an abstract system which is never presented as such. Staats' concern with speech rather than language does not get to the heart of the problem. Although there is nothing in the environment which *is* the abstract system, we acquire one nevertheless as we exist in the environment. Each stimulus is an instantiation, that is, a concrete instance of an abstraction, from a larger conceptual framework and the resulting responses are a function of the stimulus itself *and* the conceptual framework and processing characteristics of the mind of the individual. The same environmental situation (stimulus) can be conceptualized in many ways and the response to that situation depends on the conceptualization more than on the stimulus. A dime, for example, may be conceptualized as ten pennies, an infinitesimal fraction of the national debt, an object for rolling, a substitute screw driver, a likeness of FDR, or any number of other things depending on what you wish to construct from that aspect of your environment, and yet all the time it remains the same object in the environment. In summary, it does not seem possible to account for human language behavior without some understanding, first of the nature and structure of language and, second, of the processes of the mind using that language. As we shall see in later chapters, psychologists are only beginning to scratch the surface in their efforts to construct theories which will fulfill these aims, but herein lies the excitement within the field. Researchers in psycholinguistics think they are on the right track and, while the paradigm is not clear yet, it appears that the new direction in which the theory and research is moving will define the trend of the next few years.

One thing which does emerge from all this is the suggestion that there must be something unique about the human species because it is the only one that has language. In the next chapter, we will turn our attention briefly to the meaning of the statement that only humans communicate with a language system and also look at some of the evidence which suggests that we humans are built in such a way that we can naturally develop language while other animals do not.

## REFERENCES

Bloomfield, L. *Introduction to the study of language.* New York: Henry Holt, 1914.

Bloomfield, L. *Language.* New York: Holt, Rinehart & Winston, 1933.

Braine, M. D. S. On learning the grammatical order of words. *Psychological Review*, 1963, *70*, 323–48.

Bresnan, J. *Toward a realistic model of transformational grammar.* Paper presented at M.I.T.-A.T.&T. Convocation on Communications, Cambridge, Mass., March, 1976.

Carnap, R. *Meaning and necessity.* Chicago, Ill.: University of Chicago Press, 1956.

Chomsky, N. *Syntactic structures.* The Hague: Mouton, 1957.

Chomsky, N. Review of verbal behavior by B. F. Skinner, *Language*, 1959, *35*, 26–58.

Chomsky, N. *Aspects of a theory of grammar.* Cambridge: M.I.T. Press, 1965.
Chomsky, N. *Cartesian linguistics.* New York: Harper & Row, 1966.
Chomsky, N. *Language and mind.* New York: Harcourt Brace & World, 1968.
Chomsky, N. Deep structure, surface structure, and semantic interpretation.
    In D. D. Steinberg & L. A. Jakobovits (Eds.), *Semantics.* London, England:
    Cambridge University Press, 1971. Pp. 183–216.
Chomsky, N., & Halle, M. *The sound patterns of English.* New York:
    Harper & Row, 1968.
Fillmore, C. J. The case for case. In E. Bach & R. T. Harms (Eds.),
    *Universals in linguistic theory.* New York: Holt, Rinehart & Winston,
    1968. Pp. 1–88.
Fodor, J. D., Fodor, J. A., & Garrett, M. F. The psychological unreality of
    semantic representations. *Linguistic Inquiry,* 1975, *6,* 515–31.
Fodor, J., & Garrett, M. Some reflections on competence and performance. In
    J. Lyons & R. J. Wales (Eds.), *Psycholinguistic papers.* Edinburgh:
    University of Edinburgh Press, 1966.
Fries, C. C. *The structure of English: An introduction to the construction of
    English sentences.* New York: Harcourt & Brace, 1952.
Halle. M., & Keyser, J. *English stress: Its form, its growth, and its role in verse.*
    New York: Harper & Row, 1971.
Harms, R. T. *Introduction to phonological theory.* Englewood Cliffs, N.J.:
    Prentice-Hall, 1968.
Jackendoff, R. Morphological and semantic regularities in the lexicon. *Language,*
    1975, *51,* 639–71.
Jacobs, R. A., & Rosenbaum, P. S. *English transformational grammar.*
    Waltham, Mass.: Blaisdell, 1968.
Jakobson, R., Fant, C. G. M., & Halle, M. *Preliminaries to speech analysis, the
    distinctive features and their correlates.* Cambridge: M.I.T. Press, 1952.
Jakobson, R., & Halle, M. *Fundamentals of language.* The Hague: Mouton, 1956.
Jenkins, J. J., & Palermo, D. S. Mediation processes and the acquisition of
    linguistic structure. In U. Bellugi & R. W. Brown (Eds.), *The acquisition
    of language.* Monograph of the Society for Research in Child Development,
    1964, *29,* 141–69.
Katz, J. J. Interpretive semantics vs. generative semantics. *Foundations of
    Language,* 1970, *6,* 220–59.
Katz, J. J. Generative semantics is interpretive semantics. *Linguistic Inquiry,*
    1971, *11,* 313–31.
Katz, J. J. *Semantic theory.* New York: Harper & Row, 1972.
Katz, J. J., & Fodor, J. A. The structure of a semantic theory. *Language,* 1963,
    *39,* 170–210.
Kintsch, W. *The representation of meaning in memory.* New York: Wiley, 1974.
Lakoff, G. Instrumental adverbs and the concept of deep structure.
    *Foundations of Language,* 1968, *4,* 4–29.
Langacker, R. W. *Language and its structure: Some fundamental linguistic
    concepts* (2nd ed.). New York: Harcourt, Brace & World, 1973.
Liles, B. L. *An introductory transformational grammar.* New York: Prentice-Hall,
    1971.
Lyons, J. *Introduction to theoretical linguistics.* Cambridge: Cambridge University
    Press, 1969.
MacCorquodale, K. On Chomsky's review of Skinner's Verbal Behavior.
    *Journal of the Experimental Analysis of Behavior,* 1970, *13,* 83–99.
Maclay, H. Overview. In D. D. Steinberg & L. A. Jakobovits (Eds.), *Semantics.*
    London, England: Cambridge University Press, 1971.
McCawley, J. D. The role of semantics in grammar. In E. Bach & R. T. Harms

(Eds.), *Universals in linguistic theory*. New York: Holt, Rinehart & Winston, 1968. Pp. 124–169.

Mowrer, O. H. *Learning theory and the symbolic process*. New York: Wiley, 1960.

Osgood, C. E. *Method and theory in experimental psychology*. New York: Oxford University Press, 1953.

Osgood, C. E. On understanding and creating sentences. *American Psychologist*, 1963, *18*, 735–51.

Palermo, D. S. Research on language acquisition: Do we know where we are going? In L. R. Goulet & P. B. Baltes (Eds.), *Theory and research in life-span developmental psychology*. New York: Academic Press, 1970. Pp. 401–20.

Palermo, D. S. On learning to talk: Are principles derived from the learning laboratory applicable? In D. I. Slobin (Ed.), *The ontogenesis of grammar: Some facts and several theories*. New York: Academic Press, 1971. Pp. 41–62.

Ross, J. R. *Constraints on variables in syntax*. Unpublished doctoral dissertation, M.I.T., 1967.

Ross, J. R. Three batons for cognitive psychology. In W. B. Weimer & D. S. Palermo (Eds.) *Cognition and the symbolic processes*. New York: Lawrence Erlbaum Associates, 1974. Pp. 63–124.

Schane, S. A. *Generative phonology*. Englewood Cliffs, N.J.: Prentice–Hall, 1973.

Skinner, B. F. *Verbal behavior*. New York: Appleton-Century-Crofts, 1957.

Staats, A. W. Linguistic-mentalistic theory versus explanatory S-R learning theory of language development. In D. I. Slobin (Ed.), *The ontogenesis of grammar: Some facts and several theories*. New York: Academic Press, 1971. Pp. 41–62.

Straight, H. S. On representing the encoding/decoding dichotomy in a theory of idealized linguistic performance. *Papers from the seventh regional meeting of the Chicago Linguistic Society*, 1971.

Watson, J. B. Psychology as the behaviorist views it. *Psychological Review*, 1913, *20*, 158–77.

Watt, W. C. On two hypotheses concerning psycholinguistics. In J. R. Hayes (Ed.), *Cognition and the development of language*. New York: Wiley, 1970. Pp. 137–220.

Weiss, A. P. *A theoretical basis of human behavior* (2nd ed.). Columbus, Ohio: R. G. Adams & Co., 1929.

Whitehurst, G. J., & Vasta, R. Is language acquired through imitation? *Journal of Psycholinguistic Research*, 1975, *4*, 37–60.

# Biological Bases of Language

## CHAPTER 2

Nearly everyone who owns a pet has talked to the animal at one time or other. On the other hand, people seldom talk to walls and more often talk to other people than to their pets. Why should people be so selective about the recipients of their language? Clearly we can dispose of the reasons for our snobbery with respect to walls and most other inanimate objects fairly easily. Walls don't talk back and, World War II slogans to the contrary, they don't have ears to hear what we say in the first place. But neither does the dog, for example, talk back. The dog, however, often does listen and does convey messages; it communicates with us. However, the dog does not seem to have many things to talk about, and thus we spend more time talking to other persons because there are many things to say and a rather effective system for receiving (decoding) and transmitting (encoding) the ideas we wish to exchange.

As far as we can tell, people seem to have much more to say to each other than do the members of any other species. In fact, one might go so far as to say that talking to each other is a characteristic specific to the human animal or, to put it more technically, Homo sapiens is the only animal that possesses the species-specific characteristic of language. Perhaps this distinctive characteristic which differentiates human beings from other animals rests more than anything else on the difference in the number of messages humans want to convey. I do not think we should accept these statements about human characteristics, however, until we have examined, first, some evidence of the communication systems of other animals; second, evidence of the evolutionary development of human language; and, finally, some of the neuroanatomical structures which seem important to our language ability. Perhaps it may then be possible to attempt to formulate this unique human characteristic and to define language.

# ANIMAL COMMUNICATION

There is little question that many animals communicate with each other as well as occasionally with humans. The ant, for instance, communicates with its comrades about the various routes it takes by laying down a pheromone (chemical) trail which other ants, presumably using a sense of smell, may then follow and use to return to the nest. Not a very complicated message nor a very complicated system, relatively speaking, but it is communication nevertheless.

## Bees

More interesting from our point of view is the language of the bees which has been so carefully studied by von Frisch (1954, 1967), although the ancient Greeks apparently had described this phenomenon rather precisely much earlier. Observation and experimentation with bees indicate that these insects communicate food sources and possible nesting sites to other members of the hive by means of rhythmic dance movements, sounds of clapping wings, and scents. Distance is communicated by a characteristic dance and sound system (Wenner, 1964; von Frisch, 1967). If the food source is within three to one hundred meters (depending upon the species of bee), the bee that located it will merely do a round dance and the others will go out and scout around for the source. As distance from the hive increases, the dance gradually changes and greater distances yield a "wagging" form of the dance when the source is more than two or three hundred meters away. There is a good deal of variability in the dance, but Figure 2–1 illustrates the form of the circular dance, two types of dance for intermediate distance characteristic of two different species, and the form for the greatest distances. The form of the dance, the number of turns per unit of time, the number of wags or body movements, and the pattern of wing sounds are indications of the distance to the source. Direction is communicated by the orientation of the straight line portion of the waggle dance relative to the sun regardless of whether the bee is dancing on a vertical or horizontal plane. Finally, the quality and specific type of food is communicated by means of scent carried from the source on the bee's body. Nesting dances are of the same sort but are performed on the swarm (Lindaver, 1967).

Bees apparently do not learn their dance forms which are instinctive, innate behavior patterns. As Figure 2–1 shows, there are some dialectical differences from one area to another, and bees put into hives with a different species will be led astray by distance cues of the new dialect. In any case, the communication system is iconic, that is, there is a direct relationship between what is done by the bee and

Figure 2-1

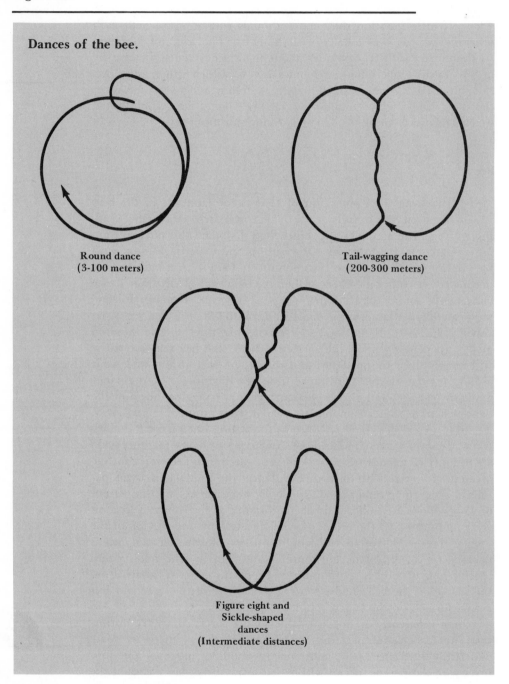

Dances of the bee.

Round dance
(3-100 meters)

Tail-wagging dance
(200-300 meters)

Figure eight and
Sickle-shaped
dances
(Intermediate distances)

what is communicated. Most human language is arbitrary in the sense that there is no relationship between the language form and the message conveyed, although some have argued that a case can be made for phonetic symbolism in human language in that certain meanings are naturally associated with certain sounds. It has also been argued that phonetic symbolism is the basis for the origin of language in man, but the relation of sound to meaning plays such a small part in human language today we will not consider it here. Those who find this topic interesting might consult Brown (1958) for an expanded discussion. We should note, however, that while the bee has nothing to tell other bees beyond the types of messages we discussed, it does have the capability of conveying an infinite number of messages since there are no limits to the number of distance-direction combinations possible for food sources, although the bee is not capable of making that many discriminations.

## Birds

Consider now the communication of birds. Here we have two phenomena to examine: the so-called talking birds and the communication among birds. In the first case, we are all familiar with mynah birds, parrots, parakeets, crows, magpies, and other birds which can be trained to produce sounds we can understand as words and phrases. While it may be obvious that these birds can talk, it is equally clear that they cannot converse. They mimic a set of utterances and cannot go beyond those specific utterances. It is even difficult to get the bird to use the utterances appropriately. There seems to be a distinct difference between the acquisition of talking by the mynah bird, for example, and the acquisition of language by the child. The bird only mimics and reproduces sound while the child seems to be doing something more than that. The child learns a particular language and uses it appropriately by recombining elements in utterances to form new, meaningfully appropriate utterances.

Birds do, however, communicate with each other. For example, the jackdaw, studied in its natural habitat by Lorenz (1952), seems to possess separate calls for courtship, nesting, flight to and from the nesting area, and anger. Other jackdaws recognize and respond appropriately to the calls. Many other birds seem to have mating calls which the males use to attract females and to warn off other males from territorial claims as well as other sorts of social communication. The number of differentiable calls, however, while used appropriately, is very limited, innate, and species specific. Additional information may be found in chapters of Lanyon and Tavolga's book (1958) and speculations about the relation of birdsongs to speech may be found in Marler (1970).

Next, let's briefly consider two special cases which deserve mention because of their notoriety. The first is a dog named Fellow and the other a horse known as Clever Hans. Fellow was a German shepherd raised and spoken to by his masters in the manner of a child. He became a stage and screen star because of his apparent ability to understand and correctly respond to spoken human words. Under careful tests it was determined that Fellow could, in fact, respond quite accurately, although not perfectly, to his master's commands such as "Go and find my keys," even when his master was out of sight (Warden, 1928). As with birds, however, Fellow could not respond correctly to novel utterances, nor, of course, could he use the language himself although there have been stage dogs who have been trained to give nearly recognizable words (barks) upon command.

Clever Hans was thought to be capable of arithmetic computation, spelling and even reading by his owner who took pride in demonstrating his horse's amazing abilities. The horse would, for example, stomp his foot six times upon request to add two and four, multiply three times two, or indicate the hundreds digit in 5,682. Unbeknownst to the owner, however, the horse was able to respond to the subtle cues conveyed by his master and others who knew the answer and who indicated their knowledge to the horse by almost imperceptible anticipatory body movements when Hans reached the correct answer. But Hans had no knowledge at all of arithmetic per se. In short, Hans was clever, but his ability to understand language and arithmetic was not the basis of his cleverness. The story of Clever Hans and the careful experiments which were required to discover his ability make fascinating reading (Pfungst, 1965).

## Dolphins

Another animal for which language has been claimed is the dolphin. Lilly, who studied the communication among captive dolphins for some years, became so convinced of the intelligence of his animals that he finally discontinued his research because of his concern that confining these animals for his studies was cruel. Lilly has argued that dolphins have a rather complex and productive language consisting of clicks, whistles, quacks, blats, and barks. He feels that dolphins communicate with each other (e.g., Lilly, 1963) and could communicate with humans, but his research did not progress far enough to demonstrate this in a convincing manner. Lilly's writings, however, make most interesting reading (e.g., Lilly, 1961).

## Apes

We come finally to our closest phylogenetic relatives, the apes. Most of the work with this group of animals has been done with chimpanzees who do vocalize a good deal and are active and lovable at least until they reach adolescence when they become so strong as to be potentially very dangerous. Many other apes, such as the gorilla and the orangutan, however, do not vocalize very much. Until very recently, evidence of the chimpanzee's ability to learn language suggested that we humans were safe in assuming that our species alone had such ability. As we shall see, however, the claims that "Anyone concerned with the study of human nature and human capacities must somehow come to grips with the fact that all normal humans acquire language, whereas acquisition of even the barest rudiments is quite beyond the capacities of an otherwise intelligent ape. . . ." (Chomsky, 1968, p. 59) must be revised at least to some extent in light of recent evidence.

The two best-known early studies of chimpanzee language acquisition come from the reports of families who took chimpanzees into their homes and reared them as children. The Kelloggs (1933) raised a female chimp named Gua with their own son Donald. At first Gua developed more rapidly than Donald on a number of dimensions. She learned to skip, kiss for forgiveness, feed herself, and so on well before Donald. Gua also learned to respond appropriately to approximately seventy verbal commands. But she never learned to utter a single word. The Hayeses (1951) reared Vicki in much the same manner but they specifically tried by all the techniques available to them to teach their adopted chimp to speak. The best Vicki could do was to approximate four words, despite all the efforts of the Hayeses. Thus, even the barest rudiments of language seemed to be out of reach of these otherwise intelligent animals.

In the past few years, two new efforts to teach language to chimpanzees have achieved considerably more success. In the first of these studies, the Gardners (1969, 1971) have, over a period of five or six years, communicated with their chimpanzee, Washoe, via American Sign Language. The Gardners reasoned that chimpanzees are not capable of spoken language, but, since they are quite facile with their hands, they may well be capable of signing which, it was assumed, has most of the properties of spoken human languages. Thus, during most of Washoe's waking hours from about one year of age she had human companions who constantly spoke to her in sign language and attempted to teach her that language by techniques ranging from operant conditioning to natural exposure. Not only has Washoe learned to use more than 85 signs appropriately, but she has learned to combine them in strings of several signs in length. Many of the combinations she has generated spontaneously. Lastly, it is of interest to note that Washoe, who has had to be returned to her colony because she has become too dangerous to continue the experiments, has attempted to sign to other chimps in her new home community (Fouts, Mellgren, & Lemmon, 1973). Thus, in some sense, Washoe has learned the bare rudiments of a language, uses it spontaneously, and has even generated new and appropriate constructions not specifically taught to her. Currently, a number of other chimps are being taught sign language by researchers at the University of Oklahoma where Washoe now resides (Fouts, 1975). The Gardners have also begun to raise another chimp in a signing environment, this time initiating the project with an infant animal.

It should be noted that when the Gardners began teaching Washoe American Sign Language, many linguists would have disagreed with their supposition that sign language has most of the properties of spoken human languages. The assumption was that signing is a loose collection of individual gestures strung together with no hierarchical structure. Since that time, however, Bellugi and Klima (1975) have presented data and argued strongly that signing is a hierarchically organized system acquired in a manner that suggests it is a language in the same sense as the spoken form—a point made earlier by others (c.f., Stokoe, 1975). It is of some interest that Fouts (1975) has found parallels between the acquisition of signing by chimpanzees and by deaf children.

The second effort to teach language to a chimpanzee is being conducted by Premack (1971a, 1971b, 1975). In these studies, Sarah, Premack's first chimp, learned a language that uses geometric-shaped objects arranged in vertical strings. Premack's approach, like that of the Gardners, avoids the problem of subword units (i.e., letters or phonemes) by using the word as the basic unit. The signs used by Washoe and the objects used by Sarah represent words. In contrast to Washoe, Sarah is being taught a grammar in which word order is important to the message. While Washoe has frequently strung together several signs, the Gardners report no apparent word order constraints in her constructions and thus on one occasion she will say, for example, "Gimme banana" and on another, "Banana gimme" with no apparent difference in meaning implied. Fouts (1975), however, has suggested that different meanings are associated with different sign orders in his chimps. In any case, Sarah is required to use a particular syntactic order and herein lies a major difference in the two languages.

Premack has used operant conditioning techniques in well-controlled situations to teach Sarah to "write" vertically arranged sentences with metal-backed plastic objects on the magnetized board in her cage where she resides and her lessons take place. Sarah, who began her language training at age six, has acquired a metalanguage for learning about language and has learned to name many objects. More impressive, however, is the fact that she has learned to answer questions about whether two objects are the same or different; answer questions requiring yes/no answers; classify on the basis of the concepts of size, color, and shape; comprehend sentences as complex as the compound sentence "Sarah insert banana pail apple dish," and sentences with a copula such as "Round is shape." She also uses pluralization, object or superordinate classes, quantifiers such as all, none, some, and several, and the logical connective If-then as in the sentence, "If Sarah take banana then Mary no give Sarah chocolate." While Brown (1973) has pointed out that we need to be cautious in interpreting the data for a number of reasons, these are rather dramatic achievements for an animal for whom it has long been thought the barest rudiments of language were out of reach. Sarah does not, however, perform perfectly. Although she is correct on about 70–80 percent of her test trials, she tends to ignore the language materials unless the experimenter stays with her, paying close attention. She also does not initiate communication, as Washoe does, but instead merely responds to statements or questions presented to her. Premack has initiated work with Elizabeth and Peony, two new chimpanzees, who may increase our knowledge of symbolic representational systems in general and language in particular (Premack, 1975). Premack has cast his research within a broad framework of understanding the mechanisms of intelligence which are preconditions to language (Premack, 1975, 1976). Recently, Rumbaugh and his colleagues (e.g., Rumbaugh & Gill, 1976) have argued that their efforts to teach language to a chimpanzee by computer may expedite our understanding of language, its etiology, and the parameters of its acquisition by human children.

In summary, we must, at the moment, be cautious with respect to making a definite statement about the species specificity of language. While we may easily dismiss the data of other animals as distinctly different in nature from human language, it is clear that Washoe and Sarah have achieved far more than was expected ten or fifteen years ago when Premack and the Gardners began their research. The question remains, how far can these animals go toward achieving language? Only the research going on today will answer that question.

## Defining Language

If we look at Hockett's (1960) criteria for defining language, however, we find that there are several important differences between the "language" of these two chimpanzees and the language of human beings. The first distinction centers about the use of the vocal-auditory channel in human language. This is not a crucial factor for we also use writing and reading as language systems. If chimpanzees can acquire a manual-visual channel system comparable to our writing-reading system, we cannot make it the basis of a definitive distinction between languages, although the advantages of the vocal-auditory channel allow communication much more efficiently and with less spacial confinement than the manual-visual system. It should be pointed out, however, that the normal human child acquires the vocal-auditory language quite naturally, spontaneously, and without specific teaching while it has required long, concentrated training to achieve the relatively little success attained with the chimpanzee.

More important is the variable Hockett calls *semanticity,* which, along with the variable of the arbitrary relation of sounds and meanings, allows us to talk of cabbages and kings and many (infinitely many) other things. This is something chimpanzees and other animals have not done, either because they cannot do so or don't want to. In addition, humans are continually capable of comprehending and producing utterances never before heard or spoken. This creativity with language, or *productivity* as Hockett calls it, seems to be a uniquely human characteristic, although Washoe has shown some rather limited productive abilities. Finally, language has allowed us to learn from other people without actually experiencing the events or ideas involved. Hockett calls this *displacement,* referring to the fact that we can know of Julius Caesar or Madame Bovary without having experienced them or being able ever to experience them. Other animals, apparently, are limited to the phenomena they experience individually.

We might then argue that language is a species-specific characteristic of Homo sapiens distinguished by vocal-auditory transmission of meaningful messages (semanticity) appropriately created (productivity) for the infinite number of situations past, present, future, and fantasized (displacement) any person may wish to convey.

## THE EVOLUTION OF HUMAN LANGUAGE

One reason we can expect that, regardless of the research outcomes with Washoe, Sarah, and other animals, there will prove to be both quantitative and qualitative differences in the language capabilities of humans and apes rests on the evolutionary history of these different species. While the ape may be our closest phylogenetic relative, and while humans and present-day apes may have evolved from a common ancestor, it does not necessarily follow that there are only quantitative differences between modern humans and apes.

Lenneberg (1967) presented these arguments very cogently in his important book which marshalled a vast amount of evidence for the biological foundations of language. The point Lenneberg makes is that evolution has not resulted in a linear development in which each successively higher animal on the phylogenetic scale adds a quantum of, for example, neurons or structures or intelligence until finally, when we arrive at Homo sapiens, we find language. Rather, Lenneberg argues, evolution is a discontinuous process of development in which branching occurs such that species on different evolutionary branches evolve in quantitatively and qualitatively different ways independently of species in other branches. Thus, there is linear continuity within branches and discontinuity between branches. Hodos and Campbell (1969) make the same general point in the broader context of a theory of comparative psychology. Figure 2–2, borrowed from Lenneberg, represents how both the common (phylogenetic) ancestry and the independent (phyletic) development of humans and apes may be represented within evolutionary theory. Thus we can see that species may share traits from their common origins and yet, as a function of the continual evolutionary process after branching, develop entirely different and independent species-specific traits. If we assume that the genetic changes which led to physiological structures that permitted the emergence of language occurred *after* the species that evolved to Homo sapiens developed (that is, after branching with respect to present-day apes), then there is no reason to believe that the experiments with chimpanzees will demonstrate that these apes can acquire a language whose properties are necessarily common to those of human language.

Let us assume then that language is species specific to Homo sapiens. Regardless of whether we assume that humans evolved as a species the way Lenneberg described or in a linear evolutionary manner, it follows that we, or our predecessors, have not always had language. Thus, one may ask how and when we attained this particular trait which has served us so well and what biological changes made it possible for language to evolve. Lieberman and his colleagues (Lieberman, Klatt, & Wilson, 1969; Lieberman, Crelin, & Klatt, 1972; Lieberman, 1973, 1975) have asked just those questions and have come up with some rather intriguing answers.

The approach taken by Lieberman's group was to examine and compare the anatomical characteristics of the adult Homo sapiens (who obviously has verbal communication) with the newborn human infant and the chimpanzee (who obviously do not have such abilities) and fossil remains of prehistoric humans, about which we have, of course, no direct knowledge. The assumption was that the anatomical similarities and differences among these four forms would be particularly revealing about the fossils. In other words, these researchers have tried to reconstruct the vocal capabilities of earlier forms of humankind by comparing the structures of their skulls and jaws with those of

**Figure 2-2**

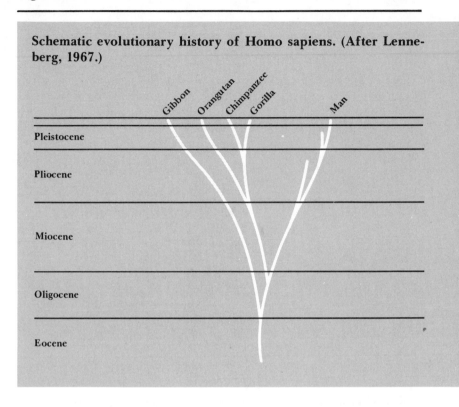

Schematic evolutionary history of Homo sapiens. (After Lenneberg, 1967.)

people and apes of today. In addition, Lieberman has incorporated further anthropological, ethological, and psychological information to formulate a theory of the evolution of human language. Lieberman defines language more broadly than most linguists do as "a communication system that is capable of transmitting new information" (Lieberman, 1973, pp. 230–31).

Lieberman's group has found fourteen specifiable common features among the fossil, chimpanzee, and infant forms, all of which differ from the adult Homo sapiens. Using the skulls, their knowledge of comparative anatomy, and the skeletal similarities between the living primates and the fossil remains, these researchers have reconstructed the supralaryngeal structures of extinct fossil hominids and compared them with the other forms. Thus, they have constructed models of the larynx, pharynx, velum, tongue, and the oral and nasal passages in each case. The differences in the supralaryngeal forms again reveal that the adult Homo sapiens is different from the other three, all of which are similar. The major commonality of the three that differs from the adult human is a relatively flat passage from the larynx to the oral cavity as opposed to the right angle passageway we possess. In the human adult, half of the supralaryngeal vocal tract is formed by the pharyngeal cavity while the opening of the larynx into the pharynx is immediately behind the oral cavity in the other three. It is important to point out that the structures of the human infant develop to the adult form by two years of age and are nearly fully developed as early as six months. It is also of some interest to note that since the human supralaryngeal pharynx serves both as a pathway for food ingestion and an airpassage for breathing, which makes efficient vocalization possible, the pharynx is less efficient for the biological functions of ingestion and breathing. Thus, we modern humans apparently have sacrificed some aspects of our abilities to eat and breathe in developing our linguistic abilities. Figure 2–3 shows a schematic diagram of the various parts of the supralaryngeal tract and the larynx of the human speech production system, adapted from Lieberman (1977).

Having established the anatomical differences between adult humans versus newborn, chimpanzee, and fossil forms, the question of the implications for speech production remains. Lieberman and his colleagues have approached this problem by determining what sounds could be produced by the various supralaryngeal vocal tracts by modeling the tract shapes on a computer programmed to determine the formant frequency patterns these tracts could produce. This is possible since there is a direct relationship between articulatory configurations of the vocal tract and formant structure and it is the formant structure which specifies the vowel sounds of speech (see Chapter 3). Specifically, they have used the vowels /i/, /a/, and /u/ for their tests because these vowels represent universal vowels, they are the extreme points defining the vowel triangle, they require less precision in articulation than other vowels, and they are the only vowels in which the acoustic pattern is determined by a unique vocal tract area function. The results of this analysis of vowel production by the four modeled tracts reveal that it would not have been possible for the Australopithecines or Neanderthal hominids and it is not now possible for human infants or chimpanzees to produce any of these vowel sounds which, of course, are easily and distinctly produced by present-day human adults. In addition, an examination of spontaneous infant and chimpanzee vocalization data shows no evidence that either infant or chimpanzee vocalize these sounds, thus providing collaborative support for the computer results. We may conclude, therefore, that Australopithecines did not have the anatomical equipment to produce vocal speech even if they had the neurological and motor capabilities. While the speech-producing anatomy of the Neanderthals was not well developed, other evidence cited by Lieberman pertaining to their tool making, for example, suggests that linguistic ability was present in at least rudi-

**Figure 2-3**

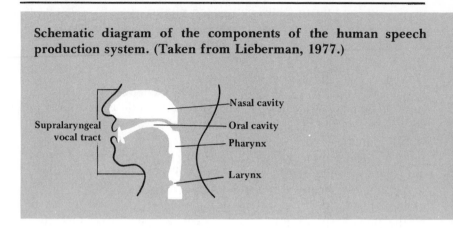

Schematic diagram of the components of the human speech production system. (Taken from Lieberman, 1977.)

Supralaryngeal vocal tract

Nasal cavity

Oral cavity

Pharynx

Larynx

mentary form. Some other fossil remains (e.g., the Steinheim fossil), however, do reflect development which would permit the vowel vocalizations studied, while still other fossil remains (Broken Hill or Rhodesian Man) represent an intermediate position between the earlier and the later developmental levels. Thus, there seems to be evidence of an evolutionary continuum to present structures.

Establishment of this apparent relationship between the anatomical characteristics and vocal speech is only one part of the development of language. Lieberman (1973, 1975), however, feels that it is an important part and fits very well with other data about prehistoric cultures, for example, which suggest that language developed gradually from one which initially combined a heavier reliance on gestures with vocalizations unlike those in present languages (perhaps phonetic symbolism was more important then). With the gradual evolution of cognitive abilities, automatization of articulatory movements and perceptual abilities, development of the supralaryngeal vocal tract anatomy, and specialized speech encoding and decoding, what we now know as human linguistic abilities developed in the relatively late stages of hominid evolution.

## NEUROANATOMICAL BASES OF LANGUAGE

Lieberman has attempted to reconstruct the past and the evolutionary development of language by comparing fossil remnants with present forms. While it is clear that the surpralaryngeal vocal tract is important to language, we must also look to the brain as an important biological support to language. In the case of contemporary humans, we can, under some circumstances, examine the structures of the brain itself which, unfortunately for those interested in evolution, disintegrates more rapidly than the skull. Our knowledge of the brain's relation to language has come from diverse sources including clinical cases of individuals who have suffered brain injuries resulting in language impairment, patients with so-called split-brain operations, electroencephalogram recordings, and research using dichotic listening tasks.

The accumulation of information from these sources has led us from the naive brain-function geography of phrenology, in which each lump on the head was believed to be associated with a particular mental faculty, to a much more sophisticated conception of brain-function relations. Yet, as we shall see, we are still very much in the dark about how our brains relate to our behaviors.

Throughout the history of inquiry into this area there has been a continuing argument which has centered about the question of whether the brain operates as a single unified whole or is composed of localized units which control various aspects of behavior. With respect to language functions at least, the localization theory had its beginnings with a series of reports given in Paris by Broca in 1861. The first of these, translated by Kann (1950), reflects Broca's efforts to refute the misconception of phrenology that language functions are located in parts of the brain behind the eyebrow and, at the same time, argues against a theory of the unity of the nervous system. Broca, who was an anthropologist and surgeon, used as evidence for his initial proposal of localized function the aphasic behavior of an epileptic patient whose disease had resulted in a lesion in one of the convolutions of the anterior lobe of the left hemisphere. Loss of speech occurred at age 30 but otherwise the patient seemed quite normal at that time. He communicated by the expression "tan-tan," which was his only speech, supplemented by hand gestures. Subsequently, further deterioration led to paralysis and loss of the senses on the right side of the body. Broca concluded cautiously that particular faculties are located in particular lobes of the brain or, more likely, in particular convolutions of the brain. In light of the autopsy results and his patient's speech, Broca argued that spoken language is controlled by either the second or more probably the third convolution of the frontal lobe. Numerous case studies since Broca's report have provided enough support for the syndrome he described for that particular part of the brain to come to be called *Broca's area*. Patients with productive speech impairments are often described as having Broca's aphasia.

A few years after Broca's report, Wernicke (1874) reported a different kind of language difficulty associated with a lesion in a different area of the brain. While Broca's area is located toward the anterior portion of the left hemisphere near the area of the motor cortex, Wernicke's area is located more toward the posterior part of the left hemisphere near the auditory cortex. In contrast to Broca's patient, who could comprehend but not produce speech, Wernicke's aphasia is characterized by the ability to produce speech but an inability to comprehend speech. The speech that is produced seems to be normal except that it is often difficult to interpret the meaning. These patients appear to have a message to convey but they fail to use correct words. Sometimes they substitute related words, but at other times, they substitute unrelated words or phrases. In addition, sound or phoneme substitution in words adds to the difficulty of comprehending their speech.

As Geschwind (1970) pointed out, Wernicke's major contribution was his proposal of how the brain is organized with respect to the language areas. Noting that Broca's area is located adjacent to that part of the cortex which controls the muscles involved in speech, he suggested that Broca's area must coordinate the speech-production functions of language. Wernicke's area, on the other hand, lies adjacent to the cortical region that receives auditory stimulation and, therefore, must coordinate the receptive aspects of language. Furthermore, Wernicke proposed that the two areas must be connected, a fact which has subsequently been verified.

In addition, Wernicke noted that comprehension of written language seems to be associated with an area behind but connected with Wernicke's area and adjacent to the visual cortex. He postulated a writing center near the motor cortex area but separate from Broca's area. Support for the latter contention was later provided by Exner after whom the writing area is named. Thus, there appear to be localized areas in the brain, located near the areas associated with motor control of the vocal tract and the hands and arms respectively, that control speaking and writing, and other localized areas in the brain that control the comprehension of vocal and written language. The relative positions of these localities may be seen in Figure 2–4 which is a schematic diagram of the left hemisphere.

Acceptance of the localization theory, however, has been resisted by many other prominent researchers in the field. Hughlings Jackson, who was a contemporary of Broca, while not denying that Broca's area was often damaged in motor aphasia cases, argued that language is a psychological rather than a physiological function and that the brain operates as a functional unit. Jackson thus clearly separated mind and body and stressed that "to locate the damage which destroys speech and to locate speech are two different things" (Jackson, 1915). Henry Head (1926), an English neurologist, argued along similar lines that the destruction of brain tissue is likely to result in interference with specific forms of behavior but the reaction that follows is an expression of the organism as a whole adjusting to the new situation. A lesion in the brain, like a break in a railroad track, disrupts service

**Figure 2-4**

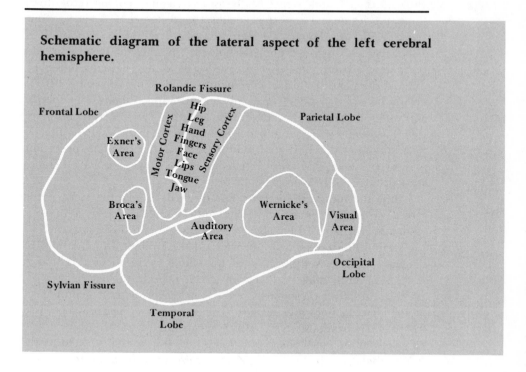

Schematic diagram of the lateral aspect of the left cerebral hemisphere.

but it does not locate the speech center. One of the most extreme opponents of the localization theory has been Kurt Goldstein (1948) whose organismic theoretical orientation emphasizes the organism as a whole and relates all specific behaviors to the concept of a functioning whole organism. The brain, of course, plays a part in the functioning total organism but Goldstein's only concession to localization is that excitation of the entire cortex may not be the same throughout all areas for each kind of behavior. Injuries lead to differentiation, or disintegration as Jackson called it, of the total brain function. Most recently, Lenneberg (1967) has argued strongly for the whole brain theory. Specifically, he notes ". . . it is not possible to assign any specific neuroanatomic structures to the capacity for language. However, this capacity may be due to structural innovations at the molecular level. Language is probably due to the particular way in which the various parts of the brain work together or, in other words, to its particular function" (p. 72).

Eisenson (1957) summarized the arguments that oppose the localization theory: (1) patients who suffer similar lesions do not always exhibit the same defect; (2) the same defects may be associated with lesions in different parts of the brain; (3) symptoms other than those with which a lesion is specifically associated may not be recognized; (4) autopsies do not consistently substantiate the pathological predictions of localizationists; (5) the various effects of brain pathology associated with physical and psychological premorbid factors are not taken into account; (6) psychological tests among patients presumed to have the same cortical involvements do not show consistent defects on psychological tests; (7) patients with presumed damage to specific and different areas of the brain are not differentiated through tests. Lenneberg adds other arguments including the evidence that there is no histological differentiation within parts of the cerebral cortex nor is there evidence that cortico-thalamic fiber-connections have demonstrated language specificity.

Still the localizationists are not quieted, as may be seen in the recent papers by Geschwind (1970) and Whitaker (1971). Whitaker, while appreciative of Lenneberg's scholarly effort to bring together all the various kinds of evidence bearing on the biological foundations of language, disagrees strongly with his whole brain theory. Whitaker notes four subsystems of language which include the tactile, verbal, graphic, and acoustic signal systems. He then proposes a neurological model that distinguishes between competence and performance (see Chapter 1) based on the central versus peripheral control of the language subsystems. The distinction allows him a sophisticated localization theory embedded within the framework of a brain conceptualized as an integrated network. Thus, he argues, one must be careful in the analysis of an adult with, say, the inability to write his or her name. Such a behavioral manifestation may result from (1) a nonlanguage, tactile system deficit, such as damage to the motor nerves of the hand; (2) a defect in the motor nerves that control the writing subsystem of language, which is a performance deficit; or, finally, (3) damage to the central language system, which is a competence deficit. One would not expect persons in the first case to have any other impairment, and, in fact, they should be able to write their names with the other hand. People with the second type of disorder should be able to say their names and recognize their own name when it is spoken although they cannot write it. In the third case, however, individuals would be unable to use their names correctly in any way. Thus, Whitaker seems able to bring within one theoretical system the relatively consistent findings of many clinical cases which suggest localization and at the same time to account for many of the objections of the whole brain theorists. In fact, at times he sounds a bit like Hughlings Jackson with more emphasis on the importance of lesion data and less on the mind-body distinction. While an integrated network of subsystems seems a reasonable framework within which to relate language to brain, at the moment we should not be too quick to take a strong stance on any position for the evidence is far from complete. It will be some time before a clear picture emerges.

## LATERALIZATION OF BRAIN FUNCTIONS

Regardless of where one stands on the localization issue, however, there is one aspect of localization on which everyone is in general agreement. Language functions seem to be controlled primarily by the left hemisphere of the brain. As Giannitrapani (1967) has noted in tracing the development of the concept of lateralization of cerebral functions, the relationship between the fact that injuries to the left side of the head affect the right side of the body and are associated with aphasia has been observed since the time of Hippocrates. Only rarely does it happen that injuries to the right hemisphere result in language impairment. According to Geschwind (1970), 97 percent of language impairment cases result from injuries to the left hemisphere. The right hemisphere, in contrast, seems to be more related to spatial tasks, visual and tactile discriminations, and music perception. With respect to the latter, it is frequently noted that aphasics with left hemisphere damage who cannot speak more than a word or two may be able to sing a melody with no difficulty.

Investigation of the lateralization phenomenon has revealed a variety of interesting insights to brain function and language. In addition to the clinical studies which consistently show language impairment only with left hemisphere injuries, studies of split-brain patients have provided other relevant information. These studies have been conducted by Sperry (1968) and his colleagues on patients who have had the two hemispheres of their brains disconnected through surgical severing of the corpus callosum. The operations were performed to control severe epilepsy unresponsive to medication. The operation essentially results in a separation of the two halves of the brain so that the person functions, in some senses, with two almost independent minds.

It is important to note that the operation does not seem to have any particular obvious effect on the everyday behavior of the individual. Only under special testing conditions does the effect of the separation of the hemispheres become evident. However, when sensory input is transmitted only to one hemisphere, which is not normally the case, it is apparent that the other hemisphere is not aware of that input in these patients. For example, the retina of the eye is vertically divided so that the left half of the visual field of both eyes is connected to the right hemisphere and the right half of the visual field to the left hemisphere. Thus, both eyes send some information to both hemispheres and since there is an overlap in the visual field of the two eyes and interconnections between the two hemispheres, both parts of the brain in normal persons receive all of the sensory input. In the case of the split-brain patient, the same result is ordinarily achieved through eye movements which compensate for the lack of interhemispheric communication and retinal transmission. However, if patients are presented the visual material in such a way that only one hemisphere receives the sensory input, then the other hemisphere is completely unaware of it. This becomes most obvious when, for example, the name of an object is flashed to the right half of the visual field and thus to the left hemisphere. Under these circumstances, the patients can readily identify the word by speaking or writing it. When the same word is flashed in the left visual field and thus to the right hemisphere, the patients deny seeing anything. They behave as if they were blind or *agnosic* (have lost their ability to recognize familiar objects) when the printed language message goes to the right hemisphere. But if the patients are asked to point to a picture or object matching the word, they will do so correctly despite the fact they have just denied seeing it. Similarly, objects placed in the right hand and out of sight are easily identified by name but objects placed in the left hand cannot be so identified. In the latter case, however, the object may be identified by touch when placed among other objects in a grab bag. To further emphasize the separation, it should be noted that objects identified by one hand cannot be identified by the other. The main point for our purposes is that tests which involve language require the left hemisphere to be brought into play. Although some very simple language comprehension and production has been evidenced by these patients using the right hemisphere, the main language center, for both vocal and written language, is in the left hemisphere. Mathematical calculations also seem to be done in the left hemisphere. Spatial construction and nonverbal ideation seems to take place primarily in the right hemisphere.

A second experimental method which has indicated lateralization of language functions in the brain involves recording the electrical activity of the two hemispheres during language processing. For example, Wood, Goff, and Day (1971) placed electrodes on their subjects at comparable points on the two sides of the skull corresponding to the language processing areas of the left hemisphere. The subjects were required to monitor the syllables /ba/ and /da/, indicating in one task whether a high or a low /ba/ occurred or, in the other task, whether a /ba/ or a /da/ occurred. In the first task, it was assumed that a nonlinguistic decision was being required because the differences in fundamental frequency of a syllable used to produce the high and low /ba/ are phonemically irrelevant in English. In the second task, a linguistically important phonemic distinction between the acoustic cues of formant transition was required. Examination of the auditory-evoked electrical responses during the two tasks revealed that an equal amount of electrical activity occurred in both hemispheres during the task which did not require linguistic analysis, but significantly greater activity occurred in the left than in the right hemisphere when linguistically relevant decisions were required. Thus, it would appear that different neural events occur in the two hemispheres during linguistic processing of this sort and that the left hemisphere is specialized for this purpose. Another interesting aspect of this specialization was reported by Papcun, Krashen, and Terbeck (1971) who found that Morse code was processed primarily in the left hemisphere by trained personnel while little or no asymmetry was evident in naive subjects. In other words, not until Morse code is processed as a language code as opposed to a series of dots and dashes does the left hemisphere become differentially involved.

The latter finding suggests that perhaps the asymmetric functioning of the brain may develop as the child acquires language. Lenneberg (1967), in fact, argued that this is the case. Noting that language is lateralized in the left hemisphere and that language does not seem to be affected by left hemisphere lesions which occur prior to age two (Basser, 1962), Lenneberg suggested that lateralization of function is not present at birth and develops sometime after age two when language is rapidly developing.

Lenneberg's hypothesis, however, seems to be contradicted by Molfese, Freeman, and Palermo (1975), who obtained auditory-evoked responses from infants, school-aged children, and adults to speech and nonspeech stimuli. The stimuli included words, syllables, a piano chord, and a mechanically produced noise. All the subjects merely listened to the stimuli while their auditory-evoked potentials were recorded from both sides of the skull at approximately the location of Wernicke's area on the left side. The infants ranged in age from one week to ten months of age. The results indicated clear hemispheric differences at all ages. Speech stimuli produced greater auditory-evoked responses in the left hemisphere. Most surprising was the evidence that the differential hemispheric responding decreased with age—the infants showed the greatest lateralization effects. Thus, the specialization of the left hemisphere for language functions appears to be present long before any of the usual evidences of language appear. More recent research using the evoked potential measure has both verified the differential hemispheric responsivity of infants to speech and nonspeech stimuli and the decrease in differential responding with age (Molfese, Nunez, Seibert, & Ramanaiah, 1976). We will discuss these findings again in Chapters 3 and 6.

Finally, in this section we should take note of the dichotic listening studies which add further support to the lateralization evidence.

The technique developed by Broadbent (1954) essentially involves placing headphones on a subject and presenting two signals at the same time, one signal to the left ear and a different signal to the right ear. The subjects are required to indicate what they hear. For example, Kimura (1964) presented her subjects with either pairs of digits, one to each ear, or pairs of melodies. The task was to recall the digits or identify the two melodies from a set of four. Kimura's results indicated that significantly more digits presented to the right ear were correctly recalled while significantly more melodies presented to the left ear were correctly identified. Kimura concludes not only that speech perception is a left hemisphere function but that melody perception is a right hemisphere function.

Kimura's research (1967) led Shankweiler and Studdert-Kennedy (1967) to somewhat more specific testing of the lateralization effects. They compared presentations of consonant-vowel (CV) syllable pairs such as /ba/ and /da/, and steady-state vowel pairs such as /a/ and /i/ to the two ears. Their results showed the ear effect for the syllables but no effect for the vowels. Their account of these results suggests that vowels in their steady-state form are halfway between speech and music and thus no ear superiority was demonstrated. On the other hand, the CV syllables engaged the speech mode associated with the left hemisphere, resulting in a right ear superiority. In later research, when vowel discriminations were made in the context of words, such as "bit" versus "bet" (Studdert-Kennedy & Shankweiler, 1970), or in unfavorable listening conditions, such as high noise level (Weiss & House, 1973), then a right ear advantage was demonstrated for vowels as well as consonants. However, the lateralization effects for vowels are consistently smaller than for consonants. The relatively steady-state nature of vowels relative to the transitional properties of consonants (see Chapter 3) may account for the differences between vowels and consonants in engaging the left hemisphere in dichotic listening tasks.

It should be made clear in this discussion that language material entering the left ear is perceived. This is clearly evidenced by the blending or fusion which occurs when, say, "pay" is put in one ear and "ray" in the other and the subject reports hearing "pray" (e.g., Cutting, 1973). The difference between the ears is a relative one in which the right ear (left hemisphere) is more efficient for speech stimuli. While it is not clear why there are such reliable ear effects, it seems likely to be related to the fact that the right ear has direct connections with the left hemisphere while the left ear input must take a longer, indirect route to the left hemisphere. The indirect route probably results in some degradation of the signal during transmission or in some decay while waiting for the right ear input to be processed in the left hemisphere in the dichotic listening situation (Studdert-Kennedy & Shankweiler, 1970). Pisoni (1975), however, has argued that such delays and degradation of the left ear input occur at the auditory rather than the phonetic processing level, suggesting that the account of these phenomena may turn out to be more complicated than currently suspected.

Thus, the dichotic listening research provides yet further evidence that the left hemisphere of the human brain is especially constructed to deal with language. There are a few other bits of information we should mention before leaving this topic. We have noted that there is a right ear advantage in dichotic listening which leads to interference or fusion with left ear input, and that other kinds of sound stimuli (e.g., music) have a left ear advantage. Day and Bartlett (1971) raised the question of the effects of putting speech in one ear and nonspeech in the other. The answer is that nothing happens. Errors occur when two speech stimuli are presented dichotically but not when speech and nonspeech stimuli are presented, adding further to the interpretation that speech and nonspeech stimuli are processed in different parts of the brain. Next it should be noted that in our common everyday experiences we perceive speech at a rate of ten or more phonemes per second, a far greater rate than that at which Morse code or any other nonspeech signal can be analyzed. When it comes to language, we humans seem to have special talents that are tied very closely to the functioning of the left hemisphere.

## SUMMARY

In this chapter we have analyzed the nature of animal communication and noted how animal "languages" differ from human language. While animals do convey messages to each other, it is clear that there are species-specific, finite limits to those messages. Lower animals do not generate new and appropriate messages when the occasion arises. Some animals can be taught to expand their communicative capabilities. Humans have, for example, been able to teach dogs to respond appropriately to a variety of commands. More impressive, however, have been the recent achievements of the chimpanzees Washoe and Sarah who have learned to communicate with people via sign language and symbolic objects. While it has been hard work for both the animal learners and the human teachers in these experiments, the achievements of the chimpanzees have been much greater than expected although hardly comparable to the human use of the symbolic language system which is acquired so naturally by children.

Our discussion of evolutionary development suggests that early hominid forms were structurally incapable of language. Their supralaryngeal vocal tracts were similar to those of present-day apes. The modifications in the supralaryngeal tract, along with the other physiological and neurological changes which allowed language to develop, probably evolved long after an evolutionary branching which separated human from ape. Thus, although the apes are our closest phylogenetic relatives, there is little likelihood that ape and human are closely related with respect to symbolic function.

Finally, we have noted the neuroanatomical bases of language. In particular, we have reviewed the data from brain-injured patients, split-brain patients, evoked-potential research, and dichotic listening studies, all of which point to the lateralization of brain function such that the left hemisphere appears to be much more intimately involved with language functions than the right hemisphere. The theoretical accounts of the relation between brain function and brain organization remain, however, a matter of considerable controversy.

## REFERENCES

Basser, L. S. Hemiplegia of early onset and the faculty of speech with special reference to the effects of hemispherectomy. *Brain*, 1965, *88*, 227–60.

Bellugi, U., & Klima, E. S. Aspects of sign language and its structure. In J. F. Kavanagh & J. E. Cutting (Eds.), *The role of speech in language*. Cambridge, Mass.: M.I.T. Press, 1975. Pp. 171–203.

Broadbent, D. E. The role of auditory localization in attention and memory span. *Journal of Experimental Psychology*, 1954, *47*, 191–96.

Brown, R. W. *Words and things*. Glencoe: Free Press, 1958.

Brown, R. W. *A first language: The early stages*. Cambridge, Mass.: Harvard University Press, 1973.

Chomsky, N. *Language and mind*. New York: Harcourt, Brace & World, 1968.

Cutting, J. E. Phonological fusion in synthetic and natural speech. *Haskins Laboratories Status Report on Speech Research*, SR–33, 1973, 19–27.

Day, R. S., & Bartlett, J. C. Separate speech and nonspeech processing in dichotic listening. *Haskins Laboratories Status Report on Speech Research*, SR–28, 1971, 93–102.

Eisenson, J. Correlates of aphasia in adults. In L. E. Travis (Ed.), *Handbook of speech pathology*. New York: Appleton-Century-Crofts, 1957, 450–67.

Fouts, R. Communication with chimpanzees. In H. Kurth & I. Eibl-Eibesfeld (Eds.), *Hominisation and behavior*. Stuttgart, Germany: Gustav Fischer Verlag, 1975. Pp. 137–58.

Fouts, R. S., Mellgren, R. L., & Lemmon, W. B. *American Sign Language in the chimpanzee*. Presented at the Midwestern Psychological Association Meetings in Chicago, 1973.

Frisch, K. von. *The dancing bees: An account of the life and senses of the honey bee*. London: Methuen, 1954.

Frisch, K. von. *The dance language and orientation of bees* (translated by L. T. Chadwick). Cambridge, Mass.: Harvard University Press, 1967.

Gardner, R. A., & Gardner, B. T. Teaching sign language to a chimpanzee. *Science*, 1969, *165*, 664–72.

Gardner, B. T., & Gardner, R. A. Two-way communication with an infant chimpanzee. In A. Schrier & F. Stollnitz (Eds.), *Behavior of nonhuman primates* (Vol. 4). New York: Academic Press, 1971, 117–84.

Geschwind, N. Language and the brain. *Science*, 1970, *170*, 940–47.

Giannitrapani, D. Developing concepts of lateralization of cerebral functions. *Cortex*, 1967, *3*, 353–70.

Goldstein, K. *Language and language disturbances*. New York: Grune & Stratton, 1948.

Hayes, K. J., & Hayes, C. Intellectual development of a home-raised chimpanzee. *Proceedings of the American Philosophical Society*, 1951, *95*, 105–9.

Head, H. *Aphasia and kindred disorders of speech* (2 vols.). London: Cambridge University Press, 1926.

Hockett, C. D. The origin of speech. *Scientific American*, 1960, *203*, 89–96.

Hodos, W., & Campbell, C. B. G. *Scala Naturae:* Why there is no theory in comparative psychology. *Psychological Review*, 1969, *76*, 337–50.

Jackson, J. H. Hughlings Jackson on aphasia and kindred affections of speech, together with a complete bibliography of his publications on speech and a reprint of some of the more important papers. *Brain*, 1915, *38*, 1–190.

Kann, J. A translation of Broca's original article on the location of speech centers. *Journal of Speech and Hearing Disorders*, 1950, *15*, 16–20.

Kellogg, W. N., & Kellogg, L. A. *The ape and the child*. New York: McGraw-Hill, 1933.

Kimura, D. Left-right differences in the perception of melodies. *Quarterly Journal of Experimental Psychology*, 1964, *16*, 355–58.

Kimura, D. Functional asymmetry of the brain in dichotic listening. *Cortex*, 1967, *3*, 163–78.

Lanyon, W. E., & Tavolga, W. N. (Eds.), *Animal Communication*. Washington, D.C.: American Institute of Biological Sciences, 1958.

Lenneberg, E. H. *Biological foundations of language*. New York: Wiley, 1967.

Lieberman, P. On the evolution of language: A unified view. *Cognition*, 1973, *2*, 59–94.

Lieberman, P. The evolution of speech and language. In J. F. Kavanagh and J. E. Cutting (Eds.), *The role of speech in language*. Cambridge, Mass.: M.I.T. Press, 1975. Pp. 83–106

Lieberman, P. *Speech physiology and acoustic phonetics*. New York: Macmillan, 1977.

Lieberman, P., Crelin, E. S., & Klatt, D. H. Phonetic ability and related anatomy of the newborn, adult human, Neanderthal man and the chimpanzee. *American Anthropologist*, 1972, *74*, 287–307.

Lieberman, P., Klatt, D. H., & Wilson, W. A. Vocal tract limitations on the vowel repertoires of Rhesus monkey and other nonhuman primates. *Science*, 1969, *164*, 1185–87.

Lilly, J. C. *Man and dolphin*. New York: Doubleday, 1961.

Lilly, J. C. Distress call of the bottlenose dolphin: Stimuli and evoked behavioral responses. *Science*, 1963, *139*, 116–18.

Lindaver, M. *Communication among social bees*. New York: Atheneum, 1967.

Lorenz, K. Z. *King Solomon's ring*. New York: Thomas Y. Crowell Co., 1952.

Marler, P. Birdsong and speech development: Could there be parallels? *American Scientist*, 1970, *58*, 669–73.

Molfese, D., Nunez, V., Seibert, S. M., & Ramanaiah, N. V. Cerebral asymmetry: Changes in factors affecting its development. In S. R. Harnad, H. D. Steklis, & J. Lancaster (Eds.), *Origins and evolution of language and speech*. New York: New York Academy of Sciences, 1976. Pp. 821–33.

Molfese, D. L., Freeman, R. B., Jr., & Palermo, D. S. The ontogeny of brain lateralization for speech and nonspeech stimuli. *Brain and Language*, 1975, *2*, 356–68.

Papcun, G., Krashen, S., & Terbeck, D. Is the left hemisphere specialized for speech, language, or something else? *UCLA Working Papers in Phonetics* (Vol. 19). 1971.

Pfungst, O. *Clever Hans, the horse of Mr. von Oste.* In R. Rosenthal (Ed.), New York: Holt, Rinehart & Winston, 1965.

Pisoni, D. B. Dichotic listening and processing phonetic features. In F. Restle, R. M. Shiffrin, N. J. Lindman, & D. Pisoni (Eds.), *Cognitive Theory* (Vol. 1). Hillsdale, N.J.: Lawrence Erlbaum, 1975. Pp. 79–102.

Premack, D. Language in chimpanzee? *Science,* 1971a, *172,* 808–22.

Premack, D. On the assessment of language competence in the chimpanzee. In A. M. Schrier & F. Stollnitz (Eds.), *Behavior of nonhuman primates* (Vol. 4). New York: Academic Press, 1971b, 186–228.

Premack, D. *Intelligence in ape and man.* New York: Holt, Rinehart & Winston, 1975.

Rumbaugh, D. M., & Gill, T. V. The mastery of language-type skills by the chimpanzee. In S. R. Harnad, H. D. Steklis, & J. Lancaster (Eds.), *Origins and evolution of language and speech.* New York: New York Academy of Sciences, 1976. Pp. 562–78.

Shankweiler, D. P., & Studdert-Kennedy, M. Identification of consonants and vowels presented to left and right ears. *Quarterly Journal of Experimental Psychology,* 1967, *19,* 59–63.

Sperry, R. W. Hemisphere deconnection and unity in conscious awareness. *American Psychologists,* 1968, *23,* 715–22.

Stokoe, W. C., Jr. The shape of soundless language. In J. F. Kavanagh & J. E. Cutting (Eds.), *The role of speech in language.* Cambridge, Mass.: M.I.T. Press, 1975. Pp. 207–28.

Studdert-Kennedy, M., & Shankweiler, D. Hemispheric specialization for speech perception. *Journal of the Acoustical Society of America,* 1970, *48,* 579–94.

Warden, C. J. The ability of "Fellow," famous German shepherd, to understand language. *Journal of Genetic Psychology,* 1928, *35,* 330–31.

Weiss, M. S., & House, A. S. Perception of dichotically presented vowels. *Journal of the Acoustical Society of America,* 1973, *53,* 51–58.

Wenner, A. M. Sound communication in honey bees. *Scientific American,* April 1964, *210,* 116–24.

Wernicke, C. Der aphasische symptomencomplex. *Eine psychologische studie auf anatomischer basis.* Breslau: Cohen & Weigert, 1874.

Whitaker, H. A. *On the representation of language in the human brain.* Edmonton, Alberta: Linguistic Research, Inc., 1971.

Wood, C. C., Goff, W. R., & Day, R. S. Auditory evoked potentials during speech perception. *Science,* 1971, *173,* 1248–51.

# The Sound System
# of
# Language

All of us have had the experience of seeing the flash of a cannon or skyrocket and a short time later hearing the sound. The explanation of the differential time between seeing and hearing rests on the difference in the rates at which the waves of light and sound travel. While we are familiar with that explanation, we often forget that different speech sounds are merely variations in the waves of air produced by the vocal tract of the speaker and impinging on the eardrums of the listener. Thus, in examining the sound system of language, we can approach the problem either by looking at the characteristics of the wave forms or by looking at (perhaps "listening to" is a better term) the nature of the sounds which are in the head. And, of course, since we brought it up, these are the two major approaches to the study of language sounds. Analysis of wave forms is called *acoustic phonetics* and analysis of sounds in the head is called *phonology*.

Notice that in the case of acoustic phonetics we are studying a physical phenomenon: the variations in air pressure produced by vocal tract movements and the consequent movements of the flexible membrane in the ear which is affected by such changes in air pressure. In the second case, however, we are concerned with the psychological problem of what goes on in the human head that enables us to make the appropriate wave forms emanate from the vocal tract and to analyze the wave forms coming to the eardrums in a manner which allows us to hear phonemes, syllables, words, and sentences. When you think about it this way, a paradox becomes immediately apparent. We hear discrete, specific sounds, such as the /m/, /a/, /n/ sounds which make up the word "man" or, if you wish, the /man/ sound that makes up the word "man" in the sentence "The man knelt." The paradoxical part of this phenomenon is that we know that waves do not come in separate units: waves are continuously flowing movements. The question of

77

speech production and perception thus turns out to be the complicated problem of how a continuous flowing movement is converted to the series of segmented discrete units we call the sounds of language. We will look first at the acoustic characteristics of speech and then at the linguistic characteristics of those acoustic forms.

## THE ACOUSTICS OF SPEECH SOUNDS

Lest you be amazed that you had not thought before now about the wave form-speech sound paradox, let me hasten to add that many people who became interested in this problem were initially almost as naive. This becomes clear when you read of the various efforts to construct reading machines for the blind (e.g., Liberman & Cooper, 1969). Obviously, all the machine must do is convert each letter to its appropriate sound and then produce that sound. Since there are twenty-six letters in the alphabet, there must be twenty-six sounds. Therefore, since we have machines that can recognize letters and machines that can produce sounds, there should be no problem. As we shall see, this is a naive approach for we still do not know all the problems and we are only beginning to find the answers!

Let's begin with a few small problems and build to the larger ones. Consider the minor problem raised by George Bernard Shaw in a slightly different context. Shaw complained that the English sound-spelling correspondences are enough to drive a schoolboy (and this author) mad. Taking the 'gh' of "cough," the 'y' of "typical," and the 'ti' of "creation," one could then, by sound-letter correspondences of English, spell the word "ghyti" and pronounce it "fish." Add to that the difference in the pronunciation of the 'a' in "cat," "tale," and "tall," and the fact that the alphabet does not represent the sounds of the language becomes clear. You can make up a phonemic alphabet, which is not entirely satisfactory either, as we discussed in Chapter 1, but let's go on to other matters more germane to the acoustic signal.

The airwave pattern produced by a speaker which results in speech sounds heard by a listener is determined by air forced from the lungs past the vocal cords in the larynx, on through the pharynx, and out through the oral or nasal cavities. The vocal cords, or laryngeal valve, may be tightened so that when the air is pushed from the lungs, the vocal cords are forced to vibrate (open and close) at a rapid rate in the same way as the reed in a clarinet or a plucked violin string. Like the musical instrument, the vocal cords produce one fundamental frequency (vibration) and harmonics (overtones) of that fundamental frequency. Harmonics are whole number multiples of the fundamental frequency. The fundamental frequency and its harmonics, actually a buzzing sound at the initiating point, then pass through the vocal tract which acts as a resonator much like the body of the clarinet or violin. The resonator, as its name implies, resonates or reinforces certain specific frequencies of the fundamental and harmonics produced by the vocal cords. The particular frequencies that are reinforced, or increased in amplitude, depend on the size and shape of the vocal tract, just as the tones you can produce by blowing across the top of a bottle vary as a function of the size of the bottle. While the bottle resonates to a restricted set of frequencies, the vocal tract can respond to a broad range of frequencies because it can assume many sizes and shapes.

The particular resonances or bands of reinforced frequencies produced by the vocal tract in speech are referred to as formants. The first formant is the lowest frequency resonance, the second formant is the next highest frequency resonance, and so on. There may be as many as six or so such formants in speech although, as we shall see, we can ignore all but the first two or three for most purposes. The formant frequencies measured in cycles per second, called hertz or Hz, are determined primarily by the vocal tract and not by the fundamental and harmonics. Thus, while the fundamental is relatively high for a child (e.g., 300 Hz), lower for the average woman's voice (200 Hz), and still lower for the average man's voice (100 Hz), the relative shape of the vocal tract may be the same for all persons and thus, according to some theorists (e.g., Joos, 1948; Lieberman, 1973), the relations among the formant frequencies, though not the frequencies themselves, remain relatively the same across speakers regardless of the fundamental frequencies of the voices (see Shankweiler, Strange, & Verbrugge, 1975, for contrary evidence). Developmentally, the frequencies of the fundamental and the formants decrease with age, particularly from three to six years. These changes correlate with the rapid anatomical changes of the vocal tract during this period (Eguchi & Hirsh, 1969).

While we shall see that the problem becomes more complicated, the simplest view of acoustics is that all the particular sounds of any language are created by varying the shape and size of the vocal tract which, in turn, produces the particular wave associated with those sounds. All vowels, for example, have a characteristic formant structure created by a combination of raising and lowering the tongue in the front and back of the mouth, and changing the postion of the lips. Note, for instance, the obvious difference in the configuration of your vocal tract as you produce the vowel sound in the word "dad" as opposed to "dude." Other language sounds may be created by allowing the vocal chords to remain open and forcing air through other constrictions in the vocal tract. The initial sounds in the word "sue," "thin," and "fan" are formed by forcing air through small constrictions in the front of the vocal tract. In such cases, there is no fundamental and therefore no formants. Instead, we have a broad frequency range, or "noise," in which the energy or amplitude is spread fairly equally over that range. In other cases, sounds are formed by a combination of vocal cord pulsation or vibration and constriction, such as in the initial sounds of "zoo," "then," and "van."

Perhaps we have put the cart before the horse, however, for you may well be asking at this point how we know about the acoustic characteristics we have been describing. We can see and feel the changes in the vocal tract, but what of the waves that are so transitory and invisible? One way to see these waves is to hook a microphone to an oscilloscope and watch the sound converted to lines of lights. While we can see the light pattern as we speak (a technique sometimes used to teach the deaf how to produce sound differences), the picture of an oscilloscope is transitory too. The development of the speech spectrograph, however, gives us a clear, permanent picture of speech. Figure 3-1, for example, shows a picture of the sentence, "Joe took father's shoe bench out." On the vertical axis is represented the frequency range from the fundamental frequency (about 100 Hz) up to about 8000 Hz. The horizontal axis is the time dimension and the relative darkness of the record reflects the amplitude at the various frequencies. It is easy to see the formants as dark bands running more or less horizontally across the record. In addition, you can see places where there is a relatively equal spread of energy over a wide range of frequencies. Finally, you should note that there are no clear boundaries between sounds nor, for that matter, between words. The spectrogram shows the ebb and flow of the waves of air which we in turn hear as sounds and words in a sentence.

Figure 3–2 shows the steady-state form for the vowel sounds /a/ (as in "cat"), the /i/ (as in "see"), and the /u/ (as in "fool") which you will recall (Chapter 2) are the point vowels that define the vowel triangle. They were the vowels Liberman used as the test for his models of the supralaryngeal tracts of early human forms, chimpanzees, infants, and present-day humans. Notice how the relationships among the well-defined formants running parallel to the horizontal vary from vowel to vowel, thus defining the differences among the vowels. Note also the evidence of the other frequencies in the signal which are less well defined and of lesser intensity. Finally, compare Figure 3-2 with 3-1 and notice that the steady-state vowels in 3-2 have a flat formant structure and the formants of the vowels in continuous speech seem to bend up and down and have no definite steady state. We will refer to the latter phenomenon (transitions) again in discussing the relationship of consonant and vowel perception.

The question, of course, arises as to how we know that the formants and their relationships define the vowels. The answer has come through the development at the Haskins Laboratories (now located in Connecticut) of another piece of apparatus called the Pattern Playback. Basically, the Pattern Playback, or speech synthesizer, is the reverse of the speech

**Figure 3-1**

**Speech spectrograph of the sentence, "Joe took father's shoe-bench out." (Courtesy of Paul Zawadski and Robert Brubaker.)**

spectrograph. While the latter takes speech and converts it to a picture, the speech synthesizer takes a picture and converts it to sound. In fact, it is possible to create quite intelligible machine-produced artificial speech by painting a speech picture and feeding it on a sleeve into the Haskins Pattern Playback or PAT (Parametric Artificial Talker), as the speech synthesizer at the University of Edinburgh is somewhat affectionately called. More recent developments in speech synthesis have allowed the creation of speech by synthesizers through computer programs rather than the now old-fashioned technique of using painted speech sleeves.

It is this facility for creating speech "pictures" which the machine can speak that allows us to investigate the acoustic parameters important to the comprehension of speech, something we cannot do with natural speech. For example, we could paint a picture, quite like the speech spectrograph, to produce a vowel but omit one of the formants and thus, on the basis of what the machine says under these circumstances, establish what the import of the omitted formant is. This is precisely the way it was discovered that the first two formants carry most of the information necessary for the comprehension of vowels in speech. The rest of the signal adds only a small amount to the intelligibility of the vowel although it does add a good deal to the voice quality. Most of the research we will discuss here on the acoustic parameters of speech perception comes from the Haskins Laboratories where apparatus has been developed and a concentrated research effort has been focused on this problem. There are, of course, other laboratories, such as the one at the University of Edinburgh, which have also been working on these and related problems.

**Figure 3-2**

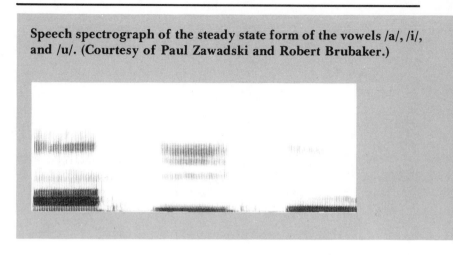

**Speech spectrograph of the steady state form of the vowels /a/, /i/, and /u/. (Courtesy of Paul Zawadski and Robert Brubaker.)**

Figures 3-1 and 3-2 represent connected discourse and single vowels, respectively. Connected discourse is too complicated to study because it involves many interrelated variables while single, isolated vowels, as we shall see, are too simple for most investigative purposes. Let's look for a moment, however, at what turns out to be a rather complex problem of consonant acoustics. Suppose we wished to know, for example, the acoustic properties of the consonant /d/. The first complication that arises is that there seems to be no isolatable acoustic entity which can be recognized as a /d/ by itself. That sounds preposterous, at first, but try to pronounce /d/ without pronouncing any other sound. You cannot do it because as soon as you release your tongue from the aveolar ridge in your mouth, a vowel of some sort comes sneaking out too. There is no /d/ or any other sound until you do release your tongue. However, if we use the speech synthesizer we might approach that /d/ in reverse. We could, for instance, take the word "do" and cut off the vowel sound to get the /d/ part alone. Figure 3–3 shows the spectrographic pattern for the word "do," showing the shape of the first and second formants which is all that is necessary to hear an intelligible version of the word "do" (Harris, Hoffman, Liberman, Delattre, & Cooper, 1958). You can see that at the beginning, for the first 50 milliseconds of the word, there is a tail on each of the formants. The tails are called transitions. There is a rising transition to the steady-state part of the first formant and a falling transition to the steady-state portion of the second formant. It would appear from what we know about vowels that all we need do is eliminate the steady-state part and we would have the /d/ sound. Unfortunately, that just does not happen. If, as has been done experimentally (see Liberman,

**Figure 3-3**

---

**Speech spectrograph of the syllable /da/. (Courtesy of Paul Zawadski and Robert Brubaker.)**

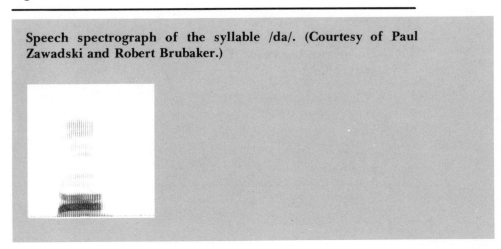

Cooper, Shankweiler, & Studdert-Kennedy, 1967), one cuts the right side of the artificial spectrographic pattern back gradually so there is less and less of the steady-state part, the sound eventually may have a discriminably shorter vowel duration but it is clearly heard as the consonant plus vowel word, "do." Finally, when the steady-state part has been eliminated, the speech sound suddenly changes to a nonspeech sound which consists of a rapidly rising and a rapidly falling whistle or glissando. The transitions seem to be only nonspeech whistles by themselves, but in combination with the steady-state formants they are heard as the consonant /d/ plus the vowel. In short, it is not possible to create a /d/ in isolation by machine any more than it is by the vocal tract. The same is true of the consonants /b/, /g/, /p/, /t/, /k/, /m/, /n/, and /ŋ/. (Liberman, Delattre, & Cooper, 1954).

The same phenomenon also occurs regardless of which vowel follows the consonant. But that raises another interesting point. Since each vowel is defined in terms of a different formant structure, and a consonant involves a transition into that formant structure, it follows that the structure of a single consonant must be different for each vowel which follows (or precedes) it. If you look at Figure 3–4, taken from Liberman, Cooper, Shankweiler, & Studdert-Kennedy (1967), which shows the spectrographic patterns for the phoneme /d/ plus seven different vowels, you can see that there is no single acoustic signal which is /d/. Very strange indeed, since we hear them all as /d/. Furthermore, the same holds true for all the other consonants mentioned above. The difference between the consonants with any particular vowel is in the form of the transitions to the steady-state vowels.

Look a little more closely now at Figure 3–4. Note first that most

**Figure 3-4**

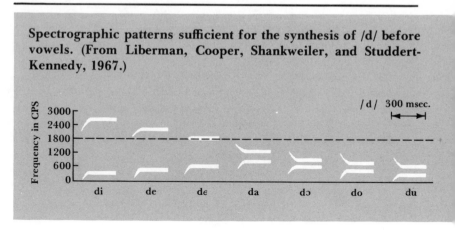

Spectrographic patterns sufficient for the synthesis of /d/ before vowels. (From Liberman, Cooper, Shankweiler, and Studdert-Kennedy, 1967.)

of the action comes in the second formant. The first formant transition is pretty much the same throughout and the frequency of the formant only moves up from about 300 Hz to about 700-800 Hz and then back down again. The second formant, however, moves steadily down from about 2500 Hz to about 600 Hz and the shape of the transition changes from rising to falling around 1800 Hz. It appears that the primary information conveyed by the first formant indicates that the preceding consonant is a voiced stop of some sort (e.g., /b/, /d/, /g/) (Delattre, Liberman, & Cooper, 1955). If the consonant were unvoiced (e.g., /p/, /t/, /k/), the first formant transition would be less pronounced (Liberman, Delattre, & Cooper, 1952) and the onset of the first formant would be delayed 20–30 milliseconds relative to the second formant (Liberman, Delattre, & Cooper, 1958; Liberman, Harris, Kinney, & Lane, 1961).

The information about which particular consonant precedes the vowel comes from the second formant. If we look at the structure of the second formant in Figure 3–4, it appears that the "locus" of /d/ is at 1800 Hz. That is, the transitions appear to emanate from 1800 Hz and move upward to the second formant for the vowels to the left of the figure and downward from 1800 Hz for the vowels to the right of the figure. There is no transition at all for the second formant at 1800 Hz. This suggested to Delattre, Liberman, and Cooper (1955) that 1800 Hz is where the second formant really begins for /d/. Therefore they constructed spectrographic representations in which the transition actually began at 1800 Hz and moved to the level appropriate for the following vowel. But when this was done the results were quite unexpected. The transitions to the highest-frequency formants resulted in a /b/, the transitions to the upper middle- and lowest-frequency formants were heard as /d/, and the transitions to low-middle formants were heard as /g/. Thus, while 1800 Hz may be the "locus" of /d/, it is not the case that the transitions begin at that frequency but, rather, only point to that frequency as their source. Furthermore, this whole line of research makes it clear that there is no acoustically specifiable /d/ independent of a vowel context. The same sort of contextual acoustic variation occurs for nearly every consonant in English. The phonemes /s/ and /š/, which occur in the initial positions of "sip" and "ship," for example, are about the only exceptions to this rule. While we have focused on variations in the second formant here, similar kinds of contextual variations also occur in the third formant (Harris, Hoffman, Liberman, Delattre, & Cooper, 1958) and in the range of the noise band caused by constrictions in the vocal tract as many of the other consonants are produced.

In sum, it becomes evident from an examination of the consonant sounds that every consonant has a different acoustic signal associated with every context in which it appears. There is no single physical stimulus which can be said to identify a particular consonantal speech sound. Furthermore, the differences between the acoustic signals of the same consonant in different contexts seem to be far larger in many cases than the differences between the acoustic signals of two different consonants in the same context. In fact, some of the transitions for different consonants are acoustically the same before different vowels. Finally, it should be pointed out that the transitions of a consonant preceding a vowel, as in the initial /d/ in "did," rise to the steady-state vowel but those for the second /d/ which follow the vowel fall from the steady-state vowel position. Thus, the same /d/ sound is produced by exactly opposite acoustic transitions.

The vowels, on the other hand, seem to have much more stability. More careful examination of the acoustic characteristics of vowels, however, demonstrates that the stability is more apparent than real. In isolation, vowels do have a characteristic acoustic form as evidenced in Figure 3–2. As pointed out by Shankweiler, Strange, and Verbrugge (1975), however, there are three factors which act to complicate the apparent simplicity of the isolated vowel when it is a part of speech. First, the coarticulation of the phonemes in a syllable frame makes it clear that the consonant environment in which the vowel occurs affects the acoustic properties of the vowel as well as the reverse, as discussed above. The duration, fundamental frequency, and formant frequencies and intensities of the same vowel are modified by the consonant context (Stevens & House, 1963). Second, the acoustic structure of the vowel is sensitive to the rate of speaking. Rapid speaking leads to what has been called articulatory "undershoot," which means that the articulators never quite reach the position for correct articulation of the vowel and, therefore, the steady-state configuration of the acoustic signal is never reached. This phenomenon can be seen in some of the vowels of Figure 3–1. Third, the vowels, of course, vary with the person speaking. Neither the absolute values nor the relations among the formants are related in any direct way between the speech of an adult and a child, for example. Thus, the acoustic characteristics of vowels are less complex than consonants only in a relative sense, if they can be isolated and compared at all.

Obviously these facts about the acoustic signal have implications for the way we produce and perceive speech. Clearly the production of a word cannot be the concatenation or simple linking of the separate sounds which make up that word. We cannot take an isolated /d/, add an isolated /i/, and then a /p/ and expect to produce the word /dip/. In fact, when this was tried with natural speech clips (Harris, 1953), the resulting sound group was unintelligible for the most part. It appears that the form of the initial sound will be determined by the second sound which in turn establishes the form of the third sound. In addition, it has been shown by physiological measures (see MacNeilage, 1970) that in producing a word like "dip," for example, the articulators actually begin to move to the position required for the last sound when the first sound is being produced. In other words, the production of a word is a complex, integrated sequence of movements which cannot be broken down either into the separate sound parts or separate physical movements.

## ACOUSTICS AND SPEECH PERCEPTION

Let's look now at the relation of these acoustic findings to some aspects of speech perception. First, although it is possible to make some discriminations among variants of /d/ (Barclay, 1972), we do not ordinarily discriminate any differences between the /d/ sounds preceding or following different vowels despite the large acoustic differences which are apparent. Like a rose, a /d/ is a /d/ is a /d/. But since a /d/ differs from a /g/ in terms of the second formant transition, we may ask the question of how our perception changes as the transition is changed. Suppose we were to vary the transition of the /d/ in small steps to the position which is appropriate to a /g/. This is a simple psychophysical experimental procedure which, if conducted with tones, would yield data indicating a gradual shift in judgments from one tone to the other with a middle area where we would have a great deal of difficulty judging which was which. In the case of speech, however, the results appear dramatically different. Instead of a gradual shift, there is a categorical shift. That is, the subjects report hearing either a clear /d/ or a clear /g/ and nothing in between (e.g., Eimas,

1963). The difference between /d/ and /g/ is one of place of articulation, i.e., the point where the tongue is placed to close the vocal tract, and similar categorical perception has been found for /b/ and /d/ (Liberman, Harris, Hoffman, & Griffith, 1957) which are also distinguished by place of articulation. The same kind of absolute identification and categorical discrimination has been found for consonants which differ in manner of articulation such as the voicing, or more technically, voice onset time, as exemplified by the difference between /t/ and /d/ (Liberman, Harris, Kinney, & Lane, 1961).

Not all speech sound discrimination functions yield categorical perception, however. Research with vowel sounds reveals that within-category discriminations are much more accurate for isolated vowels and between-category vowel boundaries are not sharp. In addition, absolute identification of vowels in isolation is much more difficult than when the vowels are in a consonantal context (Millar & Ainsworth, 1972). When vowels are presented for discrimination judgments in a language context, however, greater evidence for categorical perception becomes evident for vowels as well as consonants (Stevens, 1966).

The initial interpretation of these data (Liberman, Cooper, Shankweiler, & Studdert-Kennedy, 1967) was that categorical perception is unique to certain speech sounds when the speech mode is engaged. It is assumed that some special mechanisms are engaged to process speech differently than other auditory signals. Thus, when one processes sounds as speech, as opposed to processing vowels out of speech context, categorical perception of the linguistically relevant categories takes place. More recent work, however, has forced some rethinking of the hypothesis that speech is uniquely perceived. First, Pisoni and Tash (1974) have demonstrated that discriminations of acoustic variations can and are made within consonant categories when the appropriate measurement techniques are used. Second, Cutting and Rosner (1974) have demonstrated the same sort of categorical perception of plucked and bowed musical sounds. The latter sounds are differentiated on the basis of rise time to maximum amplitude similar to the difference in rise time of /ča/ and /ša/. Miller, Wier, Pastore, Kelly, and Dooling (1976) have shown similar categorical perception for noise-buzz distinctions. These findings suggest that categorical perception is not unique to speech and may lead to disposing of the concept of processing in the speech mode. How theoretical accounts of these new phenomena will be developed is not clear, but surely there will be an integration of theories of speech perception and theories of the perception of other acoustic signals.

Finally, it is of considerable interest to note that the same categorical perception of speech sounds is apparent in infants as young as one month of age (e.g., Eimas, Siqueland, Jusczyk, & Vigorito, 1971;

Trehub & Rabinovitch, 1972; Eimas, 1974; Lasky, Syrdal-Lasky, & Klein, 1975). Eimas et al., for example, have demonstrated that infants make discriminations between speech sounds that adults perceive as /p/ and /b/. The infants did not, however, discriminate between two forms of /p/, despite the fact that equally large acoustic differences were present in both cases. The distinction between /p/ and /b/ is one of manner of articulation. Eimas (1974) found similar results for two- and three-month-old infants for consonant stimuli varying in place of articulation. Trehub (1973) has also reported that detection of vowel differences is apparent in infants of the same age, although the procedures used did not reveal differential responsiveness to tone stimuli. Along with the Molfese, Freeman, and Palermo (1975) data on infant auditory-evoked potentials to speech stimuli, these data suggest that very young infants may be constructed in such a way as to be finely tuned to acoustic stimuli which have the characteristics of speech long before they produce speech themselves. On the other hand, the infant may be considerably less responsive to other auditory stimuli.

The results of the infant studies have led Eimas (1975) to suggest that the human organism comes equipped with linguistic feature detectors as a part of its inherent structure. Thus, speech perception is conceived as an excitation of detectors, analogous to detectors in the visual system, which respond in a relatively simple manner to the phonetic features of the linguistic information. Eimas and his colleagues have provided evidence for such detectors using a selective adaptation procedure with adult subjects. This procedure involves the repeated presentation of a speech sound assumed to affect a particular feature detector. Repetition of the sound is assumed to fatigue that detector, thus reducing its sensitivity. The reduced sensitivity would, in turn, influence the categorical perception of two sounds differing in terms of that feature. Eimas and Corbit (1973) first demonstrated this effect by testing for a voice onset time feature detector. Subjects were, for example, adapted by being presented with a /d/ or a /t/ repeatedly and then tested for their identification of /d/ and /t/ in the typical categorical perception paradigm. The results showed that the boundary between /d/ and /t/ shifted toward the adapted stimulus so that more identification judgments were classified as the unadapted stimulus. In short, the difference in voice onset time which distinguishes /d/ from /t/ had to be much larger or smaller, depending on the adapting stimulus, after adaptation in order for the usual categorical perception between the sounds to occur. The boundary between the two was shifted by the adaptation procedure. Furthermore, the same shift occurred for /b/ and /p/ after adaptation with /d/ or /t/, indicating that a general feature detector and not a particular phonetic distinction was involved. Eimas, Cooper, and Corbit (1973) demonstrated that the phenomenon is centrally rather than peripherally located by showing that adaptation in one ear and testing in the other yields similar effects. Cooper (1974) has also shown the effect for place of articulation features and Diehl (1976) has provided similar results for stops and continuants. Finally, Morse, Kass, and Turkienicz (1976) have obtained results with vowels which fit with the feature detector hypothesis. The relationship between linguistic feature detectors and the findings of Cutting and Rosner (1974) that musical sounds are categorically perceived has not been clearly worked out as yet (Cutting & Eimas, 1975). The fact that these sounds do show boundary shifts after selective adaptation, however, suggests that the feature detection theory cannot be conceived as language specific (Cutting, Rosner, & Foard, 1975).

This brief review of the acoustic properties of speech makes it abundantly clear that the airwaves we convert to speech are very complex and must require some special kind of coding mechanism in our heads which translates that complex set of stimuli into meaning-related speech sounds. Somehow we are able to convert that highly variant wave signal into a small set of sounds (about 44 sounds in English, according to Denes, 1963) which make up the words of our language. Somehow we are able to recognize those sounds as invariant in combination despite the fact that their various combinations are the result of variant acoustic signals. And somehow we are able to produce, via a set of variant muscular movements, those acoustic signals such that they are perceived by others as invariant speech components. Even the infant, long before the production process becomes manifest, seems to make at least some of the perceptual distinctions, both phonetic and intonational (Morse, 1972), which are important to speech while evidently ignoring other distinctions in the signal which are not relevant to speech. Before going into accounts of how the human organism may be able to do this, we shall turn to some of the evidence available on the acquisition of the phonological system by the young child.

## ACQUISITION OF THE PHONOLOGICAL SYSTEM

In Chapter 1 we discussed the way the linguist represents the sound system of language in terms of phonemes which are conceived as bundles of distinctive features. We can see now that those phonemes are based on an acoustic signal that shows no apparent direct relationship to many of the sounds we hear. The question immediately arises as to how the young child acquiring language is able to convert the variant, continuous flowing movements of the sound waves into recognizable categorical speech sounds and, in turn, produce sound waves others can perceive as speech sounds.

As we have noted above, the child seems capable of perceptual speech sound discrimination from early infancy. While more research needs to be done to determine the full nature of the infant's perceptual capabilities and the relation of perception to production, we will concentrate here on the way the child learns to produce speech sounds with only occasional further comments on speech perception.

The child's earliest sounds consist of a variety of cries which seem to be distinguishably different both in terms of spectrographic analyses and maternal differentiation (Lind, Truby, & Bosma, 1965), much as the cries of other animals may be distinguished and seem to reflect different states of the organism. Later, the infant coos in more contented states as well as cries in less contented states. At about six months of age and lasting into the beginnings of language, the child enters what is known as the babbling stage. During this period, it is reported (McCarthy, 1954) that the child can and does produce all the sounds that are made in all the languages of the world although it tends to produce more vowel than consonant sounds during this period (Chen & Irwin, 1946). This observation of productive capability suggests that not only can children make speech sound discriminations prior to the emergence of language but they also have the motoric capabilities of producing the sounds of language. If this is the case, the acquisition of language may depend more on factors related to general cognitive development than on variables associated specifically with speech production or perception. Before accepting this hypothesis without question, however, it should be pointed out that Lenneberg's (1967) spectrographic analysis of babbling indicates that these sounds do not have all the acoustic characteristics of true speech although adult observers may interpret the sounds as speech. Lenneberg's spectrographic records, however, seem to reflect a closer approximation to language than Shepard and Lane's (1968) analysis of earlier infant prebabbling sound production.

While we are discussing the specific sounds of the babbling period, we should also recognize the intonation contours which seem to be present during that time. Menyuk (1971) reported that Nakazima (1962) observed imitation of intonation in the utterances of six- to eight-month-old infants, followed at a later age by the spontaneous segmentation and intonation of babbling sequences. For example, some sequences are given a rising intonation, as if a question were being asked. Engel (1973) made similar comments about the babbling of his son. Tonkova Yampol'skaya (1973) also traced the development of intonation in the babbling period. Menyuk and Bernholtz (1969) found clear evidence for intonation contours of affirmative statements, imperatives, and questions in the one-word stage as well.

Thus, the babbling period seems to involve some sorts of preparatory development prior to the emergence of actual language. And yet the appearance of language seems to be preceded by a period of marked reduction in sound production followed by a systematic acqusition of the sound system of language which appears in many respects to ignore prior capabilities of producing all the language sounds. As Carroll (1960, p. 746) has put it, "It is as if the child starts learning afresh when he begins to learn to utter meaningful speech." The first language sounds to appear tend to be the reduplicated syllables "papa" or "mama" which, according to Jakobson (1962), is why these terms tend to be the nursery names of parents in a great many languages. More important, however, Jakobson's observations have led to a theory to account for the acquisition of the sounds of language (Jakobson, 1968).

Jakobson subscribes to and, in fact, was one of the earliest proponents of the distinctive feature analysis of the sound system. His theory of the acquisition of the phonological system by children therefore centers about the distinctions among features. Jakobson is not concerned with prelanguage utterances. His theory of phonological development, originally proposed in 1941 (translated in 1968) and extended in 1956 (Jakobson & Halle, 1956), applies after the period of silence when true language begins to appear. Furthermore, even as language begins, the child may make an "rrr" sound, for example, in the nonspeech context of running a toy truck long before making the feature distinctions necessary to incorporate the /r/ into the phonological system. Only when the child uses meaningful words does an active phonological system replace the unsystematic sounds that precede this stage of development.

Efforts have been made to use a distinctive feature approach to analyze the prelinguistic utterances of infants (Ringwall, Reese, & Markel, 1965), which is probably a methodological advance over trying to use a phonetic alphabet, but since most of the features used to differentiate babbling sounds are different from the features that are used to analyze language, it is not clear at this point how the results of that research will bear on language acquisition. Gruber (1973), however, has shown some systematic feature distinctions made in the babbling of one child on one day which may be worth following up. The study by Gruber, along with Weir's (1962) analysis of the child's vocal play in the crib after the onset of true language is evident, does suggest that the child is making efforts both during babbling and true speech to actively perfect the phonological system and feature contrasts through systematic practice. Perhaps there is more going on than we have yet detected. Further research will surely demonstrate previously undetected relationships between the two stages. Oller, Wieman, Doyle, and Ross (1976) have made a beginning in this direction by showing that babbled utterances reflect the phonetic elements and sequences which are most common in the production of meaningful speech when language begins. Thus, in addition to the clear evidences of perceptual differentiation of speech sounds, further research may be forthcoming to demonstrate production capacities directly related to the developing phonological system as well as the intonation contours evidenced in earlier research on babbled sequences.

Jakobson suggests that the child begins true speech by discriminating the features of the sounds used in the language he or she is acquiring. First, the child dichotomizes all sounds on the basis of one feature, giving one contrast between a group of sounds all considered alike because they are all plus on the relevant feature and a second group of sounds which are all minus on that feature. The child then adds features to the system, progressively separating the significant sounds until all the sounds of the language have been identified on the basis of their distinguishing features. In short, the child first divides the sounds in half on the basis of one feature, then further divides those sounds by a second feature, and so on. Jakobson points out that the acquisition of features in this manner implies that, since some feature differences are not made at various stages of development, there will be free variation among some sounds which contrast, or are in opposition, for the adult. For example, if the child has not acquired the voicing feature, then /p/ and /b/ may be freely alternated along with all other pairs of sounds distinguished only by this feature.

Jakobson further argues that there is an order in which the features will appear in the child's language, corresponding to the number of languages in the world which contain the feature. The most common or universal features will appear first and the features peculiar to a specific language last. In particular, Jakobson predicts that the initial language utterance will be /pa/, which from an articulatory and acoustic analysis consists of two sound elements that are polar opposites. The two constituents consist of the /p/ phoneme, in which the vocal tract is closed at the front end, and the /a/ phoneme in which the vocal tract is open as widely as possible at the front and narrowed at the back. The /p/ is a short burst of sound with no great concentration of energy in any frequency band; the /a/ is not limited in time and the energy is concentrated in a relatively narrow region of maximal aural sensitivity. This kind of utterance establishes the syllable, which is the elementary phonemic frame. The next predicted split is a consonant division on the basis of the grave-acute feature which contrasts /p/ with /t/ and subsequently differentiates /k/ from /t/. The nasal-oral feature may come in at about the same time as the /p/ and /t/ opposition, with /ma/ as the most likely syllable. Occasionally the first contrast involves the nasal bilabial /ma/ rather than the oral bilabial /pa/. The first vowel split occurs on what Jakobson calls the diffuse-compact feature, the compact /a/ contrasting with the diffuse /i/ and /u/. The /i/ and /u/ subsequently divide on the basis of the grave-acute feature. Thus, we find the vowel triangle defined before any of the other vowels within that triangular space appear.

We can see that, according to Jakobson, the development of speech sounds begins with the contrast between the optimal consonant and the optimal vowel, which is the maximal sound difference, and moves gradually to finer and finer distinctions in which the consonant sounds become more compact and more vowel-like and the vowel sounds become more diffuse and more consonant-like. The acquisition of the /l/ and /r/ sound distinction involves the finest gradations in English in that they are composed of both the vowel-like feature [+ vocalic] and the consonant-like feature [+ consonantal]. The attainment of this distinction indicates the end of the phonemic acquisition process in the English language.

Unfortunately, there is relatively little evidence bearing on Jakobson's theory at this time. Ervin-Tripp (1966) has reviewed some of the early research based primarily on scattered reports of individual children, and, in broad outline, there seems to be general support for the theory. Menyuk (1971) has reanalyzed some of the earlier normative evidence, reported additional research, and provided a comprehensive analysis of phonological development. She argues that the process of development of the phonological system represents a hierarchy of feature distinctions beginning with the consonant vowel distinction and followed by distinctions between speech sound sets including nasals, glides, stridents, and stops. Finally, distinctions are made among sounds within these sets, such as the /p/, /t/, /k/ distinctions within the stop set. Figure 3–5 shows a partial representation of this hierarchy taken from Menyuk who constructed it on the basis of Jakobson and Halle's theory (1956).

Menyuk has taken the research results of Irwin (1947), Wellman, Case, Mengert, and Bradbury (1931), and Snow (1964), all of whom used different techniques for obtaining data on phonological development, and shown that commonalities among the studies do emerge. The stops (e.g., p, t, k, b, d, g), nasals (e.g., m, n), and glides (e.g., w, h, y) are consistently found to be the earliest sounds to appear and are generally articulated correctly by age four. The voicing feature that distinguishes among stops also comes in early, but, contrary to the theory, it does not seem to be consistently applied across all stops at the same time. The sounds which are not mastered until after four years of age include the fricatives (e.g., v, s, z, š, ž) and liquids (e.g., l, r) which have in common the feature [+ continuant], and the affricates (e.g., č, j). The results of Menyuk's own research (1968a,b), involving comparisons of the phonological development of Japanese-

# Figure 3-5

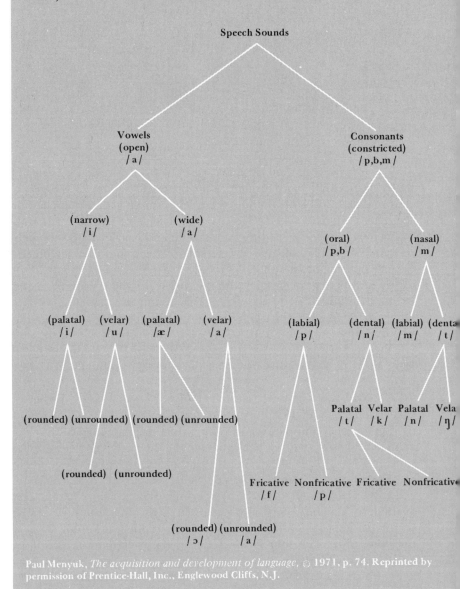

**Menyuk's schematization of an order of acquisition of speech sound distinctions with examples from English. (From Menyuk, 1971.)**

and English-speaking children, are quite comparable to the earlier studies which suggested the possible universal nature of phonological development. The features [+ nasal], [+ voice], and [+ grave] (the latter marked by closure at the peripheries of the oral cavity both front and back) are acquired early. Relative to these features [+ diffuse] (marked by closure at the midportion of the oral cavity), [+ strident] (marked by turbulence at the point of articulation), and [+ continuant] are acquired later. However, the acquisition process is rather complicated because there are interactions between the features and the task required of the child, the developmental level of the child, and among the features themselves. In the latter case, for example, the various combinations of the features continuant, strident, and grave vary considerably in difficulty and age of mastery. While sounds that involve the continuant feature seem most difficult, those which are [− continuant], [− strident] and [− grave] are more difficult than others. (See Table 1–1.)

Not only do we find contrasts interacting with other features present in a phoneme, we also find the difficulty of different feature configurations interacting with the context in which the sounds occur. We find, for example, that, as a general rule, phonemes occurring in the initial position of a word are least likely to be misarticulated while those at the end or in the middle of a word are most likely to be misarticulated (Templin, 1957). Templin's extensive developmental study of sound articulation indicates that most individual phonemes in English are correctly articulated in most positions by age five but there is considerably more difficulty in combining a series of consonants in clusters. Such consonant clusters, while less frequent in the language, certainly involve more complex phonological rules for production than consonant-vowel clusters.

Thus, the difficulties children have in sound production seem to involve (1) sounds that occur in the medial or final position of a word; (2) consonant sounds that involve the features of continuancy, especially in combination with stridency and gravity; and (3) sounds that involve a sequence or cluster of consonants as in the case of −*lfth* (as in "twelfth"), which Templin found was difficult even for eight-year-olds. Menyuk has suggested that these production difficulties may result from the fact that the sounds involved lack clear acoustic differences that children can distinguish. If children fail to perceptually discriminate the acoustic cues, they will fail, in turn, to articulate them. On the other hand, if they can make the acoustic discriminations, the production errors may result from difficulties with the articulatory gestures involved.

Systematic evidence of the perceptual errors children make is nearly nonexistent. As we have already noted, we do know that perceptual speech sound discriminations are made long before speech production occurs for both consonants (Eimas, et al., 1971) and vowels (Trehub, 1973). But efforts to study perceptual discrimination after speech has begun by Templin (1957) and Tikofsky and McInish (1968), for example, have not been very helpful because the tests used failed to yield enough errors to be particularly informative. The results of the latter study were in agreement, however, with Miller and Nicely's (1955) study with adults in demonstrating that the fewer the number of feature differences between sounds, the greater the likelihood of perceptual confusions. It is generally agreed, however, that children can and do make speech sound discriminations after true language has begun but before they can produce the distinctions consistently in their own speech. Such claims are usually based on the fact that many sounds can be produced in some contexts before others and there are many anecdotal incidents such as one reported by Berko and Brown (1960) and replicated by this writer recently. A three-year-old girl had a big bag of red candy fish which she was eating when I met her. The following conversation ensued:

"What do you have in your bag?"
"Candy fis. Would you like one?"
"Candy fis?"
"No, fis."
"I would love to have a fis."
"No, not fis, fis!"
"Oh, fish."
"Yes, fis. Here is one for you."

Clearly, the child could perceive the difference between /s/ and /š/, and, while she could not produce the difference, she insisted that I correct my articulation before she remembered to give me the candy she had offered.

Unfortunately this kind of data does not hold up in a scientific court. It would be most helpful to have some perceptual data to help resolve the question of whether lack of perceptual discrimination of acoustic cues is a part of the problem in speech production. A recent study by Eilers and Oller (1976) provides a new procedure which promises to allow the collection of more systematic data on perceptual confusions. These researchers were able to test two-year-old children on a variety of minimal phonological contrasts and obtained data suggesting that perceptual difficulties may play a role in some production errors but elements which cause production errors are not necessarily the most difficult contrasts for the child to perceive.

As has been previously suggested (Palermo & Molfese, 1972), it would seem from what little evidence we have that there are a number of reasons for believing that the difficulty in speech production resides, in part, in the articulatory gestures and not the acoustic cues alone. (1) The casual observations we have just cited, along with the infant data, suggest that speech sound perception is more advanced than production (see also Edwards, 1974). (2) The fact that sounds in the initial position cause little difficulty, while the same sounds in the medial or final position may lead to errors, suggests that articulatory factors associated with preceding articulatory contexts may be problematical. The child may have no difficulty in producing a sound from a resting position (e.g., the /θ/ in *th*umb), but when that same sound must be produced from the position of the articulators after making another sound in the sequence composing a word (e.g., the /θ/ in bir*th*day), the child finds the task more difficult. As Ingram (1974) has demonstrated, the child follows phonotactic rules in such situations so that the changes in production are not random. Even in correct articulation by adults, however, there is a great deal more variability in articulatory movements in the medial and final positions than with the initial position (MacNeilage, 1970). (3) As Menyuk has pointed out (1971), the earliest utterances are of the form CV, CVC, CVCV, and VCV consonant and vowel sequences. Children have difficulty with consonant blends that seem to involve a rapid series of complicated articulatory gestures unrelieved by the interruption of an easier vowel sound. (4) The errors which do occur in articulation seem to be near misses relative to the correct sound. According to Snow's (1964) data, for instance, stops are replaced by other stops, fricatives by other fricatives, and so on. The errors seem to result from imprecise articulation differing by only one feature rather than incorrect articulation. Finally, (5) the errors that are made after age four seem to be made on sounds such as fricatives and liquids in which partial closure in the middle of the vocal tract is required. The bilabial sounds formed with the front of the vocal tract come in earliest, the sounds made at the back of the vocal tract come in somewhat later, but when the more exacting control of the tongue shape and position from the dental ridge to the front third of the hard palate is required, production errors persist to relatively older ages. Children can identify easily, with respect to their own motor movements (as well as observe more easily at least some of the vocal tract movements of other speakers), the end points of the vocal tract. However, when partial closure of the vocal tract is required with constriction in various parts of the central region, more errors are made. Thus, the target that the articulators must hit seems to be smaller for fricatives and liquids, varies with context in the case of a broader range of sounds, and requires greater muscular control in the case of consonant blends.

It seems safe to conclude on the basis of the evidence we now have that children probably do acquire the phonological system of their own language by gradually differentiating distinctive features which are in some way hierarchically ordered. Certainly, analyses within the framework of distinctive features seem far more promising of insights than analyses in terms of phonemes. A particularly insightful analysis and discussion of the acquisition of phonology by Moskowitz (1973a), however, makes a number of cogent points about the process which may help guide future research. First, the acquisition process is far more complex than was suspected and the features do not appear to come in across the board in the straightforward fashion as was first supposed (e.g., Edwards, 1974). In addition, it appears that when a feature distinction is made, both the minus and plus values of the feature are not necessarily acquired concurrently. Furthermore, some specific sounds or phonemes seem to be learned as such by all children independent of the features involved. Second, the child is definitely following rules but those rules may be quite different from those followed by adults (Ingram, 1974, 1975). Thus, there is no reason to analyze the child's phonological system within the framework of the adult rules, as we shall also see is the case with the acquisition of syntax (Chapter 6). Third, any theory of acquisition must take into account, as Jakobson himself points out, that learning phonology is a creative process and that creativity can take many forms. The theory must also consider universal phonological phenomena which may play a basic part in stages of the acquisition process. Finally, and perhaps least considered in this area although more emphasized with respect to syntax, the child is faced with the problem of acquiring both the system of phonological representation and the phonetic representation required for production. In other words, we must look for ways of finding out what the child knows about the underlying system as well as his or her capabilities of producing that representation. The Eiler and Oller study (1976), mentioned earlier, attempts to establish that relation. Examining the surface form of production and analysis in terms of surface structure alone is not enough. We might add to Moskowitz's list that the nature of the language the child hears must surely play some part in phonological development. Ferguson (1964), for example, has pointed out the ubiquity of baby talk directed to children by adults and raises the question of its function in phonological development as well as other aspects of language acquisition.

While we have focused here primarily on Jakobson's theory of phonological development, Ferguson and Garnica (1975) provide an excellent review of other theories as well. They point out that none of the other theories can fully account for all the data either. They suggest that future research can add not only to our knowledge of the processes of language acquisition but of phonological theory as well (e.g., Moskowitz, 1973b).

## SPEECH PRODUCTION AND PERCEPTION

### Production

In the first part of this chapter we looked at the acoustic characteristics of speech and then we examined the smallest linguistic units
of speech. We also noted some of the relations of the linguistic
units, in terms of distinctive features, to the articulators which, in
turn, create the acoustic sound wave. We can now see clearly that the
sound wave is produced by a speaker who conceptualizes in terms of
linguistic units which are usually larger than phonemes. The listener
takes that sound wave and eventually conceptualizes it in terms of
linguistic units of the same size. Since there is no one-to-one correspon-
dence between linguistic unit and acoustic form, as there is in the case
of Morse code, for example, how can we account for what is going on
in this situation?

We are, as speakers and listeners, coding: encoding linguistic
messages sent and decoding linguistic messages received. We must be
coding because there are no one-to-one correspondences between analog
wave form and digital linguistic unit in those exchanges. Furthermore, we process speech signals both in production and comprehension
much more rapidly than we can process any other kind of mechanical
signal. In fact, that is one of the major stumbling blocks to building
speech recognizers and reading machines. We need to break the code
in order to use it to speed up the machines as well as to understand
the more general question of speech perception. Let's look at the
processes which allow us to code 10–15 phonemes per second into
larger units and yet be able to recover the smaller units when necessary.

Suppose you decide it is appropriate to convey from your mind
to the mind of someone else the idea, "Stop." Consider what goes on
from conceptualization to sound wave (Liberman, 1970; Cooper,
1972). Assuming that you decide you want to express your idea by
the word "Stop" rather than "Cut it out!" you must have in mind the
phonetic structure for "stop" and an analysis of the features, in appropriate linear order, which underlie that structure. That will, of
course, involve phonological rules which affect the particular configuration of features that happen to make up the phonemic units of the
word "stop." Depending on the feature configuration, commands may
then be sent in parallel to the appropriate set of neurons which are in
some way related to that feature complex. The neurons will send
messages to groups of muscles. The muscles will then respond in a
particular pattern of contractions. Some of those contractions will
result in a force of air pushed from the lungs through the supralaryngeal tract which other muscle contractions have moved into a particular
size and shape. The air will then be emitted in a wave bearing

complicated coded relationships to the phonetic representation of the idea initially conceived. In addition, during the process of production, the message being produced is monitored by the ears and that feedback is used to make adjustments in the ongoing processes and subsequent parts of the message. Thus, we begin with a semantic idea, select a form of expression, command the neurons to activate the motor mechanisms of our vocal apparatus to produce the phonemes that compose the expression, and blend those phonemes into syllabic units which result in a turbulence in the air surrounding the speaker. On completion of all this, we can say that the message has been encoded.

What do we know about that process of encoding or speech production? The answer to that question is that we know a whole lot more than we did fifty years ago but very little in terms of the final answer. We know that there is a complex one-to-one relationship between vocal tract size and shape and sound. But we also know that there is no one-to-one relationship between acoustic signal and linguistic unit. We know that there isn't even a one-to-one relationship between motor movements and linguistic unit. There is some research on electromyographic recordings of vocal tract muscles which suggests that perhaps the motor commands given to the muscles show invariant relations to the phonemes produced, although the interpretation of the results is controversial (MacNeilage, 1970). We know that the speech production unit is not the phoneme but rather is at least a consonant and a vowel and probably a syllable (Studdert-Kennedy, 1975). We also know that if we are deaf or if there is delayed auditory feedback of a few milliseconds of our own speech (Yates, 1963), our ability to speak is markedly impaired. Thus, we need immediate auditory feedback in order to carry out the process efficiently. In addition, we probably need feedback from the neuromusculature of the supralaryngeal tract (Sussman, 1972). Finally, we know that certain parts of our brains seem to have more to do with the process than other parts. All this information gives a lot of insight into the process but leaves us very much in the dark about the details of how language is converted into speech.

**Perception**

Actually, more theoretical effort has gone into conceptualizing speech perception than speech production, in part because the equipment for studying perception has been available while that for studying production has only recently been developed. In some sense the whole sequence required for production must work in reverse order for speech perception to take place. Several proposals have been made to account for speech perception but they do not differ radically. Essentially, it is assumed that in perceiving speech we use the same equipment we use for producing speech. Since we know how to produce a message and we hear what we say when we do so, we are able when we hear someone else speak to activate our own production mechanisms as we listen, and, knowing what we have in mind when we go through those producing sequences, we know what the person we are listening to is saying.

Thus, those who advance the motor theory of speech perception, as this theory is called (Liberman, Cooper, Shankweiler, & Studdert-Kennedy, 1967), argue that speech perception is closely linked to speech production. It is assumed that speech sounds are processed differently than nonspeech sounds so that when we hear speech we engage a speech mode which processes that particular kind of stimulus input. This assumption is based on the evidence that (1) different acoustic signals are heard as the same phoneme; (2) the same acoustic stimuli are heard as different phonemes in different contexts; (3) the speed of processing speech sounds is far greater (10–15 phonemes/sec.) than is possible with nonspeech sounds; (4) speech sounds are perceived categorically; (5) speech and nonspeech sound processing occurs in different hemispheres of the brain; and (6) there appear to be linguistic feature detectors.

Recent research has reinforced this position by more directly relating the perception of speech with the listener's knowledge of the production capabilities of the vocal tract (Liberman, 1975). Liberman points out first that speech is processed differently from other auditory stimuli, not only as evidenced in the kinds of phenomena noted above but also in terms of forward and backward masking. That is, in contrast to auditory stimuli which are not processed in the speech mode, Liberman presents evidence that speech stimuli are not subject to forward or backward masking. More important, however, Liberman provides evidence that when two syllables such as /bɛg/ /bɛ/ follow each other in sequence, a relatively large silent period must occur between the two syllables in order for the listener to hear the syllable-final stop in the first syllable if the same voice utters the two syllables. No interval is required to perceive the syllable-final stop of the first syllable, however, if two different voices are used for the two syllables. It appears that the listener recognizes that the vocal tract must have time to move from the postition required to produce the back consonant /g/ to the front consonant /b/, in this case, and that movement takes time. If the time is not evident in terms of a silent interval, the /g/ is not perceived unless two voices are involved, in which case it is possible, and, therefore, perceived. Thus, while the conception of the motor theory has become more abstract, the perception of speech seems intimately tied to the production processes and the listener's conception of what vocal tracts are capable of doing.

Further, it is argued that since different acoustic stimuli are perceived as the same phoneme, there can be no matching of input to a stored template for each phoneme. Nor can there be a template for syllables since there are thousands of syllables produced with different stresses, intonations, and speaker voices. Furthermore, since phonemes are psychologically real, a syllable template matching device would not work because it would not allow recovery of the phoneme. It is argued, therefore, that perception is mediated by production on the assumption that the gestures of producing the sounds, or the neuromotor correlates of these gestures, are more directly related to the acoustic wave. Thus, as the sound is received, some abstract conception of the neuromotor mechanism of production is engaged, and the parallel processing which takes place at production reconstructs the message at higher levels through processes which are the reverse of the actual production of the message. While this theory is still rather vague in detail, most theorists coming at the problem from many points of view agree that this is the general form speech perception must take. In addition, it makes some common sense that if the deaf do not acquire language production because they cannot hear, and normal speech is badly disrupted when auditory feedback is delayed for a few hundred milliseconds, there must be an intimate relation between production of speech and perception of speech.

A somewhat more specific analysis of speech perception is offered in terms of a computer analogy and referred to as the analysis by synthesis model of speech perception (Stevens & Halle, 1967; Stevens & House, 1972). Such models are removed from actual physiological processes but make clearer in terms of a mechanical model what is required of the human organism for it to behave as it does. The listener is viewed in this theory as receiving the acoustic signal and storing it while generating articulatory descriptions which would produce such an acoustical signal. Those descriptions are compared to the stored input until a match is achieved. The matched articulatory gesture set is then stored, and another part of the system generates the relationships between phonetic symbols and various articulatory gestures. These gesture sets are then compared with the input until a match is achieved and the listener is able to identify the phonetic representation of the acoustic input.

A number of variants of the analysis by synthesis models were reviewed by Cooper (1972), but at this stage these models are only sophisticated guesses about what the human organism must do in rather general terms, considering what we now know about the physical properties of acoustic signals and the psychological properties of the linguistic message. As the theorists in this area readily admit, the models of speech perception are surely wrong in detail. While the models make some sense in terms of the adult language processor, it is not clear how speech perception is acquired in the first place. They all place a good deal of emphasis on the production of speech as basic to the comprehension of speech.

The hypothesis of a speech mode which engages the speech production processes at some abstract level, thus differentiating speech perception from other auditory processing, has not, however, been accepted without challenge. Cutting, Rosner, and Foard (1975) have pointed out that music-like plucked and bowed sounds show boundary shifts after selective adaptation similar to those reported for stop consonants. They are also categorically perceived. Although there is no right ear advantage for these sounds in a dichotic listening situation, it is clear from the adaptation and categorical perception data that some modifications in presently conceived motor theory will be necessary to accommodate these findings.

Further empirical findings which bear on the motor theory of speech perception are the results of the experiments demonstrating that infants in the first month or two of life are able to perceive speech sound differences (Eimas et al., 1971; Molfese et al., 1975) long before they evidence any ability to produce sounds or even have the neurophysiological capabilities to do so (Lieberman, 1973). These findings have led to the suggestion that perhaps perception must precede production (Studdert-Kennedy, 1974; Palermo, 1975). Studdert-Kennedy has argued that the child is born with two distinct capacities: an auditory template and an articulatory template. The child must determine links between the two templates and establish their communicative significance through feedback from auditory gestures and their relation to the auditory template. Through this process the natural categories of speech are established along with the relation of the articulatory commands to the phonetic percepts.

While the Studdert-Kennedy analysis suggests that the motor theory of speech perception may be maintained once the initial links between perception and production have been establishd in infancy, Palermo's hypothesis is more radical. He suggests that a variety of data indicate that speech production is mediated by processes involved in the perception of speech rather than the reverse. Seven kinds of data to support this hypothesis are cited: the infant data that perception precedes production (Eimas et al., 1971); the evidence that the neurophysiological maturation for production lags behind perception (Lieberman, 1973); the case history of a congenitally anarthric child who has never uttered a word but who can comprehend speech with no difficulty (Lenneberg, 1962); the evidence that congenitally deaf children who cannot perceive speech never learn to speak normally; the suggestion that speech perception in the normal child may at times precede production; the evidence that tampering with the perception of a person's speech by delayed auditory feedback disrupts the pro-

duction processes (Yates, 1963) ; and the evidence that second language
speech sound production cannot proceed until perceptual discriminations can be made (Leon, 1966). While many of these phenomena
may not be crucial to a motor theory of speech perception, they all
need to be accounted for within the framework of the theory to make
the theory convincing.

It is clear that speech perception and production are intimately
tied together. They are interdependent processes which surely must
have developed in a coordinated manner from an evolutionary perspective. The precise nature of the interrelations between the two is far
from clear at the moment. How the story will unfold awaits further
theoretical and empirical developments. We are still a long way from
understanding the fascinating question of how we are able to convert
an analog wave form into a digital speech form and thus understand
how we extract a message coded according to the rules of natural
language from an acoustic signal.

## SUMMARY

In this chapter we have looked at the acoustic properties of speech
sounds and discovered that the physical properties of those sounds are
unusually complicated insofar as their relations to the phonological
components of the language system are concerned. The buzzing fundamental frequency set in motion by the vocal folds is modulated by the
size and shape of the vocal tract. The constantly changing configuration
of the vocal tract produces noise, defining some consonants, and transitions to and from relatively steady-state formants which define syllables
composed of consonants and vowels. While the vowels have fairly
constant acoustic properties, the consonants seem to have no apparent
one-to-one relation to the acoustic signal.

The phonological system is, however, abstracted in terms of discrete
segments from the continuous sound wave. It appears that we humans
have a speech mode—special mechanisms which are engaged to process
speech sounds differently than other auditory signals. We perceive
speech sounds categorically, we process them faster than other discrete
auditory signals, we engage separate parts of the brain to do the
processing, and we are able to classify different acoustic signals in very
complex ways.

The very young infant appears to have the capabilities of processing speech signals in terms of feature analyzers which are specifically
attuned to linguistically relevant acoustic characteristics of the signal.
When speech begins, the child seems to acquire the phonological system in terms of the phonological features of which the phonemes are

composed. At the same time, the child learns the phonological rules which provide for the combination of sounds into words and phrases.

The processes of encoding and decoding the speech signal appear to be intimately interrelated. Theories of speech perception are conceptualized in terms of the processes of speech production. Thus, speech perception is understood in terms of the motoric processes required to produce the sounds perceived.

## REFERENCES

Barclay, J. R. Noncategorical perception of a voiced stop. *Perception and Psychophysics*, 1972, *11*, 269–74.

Berko, J., & Brown, R. Psycholinguistic research methods. In P. H. Mussen (Ed.), *Handbook of research methods in child development*. New York: Wiley, 1969. Pp. 517–57.

Carroll, J. B. Language development in children. In C. W. Harris (Ed.), *Encyclopedia of educational research*. New York: MacMillan, 1960. Pp. 744–52.

Chen, H. P., & Irwin, O. C. Infant speech vowel and consonant types. *Journal of Speech Disorders*, 1946, *11*, 27–29.

Cooper, F. S. How is language conveyed by speech? In J. F. Kavanagh and I. G. Mattingly (Eds.), *Language by ear and by eye*. Cambridge, Mass.: M.I.T. Press, 1972. Pp. 24–25.

Cooper. W. E. Adaptation of phonetic feature analyzers for place of articulation. *Journal of the Acoustical Society of America*, 1974, *56*, 617–27.

Cutting, J. E., & Eimas, P. D. Phonetic feature analyzers and the processing of speech in infants. In J. F. Kavanagh & J. E. Cutting (Eds.), *The role of speech in language*. Cambridge, Mass.: M.I.T. Press, 1975. Pp. 127–48.

Cutting, J. E., & Rosner, B. S. Categories and boundaries in speech and music. *Perception and Psychophysics*, 1974, *16*, 564–70.

Cutting, J. E., Rosner, B. S., & Foard, C. F. Rise time in nonlinguistic sounds and models of speech perception. *Haskins Laboratories: Status report on speech research*, 1975, SR-41.

DeLattre, T. Z., Liberman, A. M., & Cooper, F. S. Acoustic loci and transitional cues for consonants. *Journal of the Acoustical Society of America*, 1955, *27*, 769–73.

Denes, P. B. On the statistics of spoken English. *Journal of the Acoustical Society of America*, 1963, *35*, 892–904.

Diehl, R. Feature analyzers for the phonetic dimension *stop* vs. *continuant*. *Perception and Psychophysics*, 1976, *19*, 267–72.

Edwards, M. L. Perception and production in child psychology: The testing of four hypotheses. *Journal of Child Language*, 1974, *1*, 205–19.

Eguchi, S., & Hirsh, I. J. Development of speech sounds in children. *Acta Otolaryngologica*, Supplementum, *257*, 1969, 5–51.

Eilers, R. E., & Oller, D. K. The role of speech discrimination in developmental sound substitutions. *Journal of Child Language*, 1976, *3*, 319–29.

Eimas, P. D. The relation between identification and discrimination along speech and non-speech continua. *Language and Speech*, 1963, *6*, 206–17.

Eimas, P. D. Auditory and linguistic processing of cues for place of articulation by infants. *Perception and Psychophysics*, 1974, *16*, 513–21.

Eimas, P. D. Speech perception in early infancy. In L. B. Cohen & P. Salapatek

(Eds.), *Infant perception: From sensation to cognition* (Vol. 2). New York: Academic Press, 1975.

Eimas, P. D., Cooper, W. E., & Corbit, J. D. Some properties of linguistic feature detectors. *Perception and Psychophysics*, 1973, *13*, 247–52.

Eimas, P. D., & Corbit, J. D. Selective adaptation of linguistic feature detectors. *Cognitive Psychology*, 1973, *4*, 99–109.

Eimas, P. D., Siqueland, E. R., Jusczyk, P., & Vigorito, J. Speech perception in infants. *Science*, 1971, *171*, 303–6.

Engle, Walburga von Raffler. The development from sound to phoneme in child language. In C. A. Ferguson & D. I. Slobin, (Eds.), *Studies of Child Language Development*. New York: Holt, Rinehart & Winston, 1973. Pp. 9–12.

Ervin-Tripp, S. M. Language development. In M. Hoffman & L. Hoffman (Eds.), *Review of child development research* (Vol. 2). Ann Arbor: University of Michigan Press, 1966.

Ferguson, C. A. Baby talk in six languages. *American Anthropologist*, 1964, *66*, 103–114.

Ferguson, C. A., & Garnica, O. K. Theories of phonological development. In E. H. Lenneberg & E. Lenneberg (Eds.), *Foundations of language development* (Vol. 1). New York: Academic Press, 1975. Pp. 154–80.

Gruber, J. S. Playing with distinctive features in the babbling of infants. In C. A. Ferguson & D. I. Slobin (Eds.), *Studies of Child Language Development*. New York: Holt, Rinehart & Winston, 1973. Pp. 4–9.

Harris, C. M. A study of the building blocks in speech. *Journal of the Acoustical Society of America*, 1953, *25*, 962–69.

Harris, K. S., Hoffman, H. S., Liberman, A. M., Delattre, D. C., & Cooper, F. S. Effect of third formant transitions on the perception of the voiced stop consonants. *Journal of the Acoustical Society of America*, 1958, *30*, 122–26.

Ingram, D. Phonological rules in young children. *Journal of Child Language*, 1974, *1*, 49–64.

Ingram, D. Surface contrast in children's speech. *Journal of Child Language*, 1975, *2*, 287–92.

Irwin, O. C. Infant speech: Consonant sounds according to the manner of articulation. *Journal of Speech Disorders*, 1947, *12*, 397–401.

Jakobson, R. Why "Mamma" and "Papa"? In *Roman Jakobson: Selected writings*. The Hague: Mouton, 1962.

Jakobson, R. Child language aphasia and phonological universals (trans. by Allan R. Keiler). The Hague: Mouton, 1968.

Jakobson, R., & Halle, M. *Fundamentals of language*. The Hague: Mouton, 1956.

Joos, M. Acoustic phonetics. *Language monographs, No. 23*. Baltimore: Linguistic Society of America, 1948.

Lasky, R. E., Syrdal-Lasky, A., & Klein, R. E. VOT discrimination by four- to six-and-a-half-month-old infants from Spanish environments. *Journal of Experimental Child Psychology*, 1975, *20*, 215–25.

Lenneberg, E. H. Understanding language without ability to speak: A case report. *Journal of Abnormal and Social Psychology*, 1962, *65*, 419–25.

Lenneberg, E. H. *Biological foundations of language*. New York Wiley: 1967.

Léon, P. Teaching pronunciation. In A. Valdman (Ed.), *Trends in language teaching*. New York: McGraw Hill, 1966.

Liberman, A. M. The grammars of speech and language. *Cognitive Psychology*, 1970, *1*, 301–23.

Liberman, A. M. How abstract must a motor theory of speech perception be? *Haskins Laboratories: Status report on speech research*, 1975, SR-44.

Liberman, A. M., & Cooper, F. S. In search of the acoustic cues. In A. Valdman

(Ed.), *Mélange à la mémoire de Pierre Delattre*. The Hague: Mouton. (Also in *Haskins Laboratories: Status Report on Speech Research*, SR-19/20, 1969.)

Liberman, A. M., Cooper, F. S., Harris, K. S., MacNeilage, P. F., & Studdert-Kennedy, M. Some observations on a model for speech perception. In W. Wathen-Dunn (Ed.), *Models for the Perception of Speech and Visual Form*. Cambridge, Mass.: M.I.T. Press, 1967. Pp. 68–87.

Liberman, A. M., Cooper, F. S., Shankweiler, D. P., & Studdert-Kennedy, M. Perception of the speech code, *Psychological Review*, 1967, *74*, 431–61.

Liberman, A. M., Delattre, P. C., & Cooper, F. S. The role of selected stimulus-variables in the perception of the unvoiced stop consonants. *American Journal of Psychology*, 1952, *65*, 497–516.

Liberman, A. M., Delattre, P. C., & Cooper, F. S. The role of consonant-vowel transitions in the perception of the stop and nasal consonants. *Psychological Monographs: General and Applied*, 1954, *68*, Whole No. 379.

Liberman, A. M., Delattre, P. C., & Cooper, F. S. Some cues for the distinction between voiced and voiceless stops in initial position. *Language and Speech*, 1958, *1*, 153–57.

Liberman, A. M., Harris, K. S., Hoffman, H. S., & Griffith, B. C. The discrimination of speech sounds within and across phoneme boundaries. *Journal of Experimental Psychology*, 1957, *54*, 358–68.

Liberman, A. M., Harris, K. S., Kinney, J. A., & Lane, H. The discrimination of relative onset-time of the components of certain speech and nonspeech patterns. *Journal of Experimental Psychology*, 1961, *61*, 379–88.

Lieberman, P. On the evolution of language: A unified view. *Cognition*, 1973, *2*, 59–94.

Lind, J., Truby, H. M., & Bosma, J. F. *Newborn infant cry*. Uppsala: Alquist & Wiesells, 1965.

MacNeilage, P. F. Motor control of serial ordering of speech. *Psychological Review*, 1970, *77*, 182–96.

McCarthy, D. Language development in children. In L. Carmichael (Ed.), *Manual of child psychology* (2nd ed.). New York: Wiley, 1954.

Menyuk, P. The role of distinctive features in children's acquisition of phonology. *Journal of Speech and Hearing Research*, 1968a, *11*, 138–46.

Menyuk, P. Children's learning and reproduction of grammatical and nongrammatical phonological sequences. *Child development*, 1968b, *39*, 844–60.

Menyuk, P. *The acquisition and development of language*. Englewood Cliffs, N.J.: Prentice-Hall, 1971.

Menyuk, P., & Bernholtz, N. Prosodic features and children's language production. *Quarterly Progress Report No. 93*, Massachusetts Institute of Technology, 1969.

Millar, J. B., & Ainsworth, W. A. Identification of synthetic isolated vowels and vowels in h-d context. *Acoustica*, 1972, *27*, 278–82.

Miller, G. A., & Nicely, P. E. Analysis of perceptual confusions among some English consonants. *Journal of the Acoustic Society of America*, 1955, *27*, 338–52.

Miller, J. D., Wier, C. C., Pastore, R. E., Kelly, W. J., & Dooling, D. J. Discrimination and labeling of noise-buzz sequence with varying noise-lead times: An example of categorical perception. *Journal of the Acoustical Society of America*, 1976, *60*, 410–17.

Molfese, D. L., Freeman, R. B., Jr., & Palermo, D. S. The ontogeny of brain lateralization for speech and nonspeech stimuli. *Brain and Language*, 1975, *2*, 356–68.

Morse, P. A. The discrimination of speech and nonspeech stimuli in early infancy. *Journal of Experimental Child Psychology*, 1972, *14*, 477–92.

Morse, P. A., Kass, J. E., & Turkienicz, R. Selective adaptation of vowels. *Perception and Psychophysics*, 1976, *19*, 137–43.

Moskowitz, A. I. The two-year-old stage in the acquisition of English phonology. In C. A. Ferguson & D. I. Slobin (Eds.), *Studies of child language development*. New York: Holt, Rinehart & Winston, 1973a. Pp. 52–68.

Moskowitz, A. I. On the status of the vowel shift in English. In T. E. Moore (Ed.), *Cognitive development and the acquisition of language*. New York: Academic Press, 1973b. Pp. 223–60.

Nakazima, S. A comparative study of the speech developments of Japanese and American English in childhood. *Studia Phonologica*, 1962, *2*, 27–39.

Oller, D. K., Wieman, L. A., Doyle, W. J., & Ross, C. Infant babbling and speech. *Journal of Child Language*, 1976, *3*, 1–11.

Palermo, D. S. Developmental aspects of speech perception: Problems for a motor theory. In J. F. Kavanagh & J. E. Cutting (Eds.), *The role of speech in language*. Cambridge, Mass.: M.I.T. Press, 1975. Pp. 149–54.

Palermo, D. S. & Molfese, D. L. Language acquisition from age five onward. *Psychological Bulletin*, 1972, *78*, 409–28.

Pisoni, D. B., & Tash, J. Reaction times to comparisons within and across phonetic categories. *Perception and Psychophysics*, 1974, *15*, 285–90.

Ringwall, E. A., Reese, H. W., & Markel, N. N. A distinctive feature analysis of pre-linguistic infant vocalizations. In K. F. Riegel (Ed.), *The development of language functions*. Center for Human Growth and Development, University of Michigan, Report No. 8, 1965.

Shankweiler, D., Strange, W., & Verbrugge, R. Speech and the problem of perceptual constancy. *Haskins Laboratories: Status reports on speech research*, 1975, SR–42/43.

Sheppard, W. C., & Lane, H. L. Development of the prosodic features of infants vocalizing. *Journal of Speech and Hearing Research*, 1968, *11*, 94–108.

Shvachkin, N. Kh. The development of phonemic speech perception in early childhood. In C. A. Ferguson & D. I. Slobin (Eds.), *Studies of child language development*. New York: Holt, Rinehart & Winston, 1973. Pp. 91–127.

Snow, K. A comparative study of sound substitutions used by "normal" first-grade children. *Speech Monographs*, 1964, *31*, 135–42.

Stevens, K. N. On the relations between speech movements and speech perception. Paper presented at the meeting of the XVIII International Congress of Psychology, Moscow, August, 1966. *(Zeitschrift fur Phonetik, Sprachwissenschaft und Kommunikations-forschung*, in press).

Stevens, K. N., & Halle, M. Remarks on analysis by synthesis and distinctive features. In W. Wathen-Dunn (Ed.), *Models for the perception of speech and visual form*. Cambridge, Mass.: M.I.T. Press, 1967.

Stevens, K. N., & House, A. S. Perturbation of vowel articulations by consonantal context: An acoustical study. *Journal of Speech and Hearing Research*, 1963, *6*, 111–28.

Stevens, K. N., & House, A. S. Speech perception. In J. Tobias (Ed.), *Foundations of modern auditory theory* (Vol. 2). New York: Academic Press, 1972.

Studdert-Kennedy, M. Speech perception. In N. J. Lass (Ed.), *Contemporary issues in experimental phonetics*. New York: Academic Press, 1974.

Studdert-Kennedy, M. From continuous signal to discrete message: Syllable to phoneme. In J. F. Kavanagh & J. E. Cutting (Eds.), *The role of speech in language*. Cambridge, Mass.: M.I.T. Press, 1975. Pp. 113–26.

Sussman, H. M. What the tongue tells the brain. *Psychological Bulletin,* 1972, 77, 262–77.

Templin, M. C. *Certain language skills in children: Their development and interrelationships.* Institute of Child Welfare Monographs, Serial No. 26, Minneapolis: University of Minnesota Press, 1957.

Tikofsky, R. S., & McInish, J. R. Consonant discrimination by seven-year-olds: A pilot study. *Psychonomic Science,* 1968, *10,* 61–62.

Tonkova-Yampol'skaya, R. V. Development of speech intonation in infants during the first two years of life. In C. A. Ferguson & D. I. Slobin (Eds.), *Studies of child language development.* New York: Holt, Rinehart & Winston, 1973. Pp. 128–38.

Trehub, S. E. Infants' sensitivity to vowel and tonal contrasts. *Developmental Psychology,* 1973, *9,* 91–96.

Trehub, S. E., & Rabinovitch, M. S. Auditory-linguistic sensitivity in early infancy. *Developmental Psychology,* 1972, *6,* 74–77.

Weir, R. H. *Language in the crib.* The Hague: Mouton, 1962.

Wellman, B. L., Case, I. M., Mengert, I. G., & Bradbury, D. Speech sounds of young children. *University of Iowa Studies in Child Welfare,* 1931, *5,* No. 2.

Yates, A. J. Delayed auditory feedback. *Psychological Bulletin,* 1963, *60,* 213–32.

# The Syntax
# of
# Language

## CHAPTER 4

Now that we know a little about the sound stream which we manage to segment into the speech sounds of language and integrate into words and phrases, we can turn our attention to "the problem of serial order in behavior" with respect to those larger units—a problem so eloquently presented by Lashley (1951). Syntax, for the psycholinguist, is the problem of serial order of language units within the framework of the sentence. At the time Lashley pointed to this problem, few psychologists were ready to listen to the important points he made about the complexity of the serial order of behavior. They were content to account for serial order in terms of the concatenation of strings of letters or words. Miller, for example, in the same year that Lashley presented his paper (Miller, 1951), had published a book which presented language as strings of stimuli and responses within the then-current and well-accepted tradition of the behavioristic S-R theoretical framework.

Shortly thereafter, in 1953, a number of linguists and psychologists got together for a summer at Cornell University in order to examine the interrelationships among the approaches to language of linguists, learning theorists, and information-processing theorists. The product of that conference was a book (Osgood & Sebeok, 1954) reflecting the behavioristic influence which was so strong in all three fields at the time. The book summarized the most advanced thinking of leaders in these fields just prior to the appearance of Chomsky's book *Syntactic Structures* (1957) which, as we saw in Chapter 1, argued so effectively against the left-to-right surface structure analyses which were the common foundation of the three theoretical groups at the Cornell conference.

## INFORMATION PROCESSING THEORY

At the time of the Cornell conference, studies of syntax were extremely limited. In fact, Miller's book devoted little space to syntax or grammar. Information theory analyses of the amount of information, noise, and redundancy in language appeared at the time to be one of the most promising approaches to an understanding of syntax. Analyses of different languages in terms of redundancy was, for example, of interest to a number of research workers. Similarly, there were many studies devoted to type-token ratios in language. Speech or written materials were analyzed in terms of the number of different words used (types) and the frequency with which each word (token) of a given type appeared in the unit analyzed. The ratio of the types to tokens was taken as an indicant of children's language development, styles of writers, and readability of written materials. Miller's book (1951) provides a good summary of this work.

Miller was at this time trying to develop somewhat more sophisticated experimental approaches to some of these problems. His attention was directed to experiments concerned with the patterns in language which facilitate comprehension, acquisition, recall, and detection of errors in language. In a study with Selfridge (Miller & Selfridge, 1950), for example, the problem was cast within the framework of contextual dependencies between sequential elements in a string of words. The experiment consisted of asking persons to recall lists of words which differed in their approximation to normal English word order. The orders ranged from a random selection of words (zero-order approximation to the statistical structure of English) up to normal text. The intermediate orders were constructed by giving, for example, a normal grammatical three-word string of words to a person and asking for a fourth word to continue the string. The first word of the string was then dropped, the new word was added, another person was then asked to add another word to that string, and so on until a string of the appropriate length using all the words had been obtained. The number of words in the initial string was designated as the order of approximation. Regardless of the length of the list, people were able to remember more from the lists as the approximation to English became higher although there was little difference in recall of passages with three or higher levels of approximation. Thus, the authors concluded, "The results indicate that meaningful material is easy to learn, not because it is meaningful per se, but because it preserves the short-range associations that are familiar to the Ss [subjects]. . . . By shifting the problem from 'meaning' to 'degree of contextual constraint,' the whole area is reopened to experimental investigation" (Miller & Selfridge, p. 183). The old bugaboo of meaning was once again discarded in the tradition of the times.

Miller was in search of an approach which would allow him to break open the problems of language, sequential kinds of behavior of all kinds, and, even more broadly, cognitive processes. The information processing theory seemed to have promise and in Miller's laboratory, research was conceived within that framework for several years. A number of enthusiastic papers seemed to suggest that this was the way to go (e.g., Miller, 1953) and his famous paper, "The Magical Number Seven, Plus or Minus Two: Some Limits on Our Capacity for Processing Information" (Miller, 1956), caught the imagination of many researchers just as Chomsky was about to influence Miller's thinking in a way that would lead him, and many others, in quite different directions.

## LINGUISTIC THEORY AND THE DERIVATIONAL THEORY OF COMPLEXITY

Chomsky's arguments in *Syntactic Structures* (1957), of course, clearly showed that information processing and the S-R behavioristic paradigm which had given birth to it were not applicable, in principle, to an understanding of language. Instead of looking at surface structure, Chomsky's linguistic analysis demanded a consideration of the underlying structure as well as the surface structure form. Furthermore, the underlying form and the surface form had to be related and that relation was to be accomplished by means of transformational rules. Chomsky's presentation in that first book was interpreted as suggesting that the number of transformational rules would vary as a function of the type and number of underlying structures which were to be combined in the surface structure form. Thus, a simple, active affirmative, declarative (SAAD) sentence was assumed to derive from a kernel underlying form which required few transformations to be converted to a surface form. Passive sentences required more transformations, passive-negatives still more, and so on.

The psychological implications of the relationship between syntactic forms and number of transformations seemed to jump out at the experimental psychologist ready to move into the laboratory. Obviously, the more transformations required to convert a sentence from deep to surface form, the greater the psychological processing effort that should be required. Tests of what came to be known as the *derivational theory of complexity* began to pour into the literature. In short, psychologists set out to test the psychological reality of transformational grammar as they interpreted it. The researchers assumed that if the number of transformations was greater for the derivation of one sentence than for another, other things being equal, it should be easier to match semantically similar sentences differing by only one transformation than sentences with more than one transformation (Miller & McKean, 1964) ; it should be easier to verify the truth or falsity of a sentence with fewer transformations in its derivation (McMahon, 1963) ; and it should be easier to recall sentences involving fewer transformations (e.g., Mehler, 1963). The initial results were encouraging. Let's look at a couple of examples.

A massive study by Clifton and Odum (1966) was designed to examine the effects of derivational complexity on judged similarity and recognition memory for sentences. In the recognition memory experiments, a set of eight sentences was presented to the subjects several times and then those eight sentences were embedded in a longer list of sentences as a recognition memory task. The original set varied in semantic content, but each of the eight was of a different syntactic form: active, passive, negative, question, passive-negative, passive-question, negative-question, and passive-negative-question. The recognition set consisted of all the other transformations of each content sentence plus some unrelated filler sentences. The confusion matrix which resulted from the errors made in recognition of the original sentences supported, in general terms, the derivational theory of complexity. Sentences which were grammatically less closely related were less frequently confused than more closely related sentences. It was clear, however, that the differences between transformations were not equally significant by the various measures used. For instance, as may be seen in Figure 4–1, the difference between negative and active constructions resulted in a greater psychological effect than the difference between a question and a negative-question, although it was assumed that there was only one transformation difference in each case. The overall results of the experiments led the authors to conclude that there is ". . . substantial evidence for the existence of some parallel between the linguistic description of a language and the reactions of a language user to his language" (p. 32).

A second experiment within this framework was conducted by Savin and Perchonock (1965), who devised a clever way to test the psychological computing space taken by the transformations required in processing sentences of differing complexity. Subjects were presented with a sentence to remember, followed by a list of eight unrelated words which were added to the memory load. Recall was requested for sentence plus word list. Scores were then computed for the number of list words recalled after the sentences which were correctly recalled. The assumption was that fewer words would be recalled after sentences of greater transformational complexity since the transformational computations would use up more of the computational "space," leaving less room for storing the unrelated words. The results were remarkably in line with the expectations of the researchers and another bit of

**Figure 4-1**

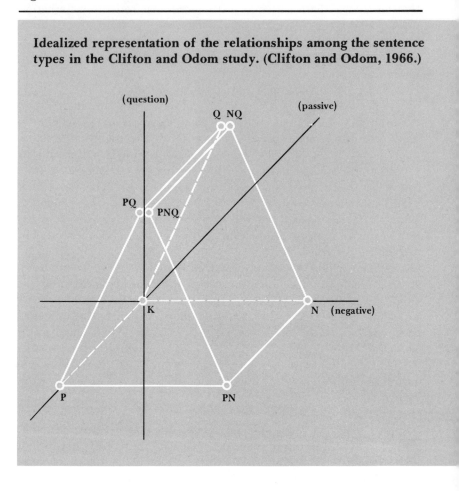

**Idealized representation of the relationships among the sentence types in the Clifton and Odom study. (Clifton and Odom, 1966.)**

support for the psychological reality of the derivational theory of complexity was recorded.

Another approach to the study of the psychological reality of the deep structure constituents should be mentioned here, although it was not directly aimed at the derivational theory of complexity. Fodor and Bever (1965) introduced a procedure, suggested by Ladefoged and Broadbent (1960), to study the segmentation of sentences into major constituent boundaries. The procedure consisted of presenting sentences to subjects with a click sound superimposed at some point during the sentence. The subject's task was to indicate where the click occurred in the sentence. The hypothesis was that the click would be identified as having occurred at a major constituent boundary regardless of where it actually occurred. For example, in the Garrett, Bever, and Fodor study (1966), a click was placed so that it occurred during the word "George" or the word "drove" in the following two sentences:

1. In order to catch his train George drove furiously to the station.
2. The reporters assigned to George drove furiously to the station.

Notice that the part of the sentences containing the critical click is exactly the same in both cases—in fact, they were made acoustically identical in the experiments. The results, however, are clear in showing that subjects indicated that they had heard the click before "George" in the first sentence and after "George" in the second sentence. In other words, the subjects reported the click as displaced into the respective major syntactic boundaries of the two sentences which, of course, was the only difference between the pertinent parts of the sentences. This result was interpreted as reflecting the active decoding of the sentences in terms of the structural analysis of the syntactic component of the grammar. Thus, the clicks were reported as having occurred outside the syntactic unit because the person decoding the sentence was too busy processing the syntax to register an irrelevant noise. Thus, further support was adduced for the psychological reality of deep structure.

In summary, the research of this period seemed to suggest that linguistic theory had opened the road to a psychological theory of sentence processing. People actively process the surface structure of sentences in a manner which allows them to recover the deep structure from the surface structure. Although some transformations may be more difficult than others, the greater the number of transformations required to convert a deep structure to a surface structure, the more psychological computational effort required to recover the deep structure from the surface structure. In addition, it was suggested that people remember the deep structure form plus a number of notations about which transformations are to be applied if someone should ask for the surface structure again (Mehler, 1963). The transformational notations seemed to be the first aspects of the sentence lost in memory, leading to the frequently observed phenomenon that derivationally complex surface structures are recalled as transformationally less complex surface forms (Mehler, 1963). In fact, Sachs (1967) reported results which suggested that the transformational notations associated with the deep structure are forgotten almost immediately and recall is limited to the semantic component alone. People can remember the surface structure if they are demanded to do so (James, Thompson, & Baldwin, 1973), but they just do not ordinarily bother.

## CRITICISMS OF THE DERIVATIONAL THEORY OF COMPLEXITY

The derivational theory of complexity looked very good as a psychological theory in the early stages but since that early research the theory has come apart at the seams. Glucksberg and Danks (1969) had difficulty replicating the Savin and Perchonock (1965) results and found alternative interpretations in terms of differences in delay of recall associated with sentences of different lengths more compatible with the data. Epstein (1969), and later Foss and Cairns (1970), found that if the word list were recalled before the sentence, the results of Savin and Perchonock completely washed out. The later results were interpreted to indicate that recall of the sentences interferes to varying degrees with word list recall. Thus, the phenomenon is a recall interference one rather than being a function of mental computation or memory storage of transformations. The impact of the studies using the click technique was markedly weakened by the finding that the click is displaced to the same boundary when no click is presented but the subject is led to believe that a click did occur (Padrick, 1973; Reber & Anderson, 1970), and by the finding that the phenomenon does not work for minor constituent boundaries (Bever, Lackner, & Kirk, 1969; Holmes & Forster, 1970). Finally, the linguistic theory was further developed and changed (Chomsky, 1965) so that the theory underlying many of the early studies, including that of Clifton and Odom (1966), was less relevant.

Perspective on the whole situation was initiated by Fodor and Garrett (1966). They took the larger issue of competence and performance in psycholinguistic research under consideration and pointed out that, among other things, the initial assumptions which led to the early research were naive. They provided an analysis of previous data along with some new data to show that the derivational theory of complexity would not hold up. The major thrust of Fodor and Garrett's position was that, "While there can be no serious doubt that a speaker who understands a sentence does so by recovering its structural description, it is by no means obvious that the processes by which he converts a wave form into a structural description are identical to (or isomorphic with) the operations by which a grammar converts an axiom string into a structural description" (1966, p. 143). The point they were making is that both linguist and psychologist must make use of the competence-performance distinction and focus on the competence aspect of the problem in either case. But the type of competence model developed by linguists for the goals they have in mind should not necessarily be the same model that psychologists would develop to account for the phenomena of interest to them. The problem with the early research of this period is that psychologists constructed their experiments assuming a direct relationship between formal features of linguistic derivations and the psychological problems of the perceptual complexity and memorial difficulty of sentences. Fodor and Garrett advanced the argument that the structural description of a sentence may be recovered in any number of ways which may or may not be related to the linguistic structural description. The grammar as the linguist constructs it may be an adequate description of our linguistic knowledge but it need not necessarily be a subcomponent of the psychological competence model which describes the mechanisms underlying the production and comprehension of speech.

Fodor and Garrett noted some of the irregularities with respect to the derivational theory of complexity in the research results up to that time. They pointed out, for example, that the length of the sentences to be recalled in memory experiments had not been controlled. The results of experiments comparing the recall of passive and active sentences, for example, could be simply accounted for by the fact that passives are longer than their respective active forms and, therefore, more difficult to recall. When length is pitted against transformational complexity, however, the results are not clear. Miller and McKean (1964) did not find a systematic relation between length and performance despite the fact that longer sentences were transformationally more complex. Slobin (1963) found performance on truncated passives equal to performance on active sentences, and performance on both was better than on full passive forms. The truncated passives were, however, derived from the full passives by additional transformations according to linguistic theory. Thus, performance was best on the shortest sentences, some of which were more and some less derivationally complex than the longer sentences.

Fodor and Garrett cite the results of some work in their own laboratory suggesting that when transformations other than those involved in the major syntactic sentence forms of active, passive, question, and negative are used, there is no support for the derivational theory of complexity. One clear case is that of particle and adverb movement. For example, "Joan called up Joe" and "Joan called Joe up" are equivalent sentences except for one transformation. No evidence of memory load problems is evidenced, however, in either case, although when recall is delayed for more than thirty seconds the untransformed version is recalled when either form has been presented. In short, the formalization of linguistic rules is not a model of psychological processing.

Fodor and Garrett were not only correct about the direction in which the theorizing should go but they also anticipated some of the data to come. The recognition that linguistic theory would not serve as a psychological theory, however, left psycholinguists in a bind. They had accepted the competence-performance distinction Chomsky had presented to them, but they had also accepted his linguistic theory as a psychological theory. Now they began to realize that they would have to construct their own abstract theory pertinent to their domain. The linguistic crutch they had been using was made of rubber. Since psychologists were not used to thinking in abstract theoretical terms and yet they recognized the trap they had fallen into with respect to linguistic theory, research on syntax became somewhat fragmentary after the Fodor and Garrett paper. Researchers went in search of empirical data that would unlock the mystery of an abstract theory relevant to psycholinguistic phenomena.

Fodor and Garrett (1967) themselves, for example, began to look at the various heuristic devices people may use as shortcuts to the structural analysis of sentences. They pointed out first that the complexity of the process of producing a sentence by converting a base structure into a surface structure does not necessarily correspond to the complexity of the perceptual process of constructing the base structure from the surface form. In other words, the grammar constrains the output but cannot in the same sense constrain the input. Having recognized that while sentence output and sentence input are both comprehended in terms of the base structure form, the question then became one of discovering how, in the case of comprehension, the base is recovered from the surface form.

Fodor and Garrett (1967) argued that the sentence perception process used in inducing the deep structure from the surface structure must involve at least two interacting processes. The person makes use of his or her knowledge about the kinds of base structure relations which lexical items in any particular sentence can enter and second, uses any clues other lexical items in the sentence may give about transformations which may have been used in constructing the sentence. In the first case, for example, the fact that some verbs are transitive and some are not can serve as an immediate clue to the deep structure of the sentences in which they are used. In the second case, the inclusion of a relative pronoun in a sentence gives an immediate clue about an embedding transformation in the sentence.

The first experimental test of these hypotheses (Fodor & Garrett, 1967) focused on the second of the factors. Subjects were presented with sentences such as the following:

1. The pen the author the editor liked used was new.
2. The pen which the author whom the editor liked used was new.
3. The green pen the old author the editor liked used was new.

The task of the subjects was to paraphrase these center-embedded sentences. The number of subject-object relations weighted by the time to respond was used as the performance measure. The results indicated a strong facilitation of sentence perception when the relative pronouns were included in the sentence. Thus, the longer sentence of the second type above was processed more easily than the shorter one. But sentence one is derivationally more complex because the relative pronouns have been deleted by two additional transformations so that the derivational theory of complexity cannot be rejected on the basis of performance on the first two sentences. However, performance on the third type of sentence was not more difficult than the first type. The third type of sentence involves at least six additional transformations because of the adjectives included which is, of course, in marked contrast to the derivational theory of complexity. Most important to Fodor and Garrett, however, was the fact that the relative pronouns appeared to act as a heuristic device for identifying the deep structure of the sentence, thus making perceptual processing of the difficult center-embedded sentences easier. Surface structure clues are a shortcut to deep structure analysis. Hakes and Cairns (1970) obtained similar results using a different experimental technique.

Fodor, Garrett, and Bever (1968) then attacked the problem in another way. This time they looked at the clues to deep structure given by the particular verb used in the sentences. They point out that while the relative pronoun signaled an embedded sentence in the previous experiment, the more important information about the relations among the nouns in a sentence is determined by the characteristics of the verb in that sentence. For example, consider this sentence:

The man whom the dog bit died.

The initial noun phrase is the object of the verb "bit" in the embedded sentence, "The dog bit the man." But now look at this sentence:

The man whom the girl knows John likes got ill.

Here the initial noun phrase is not the object of the verb "knows." The nature of the two verbs involved is a clue to the differential underlying structure of the two sentences. Since verbs can be classified in terms of the types of deep structure configurations they can dominate, Fodor, Garrett, and Bever designed their research to determine whether perceptual processing of sentences would vary as a function of the structures into which a verb could potentially enter. Thus, they point out that the greater the variety of deep structure forms the lexicon associates with the main verb of the sentence, that is, the greater the structural ambiguity of the verb, the longer it should take to process the sentence. The verb *discuss* is a pure transitive verb that denotes a single underlying structure while the verb *believe* may enter several structures:

> He believes Mary.
> He believes that Mary . . .
> He believes Mary to be . . .

Thus, the direct route to the underlying structure allowed by *discuss* should make it easier to process sentences with verbs of that sort in them relative to sentences with verbs like *believe* in them. These researchers used a paraphrase task similar to that in the previous experiment to test their hypothesis. The results confirmed the assumptions that verbs have lexical structures which denote the deep structures into which the verb may enter and that the person applies this information when attempting to understand a sentence. This preanalysis thus reduces the search for, and may even specify the underlying structure of, the perceived sentence. Of course, similar heuristics may be provided by other words in the sentence as well.

Holmes and Forster (1972), however, have demonstrated in a much more extensive examination of the perception of complement verbs that the situation is much more complex than initially thought. They found that complement sentences were no harder to process than one-clause sentences, which suggests that sentences constructed from two deep structure sentences are not necessarily perceptually more difficult than sentences with only one deep structure unit. That finding surely contradicts the derivational theory of complexity. More interesting, however, is the fact that there were marked differences among types of one-clause sentences and types of complements. Holmes (1973) has made the issue still more complicated by demonstrating that one does not necessarily perceive a two-clause sentence more easily if the main clause precedes the subordinate clause. Such a finding contradicts a hypothesis advanced by Bever (1970), who had argued that since the subordinate clause is a presupposition which is psychologically subsidiary to the main clause, the main clause, and therefore the sentence, should be perceived more easily when the subordinate clause comes second in the sentence. Fodor, on the other hand, in a later paper (Fodor, 1971), had argued that perception would be easier if the deep structure order were reflected in the surface structure order so that processing of the surface order would not require rearranging the elements of the sentence to recover the underlying structure. Both the hypothesis of Bever and that of Fodor seem intuitively reasonable but the data from the Holmes study cannot be interpreted as supporting either. She found, using the rapid visual processing task developed by Forster (1970), that the main clause-superordinate clause order does facilitate performance of adverbial clauses and noun-phrase complements but exactly the opposite effect obtains for relative constructions in right-branching and center-embedded sentences.

The resolution of the problems posed by Fodor and Garrett (1966) in this area is far from complete and looks to be highly complicated, although they have surely pointed the field in the right direction despite the fact that neither the precise form of their hypotheses nor even some of their experimental results have stood the test of additional empirical inquiry. With respect to their research results, for example, Hakes (1971) was unable to replicate the original Fodor, Garrett, and Bever (1968) results with verb types when he used a phoneme monitoring task. The latter task is an experimental procedure introduced by Foss (Foss, 1969; Foss & Lynch, 1969). Basically the method is to ask subjects to listen to sentences and press a button as soon as they hear a particular phoneme, say a /b/, in the initial position of a word. A typical sentence might be:

The man hit the ball.

In this sentence, the button should be pressed as soon as the /b/ in *ball* is perceived. In order to insure that processing of the sentence was at more than a superficial phonemic level, the subjects were required to paraphrase it as well. Foss (1969) found, for example, that if the word preceding the /b/ word was a difficult word, i.e., a low frequency word, reaction time to the /b/ word was slower than if the preceding word was an easy word. The interpretation Foss offered was that the low frequency word required more processing capacity, which made responding to the subsequent /b/ phoneme slower. The additional assumption, of course, is made that the two processes are not independent.

Hakes' (1971) assumption was that if a verb can occur in only one deep structure form, there will be less processing load in a comprehension task involving that verb than if the verb can occur in several deep structure forms. Hakes and Cairns (1970) had verified the Fodor and Garrett (1967) study of relative pronouns using this technique. The Hakes (1971) study was, therefore, an effort to extend the generality of the Fodor, Garrett, and Bever study using the same phoneme monitoring task. Two experiments were conducted using pure transitive and complement verbs followed in each case by words beginning with a /b/ phoneme. In neither experiment was any evidence found to support the earlier study. Hakes points out that rejecting the idea that the verb structure has any effect on comprehension seems inappropriate. It may be, as he suggests, that the verb structure effect does not occur during comprehension per se, but during later processing, as in the paraphrasing task used by Fodor et al. Alternatively, the task used by Hakes may have been too easy and thus the effect did not appear. Finally, it could be that structure decisions are made at the end of a clause and not within a clause. If the latter is the case, the phoneme was in the wrong place and the monitoring effect would only be detected if the /b/ occurred at the beginning of the next clause rather than in the immediately following word. In any case, the verb structure effect on processing seems less than clear at this stage.

Regardless of the outcome of the specific hypotheses which were made by Fodor and Garrett (1966), their paper should be considered a milestone in the field because it opened up psycholinguistic research on syntactic problems to many new hypotheses. It released other researchers to look at all kinds of variables which might be relevant to discovering the deep structure from the surface structure. In short, anything which could be shown to facilitate comprehension had to be incorporated into a new theory of performance in language comprehension situations. No longer were psycholinguists tied to linguistic theory as they had been prior to that time.

## RULE ACQUISITION

One aspect of the linguistic syntactic theory which caught the attention of psychologists early was the interpretation that language is a system of rules. If the acquisition and use of language is a matter of acquiring and using a system of rules, then the study of rule learning, it was argued, would surely provide some insight into the nature of language processing. Miller (1966) took this position first in initiating his Grammarama Project. He and his students tried in various ways to determine how college students formulate language-like rules. Some experiments were conceived in which subjects were asked to generate instances in a specified domain and those instances were identified as correct or incorrect with respect to some arbitrary rule established by the experimenter (a computer). In other experiments the experimenter provided a sample of instances of the rule and the subject tried to formulate the rule or rules from the instances. In either case some sort of test was given to determine whether the precise rule had been properly induced by the subject. Little of this research was ever published, but the rediscovery of Esper's (1925) much earlier rule learning research on miniature linguistic systems led to a flurry of experiments on rule acquisition from other laboratories.

Esper (1925) had demonstrated that, given a paired-associate type of task in which subjects were required to learn two-syllable nonsense names for shapes of different colors, learning was quite possible and easily generalized to new instances when a systematic relationship (rule) existed between the color-shape combination and the first and second syllable of the name. In contrast, random pairing of name and color-shape combination resulted in a nearly impossible learning task. As may be seen in Figure 4–2, Esper's stimuli consisted of four different shapes of four different colors. Fourteen of the sixteen possible stimuli obtained by combining all colors with all shapes were presented in a random order and the subjects were required to learn the names. Once the names had been acquired, a test was given which included both the fourteen training stimuli and the two stimuli which had never been presented during acquisition. The subjects had no difficulty with the old stimuli, of course, but the evidence that rule learning had been involved, rather than rote learning of individual stimulus-name pairs, came from the fact that the subjects had no difficulty in appropriately generating the names of the new stimuli from the rule for the old stimuli. In fact, most of the subjects did not even notice that they had never before seen the new stimuli. Esper's results were robust and found to be easily replicable (e.g., Foss, 1968a; Palermo & Eberhart, 1968).

Smith (1966) took the Esper technique and modified it for use in a memory task in order to examine "the kind of rule-governed creativity which is analogous to at least one type of creativity displayed by all native speakers" (p. 447). Smith created a set of letter pairs conforming to the rules of a simple generative grammar and presented a subset of the total set for subjects to recall. The rules used to generate the letter pairs were phrase structure rules of the following form:

(1) Pair → I + II
(2) I → D, V, H, R, X
(3) II → M, F, G, K, L

There were, therefore, 25 possible pairs in which each of the five letters in the first position could be paired with each of the five letters in the second position. Only 20 of these pairs were actually presented to the subjects. Recall of the 20 presented pairs was, of course, quite good, but it was the errors in recall which were of most interest in Smith's experiments. If the subjects were using the phrase structure rules to generate the letter pairs, then one would expect a significant number of errors involving the pairs generated by the rules but not actually presented. In fact, that is exactly what happened. The subjects did make errors and the errors were consistent with the rule. Other kinds of errors seldom occurred. Smith extended this research

Figure 4-2

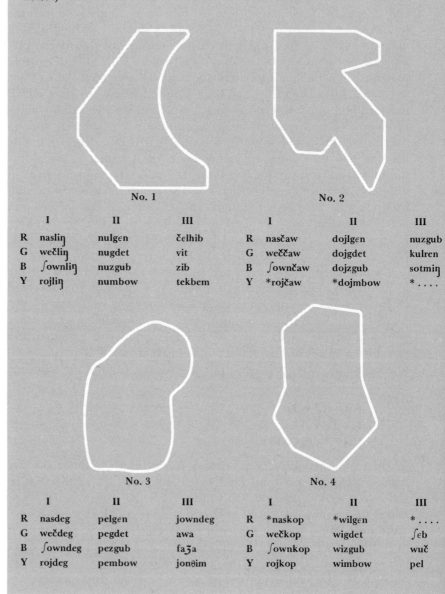

Four shapes and four colors (red, green, blue, and yellow) with the names used in three different experiments. (From Esper, 1925.)

No. 1

| | I | II | III |
|---|---|---|---|
| R | naslɪŋ | nulgɛn | čɛlhib |
| G | wečlɪŋ | nugdet | vit |
| B | ʃownlɪŋ | nuzgub | zib |
| Y | rojlɪŋ | numbow | tekbem |

No. 2

| | I | II | III |
|---|---|---|---|
| R | nasčaw | dojlgɛn | nuzgub |
| G | weččaw | dojgdet | kulren |
| B | ʃownčaw | dojzgub | sotmɪŋ |
| Y | *rojčaw | *dojmbow | * . . . . |

No. 3

| | I | II | III |
|---|---|---|---|
| R | nasdeg | pelgɛn | jowndeg |
| G | wečdeg | pegdet | awa |
| B | ʃowndeg | pezgub | faʒa |
| Y | rojdeg | pembow | jonθim |

No. 4

| | I | II | III |
|---|---|---|---|
| R | *naskop | *wilgɛn | * . . . . |
| G | wečkop | wigdet | ʃɛb |
| B | ʃownkop | wizgub | wuč |
| Y | rojkop | wimbow | pel |

to demonstrate that transformational rules can be learned in these artificial miniature linguistic systems (Smith & Gough, 1969) and that the introduction of irregular pairs (i.e., letter pairs which do not conform to the rule) in the acquisition task does not seriously impair rule learning of the regular pairs (Smith, 1973). The irregular pairs are acquired separately by rote learning and the rule for the regular pairs is acquired at the same time or shortly thereafter. Similar results have been reported by Foss (1968b) and by Palermo and his students (Palermo & Howe, 1970; and Palermo & Parrish, 1971) using a paired-associates task similar to Esper's rather than the recall procedure used by Smith. Smith and Braine (1971) have provided a comprehensive summary of the research in this area.

All these studies of artificial miniature linguistic systems began by making explicit reference to the natural language system. All of the researchers felt that the study of rule systems in a well-controlled laboratory task would provide insights into the rule systems of language. In the case of Miller and Smith, the analogies were to phrase structure and transformation rules, and in Palermo's case, the analogy was to the acquisition of morphological rules by children. Certainly these studies do add to our knowledge of the way rules are acquired and used by the human organism faced with regularities in the materials we must deal with in acquiring and using language. But, two problems are of concern. First, the human organism is an unusual information processing machine, capable of formulating many kinds of rules, giving them up for others in the middle of a task, using rules for generating some responses and suppressing others, and, in general, formulating more ways to solve a problem than an experimenter can anticipate in creating the research problem. It is difficult to know what a person may be doing in any given task, although analyses of error patterns allow us to gain considerable insight into the processes involved. Experimental ingenuity may be all that is required to solve that problem. The second problem is that all of these rule learning tasks have required adults who already know a language to learn a meaningless relation between letter pairs or letter-number pairs. Such a task may differ in significant ways from the processes inherent to acquiring a first language. The question of semantics has been ignored in these experiments and thus the relation of the results to language is not clear until we know how semantics relates to syntactic rules. A recent study by Moeser and Bregman (1973) makes it clear that when meaning is a part of the rule acquisition process, there are important differences in the nature of rule learning. Syntax is most difficult to learn without a referential field to which it relates. It is obvious that children learn rules in acquiring language, but it is equally obvious that they do it in connection with a semantic system.

It may not be possible to study one without taking the other into account.

## YNGVE DEPTH HYPOTHESIS

Another line of research which began at about the same time as the rule learning studies was stimulated by a sentence production model proposed by Yngve (1960). He was engaged at that time in attempting to develop a system for the mechanical translation of languages. The grammar Yngve devised consisted of a finite, unordered set of constituent structure rules. The rules could be mechanically applied to any language construction to provide the structure of that construction in terms of the relations among the constituents of which it was composed. While Yngve was aware of the limitations of a phrase structure analysis of language, he felt that, at least for his purposes, those limitations could be overcome. In order to avoid the problem of an infinitely large memory, Yngve hypothesized that the structure of language is such as to require only a limited, temporary memory. This hypothesis took the form of postulating what has come to be known as the Yngve depth hypothesis, or depth limitation in language.

Yngve (1960) argued that the human has a temporary, or working, memory of about seven items (Miller, 1956) and that sentences are produced so as to take into account this memory limitation. The units of depth, as indicated under each word in the sentences below, are defined in terms of the constituents which must be held in memory during the production of any particular part of the sentence. Take, for example, the production of the first word in the sentence:

> The boy hit the girl.
>  2    1    1   1   0

This involves holding in mind two things: the other word in the initial noun phrase plus the verb phrase. Once *boy* has been produced, completing the noun phrase, then only the verb phrase need be in temporary memory. Utterance of the verb requires holding the noun phrase in memory and so on until the last word is produced which requires no further memory load.

Now look at this sentence:

> The friendly young boy hit the girl.
>  2      2       2    1   1   1   0

This one is more complicated, requiring a greater memory load, because the initial noun phrase is longer. But notice that it does not involve great depth because there is merely a right branching of the initial noun phrase and that is not, according to this model, a difficult memory load. Left branching on the other hand is more taxing on memory as in the case of:

A not very pretty girl is here.
2   4   4      2     1  1   0

In this case, greater depth and thus greater memory load is required despite the fact that the sentence has the same number of words as the previous one. Thus, Yngve analyzed sentences in terms of the surface structure constituents which have to be stored at any particular point in the sentence. The points of difficulty in the sentences can be determined in terms of the model and the mean depth of a sentence can be computed to establish the relative difficulty of processing that sentence. The implications for psychology were obvious and research started in two directions.

The first research approach using the depth metric was taken by E. Martin and Roberts (1966). They conducted an experiment in which they required subjects to recall a list of sentences which differed in depth according to the Yngve measure. All sentences were of the same length and included active, passive, negative, and negative-passive forms. The results appeared to show that Yngve's depth measure of surface structure was a much more powerful variable than transformational complexity for predicting sentence memory. The greater the mean depth of a sentence, the more difficult it was to remember. The results not only failed to support the derivational theory of complexity, but they also appeared to suggest that a surface structure analysis was sufficient to account for sentence memory results. The results of that first study were replicated in subsequent experiments (Martin, Roberts, & Collins, 1968; Roberts, 1968).

Rohrman (1968), however, pointed out a number of difficulties with the Yngve measure and its application in the earlier studies. As Rohrman noted, given any word in English there is no limitation on the word or words which may follow. Only in a very broad sense may one predict a following word, or class of words, knowing the previous word in a sentence. A listener cannot know at each word juncture the memory load ahead and would have to revise at various points as the sentence is heard. In other words, the Yngve analysis seems to be a variant of the information processing approach which Miller (1953) had used to guide the work we discussed earlier.

Second, Rohrman pointed out that there are some ambiguities in establishing the depth metric as Yngve (1960) presented it. Thus, some sentences used in the Martin and Roberts research could be given other depth evaluations. Most important, however, is the problem that, in controlling the length of the sentences in the earlier research, Martin and his collaborators had markedly varied the underlying deep structure of the sentences. While sentence type had been carefully controlled in terms of the major structures such as active and passive, many other structures within these forms had been widely varied, implicating many other kinds of transformations. Rohrman's series of experiments controlled length of sentence and pitted deep structure complexity against Yngve's depth measure. The subjects were required to recall lists of sentences such as the following two types:

1.  They are raising flowers.
     1    2    1      0

2.  They are growling lions.
     1    1    1      0

By the Yngve measure, sentences of the first type, as indicated, have slightly greater depth than sentences of the second type. A deep structure analysis, however, shows the latter to be far more complicated than the former. The first is a simple declarative sentence with a deep structure much like the surface structure. The second, however, has a deep structure which includes the two underlying sentences, "They are lions" and "Lions growl." Rohrman found recall to be a function of deep structure complexity and not Yngve depth. Rohrman's experiments did not, however, support the derivational theory of complexity. It proved not to be the number of transformations in the derivation but rather the complexity of the underlying phrase structure or some aspect of the semantic characteristics of the words as represented in the lexicon which appeared to be most important (Rohrman, 1970).

The second line of research growing out of the Yngve depth model was initiated by Johnson (1965). His approach was to total the number of operations required to decode the constituents of a sentence and make the assumption that a person who is producing or decoding a sentence is holding all of the subsequent decoding operations in short-term memory while producing any particular word in the sentence. Consider the following sentence:

The tall boy saved the dying woman.

Here it is assumed that the sentence is first decoded into a subject and a predicate; the predicate is held in memory while the subject is decoded into modifier and noun; the noun is held in memory while the modifier is decoded into article and adjective; the adjective is held in memory while the article is decoded to the terminal node which is the word *the*. The adjective must then be recalled from memory and decoded as *tall* and the noun recalled and decoded as *boy*. The predicate is then recalled from memory and all of the subsequent decoding operations must be performed before *saved*, which is the next word in the sentence, may be produced. Obviously, according to this hypothesis, it takes more decoding operations to get from *boy* to *saved* than from *tall* to *boy*. Johnson reasoned that if a person had to learn to produce a sentence on cue, the transitional difficulties associated with the number of decoding operations should allow prediction of error patterns. For example, if the word *boy* was produced, the likelihood of there being an error in producing *saved* should be far greater than would be the case for producing *boy* given *tall*. Thus, subjects were required to learn lists of sentences and the predictions of transitional error probabilities during learning were based on the number of decoding operations, determined by using the surface structure constituent analysis proposed by Yngve. Johnson has summarized a number of studies conducted in his laboratory (Johnson, 1968) which tend to support his hypothesis, especially for the major constituent boundaries. The results were not as consistent when lesser constituent boundaries were concerned, a finding which is reminiscent of the click studies we discussed earlier. Johnson has been particularly successful in producing the effect when using letter strings divided into units by spacing. The latter finding suggests that some chunking is taking place in the surface structure units, but the relation of the experiments with letters to the production of sentences is not clear. Certainly the criticisms made by Rohrman (1968) relating to the Yngve hypothesis are relevant to the Johnson experiments as well, although the deep structure account does not apply to the letter string experiments.

While the particular hypothesis of Yngve has not proven to be a satisfactory account of the psychological processing of sentences, it is likely that some of Yngve's ideas about sentence processing may be relevant to theoretical accounts of this phenomenon. We certainly do have psychological limitations on sentence processing and we probably do use surface structure cues at the beginning of a sentence as probabilistic predictors of the structure of the complete sentence in at least some circumstances. The latter is, of course, the same type of hypothesis which Fodor and Garrett (1966) were advancing several years after Yngve (1960). Ignoring the underlying structure, however, especially as it relates to the meaning of a sentence as opposed to the syntactic analysis of a sentence, makes this approach less than satisfactory in principle. A more recent account of sentence parsing has been advanced by Kimball (1973), who has suggested seven principles used by a listener in decoding sentences. He begins with the same assumption made by Yngve that sentence processing proceeds from top to bottom of the phrase structure tree, but he then diverges in his additional principles to take advantage of the advances in linguistics and psycholinguistics since 1960. Kimball's principles, however, must be subjected to the same type of systematic research program as was initiated by Martin and Johnson on the Yngve hypothesis to determine whether the principles he has suggested as important are used by persons actually processing sentences.


## AMBIGUITY

Yet another approach to the study of syntax has centered on the ambiguity of some sentences. MacKay and Bever (1967) were the first to examine this problem. They pointed out that ambiguity may take at least three forms: (1) *lexical ambiguity,* produced by a word in the sentence which has more than one meaning; (2) *surface structure ambiguity,* produced by differences in the grouping of words into phrases within the sentence, resulting in different meanings; and (3) *underlying structural ambiguity,* produced when there is more than one set of logical relations among the words in the sentence, thus resulting in different meanings. The three types of ambiguity are illustrated in the following three sentences taken from their study:

(1) He wears a light suit in the summer.
(2) They sent the requisition over a week ago.
(3) The mayor requested the police to stop drinking.

The question arises, of course, as to what ambiguity does to sentence processing and how the different kinds of ambiguity may differentially affect sentence comprehension. The authors of the early studies, taking their cue from linguistic theory, assumed that, since sentence comprehension was supposed to begin with the recovery of the underlying structure, followed by recovery of the surface structure, and finally the lexical items, ambiguities should be identified in the order in which the structures are recovered. The experiment of MacKay and Bever consisted of asking subjects to indicate as quickly as possible the two meanings of sentences containing one of the three types of ambiguity. The amount of time it took to respond with both meanings was taken to indicate the difficulty of processing each ambiguity type. The results were exactly the opposite of those predicted by linguistic theory: lexical ambiguities were most quickly perceived and the underlying structural ambiguities took longer to process than those with only surface ambiguities. MacKay (1966) obtained similar results with a sentence completion task in which an ambiguity was put in the stem of the sentence to be completed. It is clear from these early studies of ambiguity that the results were in line with arguments put forward by Fodor and Garrett (1966) that linguistic theory did not necessarily reflect an account of psychological processing.

Subsequent research has been directed toward determining how ambiguities are resolved. Does a person analyze all the possible interpretations of a sentence and then in some way choose the appropriate one from among them? Does the person recognize an ambiguity and hold off interpretation until it is resolved at a later point in the sentence? Or, does the individual accept one meaning of the ambiguous sentence, either with or without recognizing that it is an ambiguous sentence, and consider another meaning only when conflicting information is processed which requires that a change in interpretation is necessary? Foss, Bever, and Silver (1968) used a picture-sentence verification task to test these alternative hypotheses. The task consisted of presenting a sentence to the subject, followed by a picture of the correct or an incorrect interpretation of the sentence. Response time was measured for the verification decision that the sentence described the picture. In the case of the ambiguous sentences, the picture either depicted a frequent interpretation of the ambiguity or an infrequent interpretation. The meaning bias of the ambiguities was pretested so that it was known which meaning was most often assigned to each sentence. An example of the kind of ambiguities used is this statement:

The boy is looking up the street.

This was most often interpreted as gazing up the street and less often as looking up the street on a map.

The results indicated that response time was fastest for unambiguous sentences but equally fast for ambiguous sentences when the frequent interpretation was depicted in the picture. Responses to the less frequent interpretation of the ambiguity were significantly slower. The results seemed to support the third model of ambiguous sentence comprehension, i.e., the usual interpretation is assigned to a sentence and rejected for another interpretation only if an unexpected conflict occurs between the first interpretation and subsequent information.

The finding that frequency of interpretation, or meaning use, is relevant was also demonstrated for isolated words by Rubenstein, Lewis, and Rubenstein (1971). They found, however, that *homographs,* words which are spelled the same but have multiple unrelated meanings, are more easily recognized as words than words with a single meaning. Thus, ambiguity facilitated word recognition in the Rubenstein et al. study but impaired comprehension in the Foss et al. study. Since Foss (1970) had used the phoneme monitoring task earlier to demonstrate that ambiguity in sentences requires more time be allowed to process a sentence, Foss and Jenkins (1973) decided to use the same task to try to determine which of the various interpretations of what is happening when one attempts to comprehend an ambiguous sentence may be correct. They assumed that if a *disambiguating context* were provided early in a sentence, one of the meanings of the ambiguous lexical items would be identified and the context would help to facilitate processing of the sentence by resolving the ambiguity. The critical phoneme was placed after the lexically ambiguous word in the sentences. The sentences were constructed so that half of the ambiguities were contextually disambiguated early in the sentence, while in the other half the context of the initial part of the sentence was neutral with respect to the two meanings of the lexically ambiguous items.

The results indicated that phoneme monitoring was slower after ambiguous words regardless of the preceding context. It would seem that contextual effects do not operate to reduce the ambiguity-caused processing load. Since prior decisions about the ambiguous word do not seem to be made before the ambiguous word is encountered, the notion that a single meaning is settled on until conflicting information occurs was not supported. Rather, it appears that all meanings known to the person are activated to working memory and some choice is made among the many meanings after the time the word is encountered in the sentence. Olson andMacKay (1974) have provided further evidence using other experimental procedures that this is the case. Cairns and Kamerman (1975) provided data which indicates that the decision stage following retrieval of the various meanings is very short. Phoneme monitoring is unaffected by ambiguity if the phoneme occurs three words rather than immediately after the ambiguous word. Data from Hogaboam and Perfetti (1975), however, support a model based on a sequentially ordered search through meanings of words and raise questions about whether lexical, as opposed to structural, ambiguities actually increase the complexity of processing. The uncertainty about how ambiguous sentences are processed, however, is clearly not solved by the current research, and we shall have to look to further studies before we may be able to understand which of the alternative theoretical accounts may be most nearly correct.

## RHYTHM

An entirely different kind of variable that may play an important part in speech production and perception is rhythm. J. G. Martin (1972) has been particularly interested in this phenomenon. He has argued that rhythm, or temporal patterning, is an important aspect of sentence processing. As we noted in Chapter 3, speech is not a mere string of concatenated sounds in a time sequence; Martin argues that these sounds are a hierarchically organized rhythmic structure of stressed and unstressed patterns much like a musical score. The sound elements which make up a sentence are organized in such a way as to be redundant with respect to linguistic message elements, and tracking the sound pattern allows anticipation of elements without the necessity of continuous monitoring of the pattern itself. Syntactic units, for example, can be identified not by words or syntactic boundaries alone, but by rhythmic patterns of the structures as well (Dooling, 1974). Such patterns will point to parts of the message to which attention must be directed and in this way facilitate strategies of sentence perception (as opposed to syntactic processing, for example). Martin has shown how speech does follow hierarchically organized rhythmic patterns which describe the timing of syllabic elements in natural temporal patterns and has shown how modifications of these patterns may affect speech perception (Martin, 1970).

The idea of rhythm in language actually grew out of some earlier work dealing with pauses and hesitations in speech (Maclay & Osgood, 1959). Goldman-Eisler (1968) stimulated much of this research in a number of experiments which demonstrated that hesitations and pauses in speech appear to be related to the amount of what might loosely be called the mental effort necessary to produce the utterance. She found that hesitations tend to occur most frequently just prior to high information words—those occasions in sentence production which involve selection from the lexicon of the precise word which will convey the idea the speaker has in mind (e.g., Goldman-Eisler, 1958). Furthermore, pauses tend to be longer and more frequent when a person is discussing the meaning of some event as opposed to merely describing the event (Goldman-Eisler, 1961). If the person who abstracts the meaning of an event is asked to repeat the content of the same utterance, the frequency and length of pauses decreases significantly. The latter finding suggests that the mental effort or semantic decisions had been made in the initial construction of the sentence so that in the second production the person merely needed to describe what was said before.

While Goldman-Eisler has shown that hesitations in speech production are placed at points of transition to high information within constituent boundaries of sentences, J. G. Martin and Strange (1968) have demonstrated that when the message is decoded by a listener, the hesitations are reported to occur at points between constituent boundaries. There appears to be a perceptual shift of the hesitation from the actual position of the pause within constituent boundaries in encoding to a position between constituent boundaries at decoding. The shift of pauses to constituent boundaries is reminiscent once again of the shift in identification of the click placements in the Fodor and Garrett (1967) research mentioned earlier. While hesitations in natural speech production seem to occur most frequently within constituents and listeners tend to displace them between the boundaries, Fillenbaum (1970a) has shown that pauses are more likely to be noticed and judged longer by listeners when they occur within rather than between constituent boundaries. Such a finding suggests that sentence perception and the decoding process may be made more difficult by pauses that occur at the natural places *within* constituents during production rather than *between* constituents, which is the natural place for perception. In other words, hesitations within constituent boundaries distract attention while those between boundaries do not. (Public speakers should take note.) While J. G. Martin and Strange (1968) demonstrated the pause shift phenomenon, it still seems to be the case that if breaks in the speech signal actually coincide with major constituent boundaries then speech perception may be facilitated. The latter prediction was confirmed by Wingfield and Klein (1971). That study also suggested that intonation pattern is another aid to speech perception which is, of course, a component of the rhythm phenomenon and brings us full circle to the point that J. G. Martin has emphasized as being so important.

The problem becomes even more complicated, however, when we consider the study of J. E. Martin, Kolodziej, and Genay (1971), who demonstrated that segmentation of sentences appears to be dependent not so much on the major constituent boundaries of the syntactic surface structure as it is on the *phonologically interpreted readjusted surface structure,* by which they mean the units defined in terms of perceived intonation that are chunked in language processing. Such units often coincide with the syntactic surface structure, but as the Martin et al. data demonstrate, long subject, verb, or object parts of sentences lead to different segmentation of a sentence in terms of the phonological phrase. For example, the segmentation of the following sentences would be quite different:

The boy went on a very long trip to the market.

The very tall, handsome, young boy went to the market.

In the first case, the long phrase after the verb leads to putting the subject and the verb together in terms of phonological phrasing; in the second sentence, the break in phonological phrasing is after *boy* rather than after *went*. The major syntactic surface structure boundary is, of course, in the same place in both cases, but the rhythm which J. G. Martin (1972) has pointed to is based on the phonological phrase rather than the syntactic phrase. Thus, in addition to syntactic variables, we find that intonation, pausing, and rhythm associated with the phonological phrase play a part in sentence processing, both productive and receptive.

## ASSOCIATIVE RELATIONS

The influence of meaning on syntactic processing could not, however, be ignored. Some researchers had for various theoretical reasons looked at variables related to meaning and their effects on syntactic issues in connection with sentence processing. Rosenberg (1968, 1969), for example, has demonstrated that the type of syntactic errors made in recalling sentences can be markedly influenced by the associations among the words within the sentence. Sentences which are semantically well integrated, i.e., constructed of associatively related words, are recalled in larger chunks (Rosenberg, 1968); associations facilitate recall of other unrelated parts of complex sentences (Rosenberg, 1969); and associations facilitate sentence perception in noise (Rosenberg & Jarvella, 1970).

## IMAGERY

Paivio has extended his well-known work on imagery (1971a) to problems of sentence memory. He argues that imagery is a significant component of meaning and that sentence processing is strongly affected by the image-arousing characteristics of the words in sentences. Begg and Paivio (1969), for example, replicated parts of the Sachs study (1967), showing that if high-imagery words were used in sentences, the meaning of the sentences was well remembered but the syntax was poorly retained, exactly as Sachs had found. When abstract or low-imagery materials were used, however, modifications in meanings were not as frequently noted and syntactic structure was better retained. Paivio (1971b) also reported that a replication of the Rohrman (1968) study revealed that the subject nominalizations used in that study were of higher imagery value than the object nominalizations, suggesting that imagery rather than deep structure complexity may account for those results.

The Begg and Paivio results were confirmed by Jorgenson and Kintsch (1973), but problems with the equivalence of meaning of the synonyms used in the Paivio study and the verbs used in the Jorgenson and Kintsch study make the role of imagery unclear in these studies. For example, Johnson, Bransford, Nyberg, and Cleary (1972) have shown that the abstract sentences used by Begg and Paivio were more difficult to understand and the meaning changes were not as great as in the concrete sentences which Begg and Paivio used. Pezdek and Roger (1974) have also shown that context greatly facilitates recognition of meaning changes for abstract materials while having no effect on concrete materials. In short, neither the influence of imagery on sentence processing nor its relation to meaning is at all clear on the basis of the evidence we have at this point. The difficulty of equating materials which are high and low in terms of imagery on all the other variables makes it unlikely that the relative importance of imagery will be determined for some time.

## VERIFICATION TASKS

Actually, the study of the relation of meaning and syntax began much earlier when Wason initiated some research on the processing time for affirmative and negative statements (Wason, 1959). He found that a statement about some referent takes longer to verify if it is a negative statement than if it is a positive statement. Furthermore, it takes longer to respond if the sentence is false rather than true with respect to the referent. Wason (1961) suggested that when a person perceives a sentence in a referential context, both the sentence and the referent must be processed. Once both have been processed, i.e., the meaning has been determined for each, then a match between referent and sentence must be determined, followed by the appropriate response. When the sentence is affirmative and true relative to the referent, the match is simple and direct. When the sentence is false, the mismatch takes longer to verify than when it is true. When the sentence contains a negative, however, the person may convert the negative to some sort of an affirmative form and then check against the referent. For example, if a statement such as "The number is not odd" is presented in the presence of some specific number, the statement may be changed to the positive form, "The number is even," and then a comparison made with the number. The extra step in processing, of course, takes time and, therefore, slows the verification process. Wason's results were replicated in other situations (e.g., Wason, 1965; Gough, 1965; Slobin, 1966), although Wales and Grieve (1969) have demonstrated that we must be cautious in generalizing these hypotheses from binary choices to all cases of negative constructions since contradictory binary events (e.g., odd-not odd) are not the same as contrary ones (e.g., cold-not cold). Gough (1966) threw additional light on the situation by delaying for three seconds the time from sentence presentation to picture verification. This procedure guaranteed that the sentence had been processed before the verification process took place. The results of his experiment showed the same effects as the previous studies, indicating that it is not the sentence comprehension processing alone but the verification procedure as well which takes longer in the case of negative and false statements.

The literature in this area was examined by Chase and Clark (1970) and by Trabasso (1970) independently at about the same time and they proposed essentially the same theory to account for the data then available. They both noted that when an individual is presented with linguistic and nonlinguistic materials to process and compare, the task involves comparing the coding of the features or propositions of the input in the two cases. Negative input is coded as a set of affirmative features or propositions plus a negative marker. In the case of binary features, the negative feature may be recoded as the affirmative contradictory feature. The second task of the person becomes one of comparing features of the two sets of input. Identical codes prime responses of "true" or "same," while mismatches prime "false" or "different" responses. In the latter case, a recheck of the features is made. Finally, a check is made on negative markers and if both codes are marked for affirmative or both are negated then no changes are made in the initial response decision, but if one is negative and the other is affirmative, the response decision is changed. The actual response is then made. Each of these steps is assumed to take time so that true affirmative statements should take the least time and false negatives the most time because the steps necessary to determine the appropriate responses are fewest in the first case and greatest in the latter. Both Trabasso (Trabasso, Rollins, & Shaughnessy, 1971) and Clark and Chase (1972) have provided extensive data to support their respective models which differ in little but terminology.

Clark and his colleagues have continued research in this area with studies designed to extend the generality of the model for the comprehension of negation to other semantically related sentence comprehension and verification phenomena. Clark and Chase (1972), for example, have shown that the model may be modified to include picture-sentence as well as sentence-picture verification. Furthermore, the latter studies appear to suggest that people are able to respond more rapidly to the unmarked version of prepositional pairs such as *above* and *below*. Verification of sentences involving *above*, which is the unmarked form, is faster than sentences using *below*. (You will find more on markedness in the next chapter.) Just and Carpenter (1971) have reported a series of experiments which indicate that the implicit negative characteristics of *few* and *scarcely any*, for example, also result in affecting sentence processing in much the same way as the syntactic *not* sentence forms. Yet another extension of the model (Just & Clark, 1973) relates to the presuppositions and the implications of sentences involving verbs which are positive or inherently negative. For example, *remember* and *thoughtful* are positive verbs while *forget* (not remember) and *thoughtless* (not thoughtful) are inherently negative. Just and Clark point out that the presuppositions of both the positive and the negative verbs in each of these cases is the same. On the other hand, the implication of the positive one is positive while the implication of the negative verb is negative. The latter characteristic of the verb reveals the basis of the inherent negative aspect of the verb. The following examples illustrate the similarities and differences of the verbs *remember* and *forget*.

1. (a) John remembered to let the dog out.
1. (b) John was supposed to let the dog out. (Presupposition)
1. (c) John let the dog out. (Implication)

2. (a)  John forgot to let the dog out.
2. (b)  John was supposed to let the dog out. (Presupposition)
2. (c)  John didn't let the dog out. (Implication)

As in all the previous studies, the experiment consisted of determining the reaction time for processing the sentences. It is assumed that longer reaction times are required for greater numbers of processing steps. In the Just and Clark study, the subjects were presented with the initial statement (a) and their reaction times to questions about the truth or falsity of the presupposition or implication of the sentence were measured. For example, "John forgot to let the dog out," "The dog is in (out)?" (Implication); "The dog is supposed to be in (out)?" (Presupposition). As predicted by the model, both presupposition and implication reaction times were slower when the negative verbs appeared in the statements. Furthermore, positive sentences were verified more quickly when true, and negative sentences were verified more quickly when false. The interesting results, however, pertain to the relationship between reaction times to presuppositions and the implications relative to the sentences. Regardless of whether the statement contains *remember* or *forget*, the presuppositions are positive, which means that a true response should be faster than a false response—this is exactly the result obtained in both cases. The implication of *forget*, however, is negative. Therefore, slower reaction times to true implications of *forget* should occur than to false implications. Again, the model was supported by the data. The model and the data nicely separate the negative from the positive components in these sentences with inherently negative verbs. Clark (1971) has reported similar results for sentences including words such as *absent, different,* and *conflict.* Data presented by Sherman (1975) for multiply-negated sentences including *sad* and *unhappy* do not, however, fit so nicely with the model.

Haviland and Clark (1974) have extended the general model which has guided this research still further to performance with sentences involving the acquisition of new information. The fact that sentences usually provide a context of given or already-known information followed by some new information led Haviland and Clark to assume that without the given information the new information would take longer to process. Their experiments using the same reaction time technique demonstrated that comprehension of a target sentence was, in fact, faster when a preceding contextual sentence was compatible with the given part of the target sentence. For example, the first context led to faster comprehension than the second for the target sentence below:

1.  We got some beer out of the car.

2. Andrew was especially fond of beer.
Target: The beer was warm.

Clearly the target sentence presupposes that some beer was present, i.e., that is a given, and the first context sentence indicates that presupposition while the second sentence does not. When the presupposition has been made explicit in the preceding context, the target sentence is easier to process. This is an interesting result, especially when one remembers that the preceding context did not reduce the processing time of ambiguous sentences using the phoneme monitoring task.

Extending the model out of the immediate referential relationship inherent in its development, Just (1974) has shown that the same types of processing differences which obtain for picture verification tasks may also apply to semantic memory, i.e., "Is it true or false that dogs are animals?" Not surprisingly, the verification of statements which must be compared to semantic memory as opposed to a presented picture involves the same processing and reflects the effects of the same variables.

## SUMMARY

In summary, those doing research on syntax began with the assumption that linguistic theory was a psychological theory, and, having demonstrated the falsity of that assumption, they have begun to search for a psychological theory. The search has led to the development of a host of hypotheses and a number of techniques to test them. The simplest of the hypotheses have been rejected one by one, and the complexity of sentence production, perception, and memory has become more and more apparent. No simple account will do and it seems unlikely at this stage that even complex hypotheses which seem to hold for one task will have any generality from one situation to the next.

One reason for the latter difficulty is that there has been no clear differentiation among tasks or experimental techniques and the processing requirements demanded of the subject. Fillenbaum (1970) has made this point with respect to memory tasks used to assess the nature of processing syntax. As he notes, syntactic confusions or errors in a memory task are a function of syntactic processing of the structures involved plus memorial processes. The assumption that the two processes are independent is a tenuous one. Fillenbaum presents some data to show that different results may be obtained when different techniques are used to assess sentence processing. Craik and Lockhart (1972) have made a related point in a different context. They argue that there are levels of processing material whether it be drawings, words, or sentences. Depending on the task requirements, the subject may process a sentence, for example, as a series of sounds, phonemes, words, syntactic forms, or meanings. The level at which the material is processed will be reflected in the measure taken. To take an extreme example, if you ask a person to listen for sounds in a sentence and then ask for the meaning of the sentence, the processing of meaning is likely to be small relative to a subject asked to consider the meaning of the words.

Experiments proposing to examine syntactic processing have not always been designed with these problems in mind. We are often faced with the problem of comparing results obtained by different techniques which involve different kinds of psychological processing, due to the kind of task and the different requirements of the subject in the task. More attention needs to be given to these problems in future research in this area.

Finally, we should note another shift in the emphasis of research on syntax. While early research focused on the major optional syntactic transformations associated with passives, questions, and negatives and then shifted to some of the transformations within these sentence form types, there has been a gradually increasing concern with the influence of meaning on syntactic processing. The neat line between syntax and semantics has eroded so that the early work on negative syntactic forms, for example, has become more and more concerned with the semantic problems of implication, presupposition, and context, along with the more general cognitive processing of the referential field on which the linguistic material bears. Although there is some evidence that a clear distinction between the effects of syntax and semantics on sentence processing may be maintained (Forster & Olbrei, 1973), the question of where this chapter should end and the next one begin has grown a bit fuzzy.

## REFERENCES

Begg, I., & Paivio, A. Concreteness and imagery in sentence meaning. *Journal of Verbal Learning and Verbal Behavior*, 1969, *8*, 821–27.

Bever, T. G. The comprehension and memory of sentences with temporal relations. In G. B. Flores d'Arcais & W. J. Levelt (Eds.), *Advances in psycholinguistics*. Amsterdam: North-Holland, 1970.

Bever, T. G., Lackner, J. R., & Kirk, R. The underlying structures of sentences are the primary units of immediate speech processing. *Perception and Psychophysics*, 1969, *5*, 225–34.

Cairns, H. S., & Kamerman, J. Lexical information processing during sentence comprehension. *Journal of Verbal Learning and Verbal Behavior*, 1975, *14*, 170–79.

Chase, W. G., & Clark, H. H. Mental operations in the comparison of sentences and pictures. In L. Gregg (Ed.), *Cognition in learning and memory*. New York, Wiley, 1970.

Chomsky, N. *Syntactic structures.* The Hague: Morton, 1957.

Chomsky, N. *Aspects of a theory of syntax.* Cambridge: M.I.T. Press, 1965.

Clark, H. H. The chronometric study of meaning components. Presented: C.R.N.S. Colloque International sur les Problèmes Actuels de Psycholinguistique. Paris, December 1971.

Clark, H. H., & Chase, W. G. On the process of comparing sentences against pictures. *Cognitive Psychology,* 1972, *3,* 472–517.

Clifton, C., Jr., & Odom, P. Similarity relations among certain English sentence constructions. *Psychological Monographs,* 1966, *80,* No. 5, 1–35.

Craik, F. I. M., & Lockhart, R. S. Levels of processing: A framework for memory research, *Journal of Verbal Learning and Verbal Behavior,* 1972, *11,* 671–84.

Dooling, D. J. Rhythm and syntax in sentence perception. *Journal of Verbal Learning and Verbal Behavior,* 1974, *13,* 255–64.

Epstein, W. Recall of word lists of following learning of sentences and of anomalous and random strings. *Journal of Verbal Learning and Verbal Behavior,* 1969, *8,* 20–25.

Esper, E. A. A technique for the experimental investigation of associative interference in artificial linguistic material. *Language Monographs,* 1925, No. 1.

Fillenbaum, S. Syntactic locus as a determinant of judged pause duration. *Perception and Psychophysics,* 1970a, *9,* 219–21.

Fillenbaum, S. On the use of memorial techniques to assess syntactic structures. *Psychological Bulletin,* 1970b, *73,* 231–37.

Fodor, J. A. Current approaches to syntax recognition. In D. L. Horton & J. J. Jenkins (Eds.), *Perception of language.* Columbus, Ohio: Charles E. Merrill, 1971.

Fodor, J. A., & Bever, T. G. The psychological reality of linguistic segments. *Journal of Verbal Learning and Verbal Behavior,* 1965, *4,* 414–20.

Fodor, J. A. & Garrett, M. Some reflections on competence and performance. In J. Lyons & R. J. Wales (Eds.), *Psycholinguistic papers.* Edinburgh: Edinburgh University Press, 1966. Pp. 135–54.

Fodor, J. A., & Garrett, M. Some syntactic determinants of sentential complexity. *Perception and Psychophysics,* 1967, *2,* 289–96.

Fodor, J. A., Garrett, M., & Bever, T. G. Some syntactic determinants of sentential complexity. II: Verb structure. *Perception and Psychophysics,* 1968, *3,* 453–61.

Forster, K. I. Left-to-right processes in the construction of sentences. *Journal of Verbal Learning and Verbal Behavior,* 1966, *5,* 285–91.

Forster, K. I. Visual perception of rapidly presented word sequences of varying complexity. *Perception and Psychophysics,* 1970, *8,* 215–21.

Forster, K. I., & Olbrei, I. Semantic heuristics and syntactic analysis. *International Journal of Cognitive Psychology,* 1973, *2,* 319–47.

Foss, D. J. An analysis of learning in a miniature linguistic system. *Journal of Experimental Psychology,* 1968a, *76,* 450–59.

Foss, D. J. Learning and discovery in the acquisition of structured material: Effects of number of items and their sequence. *Journal of Experimental Psychology,* 1968b, *77,* 341–44.

Foss, D. J. Decision processes during sentence comprehension: Effects of lexical item difficulty and position upon decision times. *Journal of Verbal Learning and Verbal Behavior,* 1969, *8,* 457–82.

Foss, D. J. Some effects of ambiguity upon sentence comprehension. *Journal of Verbal Learning and Verbal Behavior,* 1970, *9,* 699–706.

Foss, D. J., Bever, T. G., & Silver, M. The comprehension and verification of ambiguous sentences. *Perception and Psychophysics,* 1968, *4,* 304–6.

Foss, D. J., & Cairns, H. S. Some effects of memory limitation upon sentence comprehension and recall. *Journal of Verbal Learning and Verbal Behavior*, 1970, *9*, 541–47.

Foss, D. J., & Jenkins, C. M. Some effects of context on the comprehension of ambiguous sentences. *Journal of Verbal Learning and Verbal Behavior*, 1973, *12*, 577–89.

Foss, D. J., & Lynch, R. H., Jr. Decision processes during sentence comprehension: Effects of surface structure on decision times. *Perception and Psychophysics*, 1969, *5*, 145–48.

Garrett, M., Bever, T. G., & Fodor, J. A. The active use of grammar in speech perception. *Perception and Psychophysics*, 1966, *1*, 30–32.

Glucksberg, S., & Danks, J. H. Grammatical structure and recall: A function of the space in immediate memory or recall delay? *Perception and Psychophysics*, 1969, *6*, 113–17.

Goldman-Eisler, F. Speech production and the predictability of words in context. *Quarterly Journal of Experimental Psychology*, 1958, *10*, 96–106.

Goldman-Eisler, F. The distribution of pause durations in speech. *Language and Speech*, 1961, *4*, 232–37.

Goldman-Eisler, F. *Psycholinguistics: Experiments in spontaneous speech*. London: Academic Press, 1968.

Gough, P. B. Grammatical transformations and speed of understanding. *Journal of Verbal Learning and Verbal Behavior*, 1965, *5*, 107–11.

Gough, P. B. The verification of sentences: The effects of delay of evidence and sentence length. *Journal of Verbal Learning and Verbal Behavior*, 1966, *5*, 492–96.

Hakes, D. T. Does verb structure affect sentence comprehension? *Perception and Psychophysics*, 1971, *10*, 229–32.

Hakes, D. T., & Cairns, H. S. Sentence comprehension and relative pronouns. *Perception and Psychophysics*, 1970, *8*, 5–8.

Haviland, S. E., & Clark, H. H. What's New? Acquiring new information as a process in comprehension. *Journal of Verbal Learning and Verbal Behavior*, 1974, *13*, 512–21.

Hogaboam, T. W., & Perfetti, C. A. Lexical ambiguity and sentence comprehension. *Journal of Verbal Learning and Verbal Behavior*, 1975, *14*, 265–74.

Holmes, V. M. Order of main and subordinate clauses in sentence perception. *Journal of Verbal Learning and Verbal Behavior*, 1973, *12*, 285–93.

Holmes, V. M., & Forster, K. I. Detection of extraneous signals during sentence recognition. *Perception and Psychophysics*, 1970, *7*, 297–301.

Holmes, V. M., & Forster, K. I. Perceptual complexity and underlying sentence structure. *Journal of Verbal Learning and Verbal Behavior*, 1972, *11*, 148–56.

Holyoak, K. J. The role of imagery in the evaluation of sentences: Imagery or semantic factors? *Journal of Verbal Learning and Verbal Behavior*, 1974, *13*, 163–66.

James, C. T., Thompson, J. G., & Baldwin, J. M. The reconstructive process in sentence memory. *Journal of Verbal Learning and Verbal Behavior*, 1973, *12*, 51–63.

Johnson, M. K., Bransford, J. D., Nyberg, S. E., & Cleary, J. J. Comprehension factors in interpreting memory for abstract and concrete sentences. *Journal of Verbal Learning and Verbal Behavior*, 1972, *11*, 451–54.

Johnson, N. F. The psychological reality of phrase structure rules. *Journal of Verbal Learning and Verbal Behavior*, 1965, *4*, 469–75.

Johnson, N. F. Sequential verbal behavior. In T. R. Dixon & D. L. Horton (Eds.), *Verbal behavior and general behavior theory*. Englewood Cliffs, N.J.: Prentice-Hall, 1968. Pp. 421–50.

Jorgensen, C. C., & Kintsch, W. The role of imagery in the evaluation of sentences. *Cognitive Psychology*, 1973, *4*, 110–16.

Just, M. A. Comprehending qualified sentences: The relation between sentence-picture and semantic memory verification. *Cognitive Psychology*, 1974, *6*, 216–36.

Just, M. A., & Carpenter, P. A. Comprehension of negation with quantification. *Journal of Verbal Learning and Verbal Behavior*, 1971, *10*, 244–53.

Just, M. A., & Clark, H. H. Drawing inferences from the presuppositions and implications of affirmative and negative sentences. *Journal of Verbal Learning and Verbal Behavior*, 1973, *12*, 21–31.

Kimball, J. Seven principles of surface structure parsing in natural language. *International Journal of Cognitive Psychology*, 1973, *2*, 7–14.

Ladefoged, P., & Broadbent, D. Perception of sequences in auditory events. *Quarterly Journal of Experimental Psychology*, 1960, *12*, 162–70.

Lashley, K. The problem of serial order in behavior. In L. Jeffriess (Ed.), *Cerebral mechanisms in behavior*. New York: Wiley, 1951. Pp. 112–38.

MacKay, D. G. To end ambiguous sentences. *Perception and Psychophysics*, 1966, *1*, 426–36.

MacKay, D. G., & Bever, T. G. In search of ambiguity. *Perception and Psychophysics*, 1967, *2*, 193–200.

Maclay, H., & Osgood, C. E. Hesitation phenomena in spontaneous English speech. *Word*, 1959, *15*, 19–44.

Martin, E., & Roberts, K. H. Grammatical factors in sentence retention. *Journal of Verbal Learning and Verbal Behavior*, 1966, *5*, 211–18.

Martin, E., Roberts, K. H., & Collins, A. Short-term memory for sentences. *Journal of Verbal Learning and Verbal Behavior*, 1968, *7*, 560–66.

Martin, J. E., Kolodziej, B., & Genay, J. Segmentation of sentences into phonological phrases as a function of constituent length. *Journal of Verbal Learning and Verbal Behavior*, 1971, *10*, 226–33.

Martin, J. G. Rhythm-induced judgments of word stress in sentences. *Journal of Verbal Learning and Verbal Behavior*, 1970, *9*, 627–33.

Martin, J. G. Rhythmic (hierarchical) versus serial structures in speech and other behavior. *Psychological Review*, 1972, *79*, 487–509.

Martin, J. G., & Strange, W. Determinants of hesitations in spontaneous speech. *Journal of Experimental Psychology*, 1968, *76*, 474–79.

McMahon, L. E. Grammatical analysis as a part of understanding a sentence. Unpublished doctoral dissertation, Harvard University, 1963.

Mehler, J. Some effects of grammatical transformations on the recall of English sentences. *Journal of Verbal Learning and Verbal Behavior*, 1963, *2*, 346–51.

Miller, G. A. *Language and communication*. New York: McGraw-Hill, 1951.

Miller, G. A. What is information measurement? *American Psychologist*, 1953, *8*, 3–11.

Miller, G. A. The magical number seven, plus or minus two: Some limits on our capacity for processing information. *Psychological Review*, 1956, *63*, 81–97.

Miller, G. A. *Grammarama: II. Review and statement of the problems*. Scientific Report #CS-6 Center for Cognitive Studies, Harvard University, 1966.

Miller, G. A., & McKean, K. A chronometric study of some relations between sentences. *Quarterly Journal of Experimental Psychology*, 1964, *16*, 297–308.

Miller, G. A., & Selfridge, J. Verbal context and the recall of meaningful material. *American Journal of Psychology*, 1950, *63*, 176–85.

Moeser, S. D., & Bregman, A. S. Imagery and language acquisition. *Journal of Verbal Learning and Verbal Behavior*, 1973, *12*, 91–98.

Olson, J. N., & Mackay, D. G. Completion and verification of ambiguous sentences. *Journal of Verbal Learning and Verbal Behavior,* 1974, *13,* 457–70.

Osgood, C. E., & Sebeok, T. A. (Eds.). *Psycholinguistics: A survey of theory and research problems.* Bloomington, Indiana: Indiana University Press, 1954.

Padrick, T. A. *An investigation into the unit of immediate speech perception.* Unpublished master's thesis. Pennsylvania State University, 1973.

Paivio, A. *Imagery and verbal processes.* New York: Holt, Rinehart & Winston, 1971a.

Paivio, A. Imagery and language. In S. J. Segal (Ed.), *Imagery: Current cognitive approaches.* New York: Academic Press, 1971b. Pp. 7–32.

Paivio, A., & Begg, I. Imagery and comprehension latencies as a function of sentence concreteness and structure. *Perception and Psychophysics,* 1971, *10,* 408–12.

Palermo, D. S., & Eberhart, V. L. On the learning of morphological rules: An experimental analogy. *Journal of Verbal Learning and Verbal Behavior,* 1968, *7,* 337–44.

Palermo, D. S., & Howe, H. E., Jr. An experimental analogy to the learning of past tense inflection rules. *Journal of Verbal Learning and Verbal Behavior,* 1970, *9,* 410–16.

Palermo, D. S., & Parrish, M. Rule acquisition as a function of number and frequency of exemplar presentation. *Journal of Verbal Learning and Verbal Behavior,* 1971, *10,* 44–51.

Pezdek, K., & Roger, J. M. The role of comprehension in learning concrete and abstract sentences. *Journal of Verbal Learning and Verbal Behavior,* 1974, *13,* 551–58.

Reber, A. S., & Anderson, J. R. The perception of clicks in linguistic and nonlinguistic messages. *Perception and Psychophysics,* 1970, *8,* 81–89.

Roberts, K. H. Grammatical and associative constraints in sentence retention. *Journal of Verbal Learning and Verbal Behavior,* 1968, *7,* 1072–76.

Rohrman, N. L. The role of syntactic structure in the recall of English nominalizations. *Journal of Verbal Learning and Verbal Behavior,* 1968, *7,* 904–12.

Rohrman, N. L. More on the recall of nominalizations. *Journal of Verbal Learning and Verbal Behavior,* 1970, *9,* 534–36.

Rosenberg, S. Association and phrase structure in sentence recall. *Journal of Verbal Learning and Verbal Behavior,* 1968, *7,* 1077–81.

Rosenberg, S. The recall of verbal material accompanying semantically well-integrated and semantically poorly integrated sentences. *Journal of Verbal Learning and Verbal Behavior,* 1969, *8,* 732–36.

Rosenberg, S., & Jarvella, R. J. Semantic integration and sentence perception. *Journal of Verbal Learning and Verbal Behavior,* 1970, *9,* 548–53.

Rubenstein, H., Lewis, S. S., & Rubenstein, M. A. Homographic entries in the internal lexicon: Effects of systematicity and relative frequency of meaning. *Journal of Verbal Learning and Verbal Behavior,* 1971, *10,* 57–62.

Sachs, J. S. Recognition memory for syntactic and semantic aspects of connected discourse. *Perception and Psychophysics,* 1967, *2,* 437–42.

Savin, H. B., & Perchonock, E. Grammatical structure and immediate recall of English sentences. *Journal of Verbal Learning and Verbal Behavior,* 1965, *4,* 348–53.

Sherman, M. A. Adjectival negation and the comprehension of multiply negated sentences. *Journal of Verbal Learning and Verbal Behavior,* 1976, *15,* 143–57.

Slobin, D. I. Grammatical transformations and sentence comprehension in childhood and adulthood. *Journal of Verbal Learning and Verbal Behavior,* 1966, *5,* 219–27.

Smith, K. H. Grammatical intrusions in the free recall of structured letter pairs. *Journal of Verbal Learning and Verbal Behavior*, 1966, *5*, 447–54.

Smith, K. H. Effect of exceptions on verbal reconstructive memory. *Journal of Experimental Psychology Monograph*, 1973, *97*, No. 1, 119–39.

Smith, K. H., & Braine, M. D. S. Miniature languages and the problem of language acquisition. In T. G. Bever & W. Weksel (Eds.), *The structure of psychology of language* (Vol. 2). New York: Holt, Rinehart & Winston, 1971.

Smith, K. H., & Gough, P. B. Transformational rules in the learning of miniature linguistic systems. *Journal of Experimental Psychology*, 1969, *79*, 276–82.

Trabasso, T. Reasoning and the processing of negative information. Invited Address, Division 3, 78th Annual Convention of the American Psychological Association, 1970.

Trabasso, T., Rollins, H., & Shaughnessy, E. Storage and verification stages in processing concepts. *Cognitive Psychology*, 1971, *2*, 239–89.

Wales, R. J., & Grieve, R. What is so difficult about negation? *Perception and Psychophysics*, 1969, *6*, 327–32.

Wason, P. C. The processing of positive and negative information. *Quarterly Journal of Experimental Psychology*, 1959, *11*, 92–107.

Wason, P. C. Response to affirmative and negative binary statements. *British Journal of Psychology*, 1961, *52*, 133–42.

Wason, P. C. The contexts of plausible denial. *Journal of Verbal Learning and Verbal Behavior*, 1965, *4*, 7–11.

Wingfield, A., & Klein, J. F. Syntactic structure and acoustic pattern in speech perception. *Perception and Psychophysics*, 1971, *9*, 23–25.

Yngve, V. H. A model and an hypothesis for language structure. *Proceedings of the American Philosophical Society*, 1960, *104*, 444–66.

# The Meaning
# in
# Language                            CHAPTER 5

In the previous two chapters we have examined the sound system of language and the syntactic system of language. We now come to the heart of the language problem—the semantic system. If you consider the obvious fact that language is a vehicle for transferring a message or idea from one person to another and that message transference of this sort would never have developed if there were no meaning to the message, it is strange to note that neither linguist nor psychologist has spent much time studying meaning relative to their concerns with sounds and syntax. The behavioristically oriented linguist Bloomfield (1933) avoided the problem by assigning the study of meaning to other sciences. In his words, "The statement of meanings is therefore the weak point in language-study, and will remain so until human knowledge advances very far beyond its present state. In practice, we define the meaning of linguistic form, wherever we can, in terms of some other science" (Bloomfield, 1933, p. 140). In Bloomfield's book, psychology was most often referred to as the likely other science.

Psychologists have not been entirely unwilling to undertake the task assigned to them by Bloomfield. In fact, as Blumenthal (1970) pointed out, Wundt had been concerned with the problem of meaning long before Bloomfield's book appeared. The relation between the linguistic utterance and the cognitive processes or mental activity which language reflects were central concerns of Wundt's psycholinguistic interests. He was, to quote Blumenthal, ". . . concerned with the nature of the mental representation that underlies the sentence" (Blumenthal, 1970, p. 243). Blumenthal suggested that the bridge between the present-day psycholinguistics stimulated by Chomsky and the Wundtian tradition has now been cemented after the long interruption of the behavioristic tradition in both linguistics and psychology.

## BEHAVIORIST APPROACHES TO MEANING

The behaviorists had, however, been willing to tackle the problem of meaning within the framework of their own paradigm. Mowrer (1954), for example, argued that the traditional principles of conditioning plus mediating responses can account for the acquisition of meaning (Mowrer, 1952) and the transmission of meaning by language. Mowrer argued, in the latter case, that meaning is not conveyed from speaker to listener by sentences but rather sentences act to shift meanings from sign to sign within the mind of the listener by the process of conditioning in which ". . . the sentence subject is analogous to the conditional stimulus and the predicate to the unconditional stimulus" (Mowrer, 1954, p. 691).

Osgood, Suci, and Tannenbaum (1957) stimulated a great deal of research on meaning by providing an instrument for measuring meaning and a theoretical account of meaning. The semantic differential, as the measuring instrument came to be known, consisted of a series of rating scales each of which was anchored at its two ends by one of a pair of bipolar adjectives. Words could be rated on the set of scales so that a profile of the meaning of each word could be obtained or the meaning could be conceptualized as located in the N-dimensional semantic space defined by the scales. Factor analyses of the ratings of various words against a large number of scales in a number of different languages consistently resulted in a set of three major dimensions of denotative meaning: *evaluation* (e.g., good-bad, fair-unfair, beautiful-ugly), *potency* (e.g., strong-weak, hard-soft, heavy-light), and *activity* (e.g., active-passive, quick-slow, excitable-calm). An excellent sample of the research using the semantic differential, the theory related to it, and some critical evaluations of it may be found in Snider and Osgood (1969).

Although Osgood's research interests have shifted away from the use of the semantic differential to other approaches to the study of language (e.g., Osgood, 1971) and to other techniques for studying meaning (e.g., Osgood, 1968), his theoretical position has remained unchanged since the first presentation of his conception of the nature of meaning (Osgood, 1952). The latter is based on a more general theory of learning and specifically on his concept of mediation. He argues that people acquire the meaning of words or signs through learning to make mediating representational responses to the words. The mediating responses are assumed to be some form of replica of the actual behavior toward the things represented by the words. Words are signs for the stimuli to which people respond. As Osgood puts it, ". . . a pattern of stimulation which is not the object is a sign of the object if it evokes in an organism a mediating reaction, this (a) being some functional part of the total behavior elicited by the object and

(b) producing distinctive self-stimulation that mediates responses which would not occur without the previous association of nonobject and object patterns of stimulation" (Osgood, 1952, p. 204). In other words, a sign occurs in the presence of an object and a part of the total set of responses to the object are conditioned to the word sign and act as a mediating response ($r_m$) which has stimulus consequences ($s_m$) to which other responses may be made. (A schematized version of these relations is shown in Figure 5–1.) It is the mediating response which Osgood calls the meaning of the word sign. The meaning of the earliest signs must come through direct experience but most signs acquire meaning via association with other signs rather than by direct learning. The latter principle accounts for the assigning of meaning to words associated with objects not directly experienced. Meanings will differ from person to person depending on the behaviors toward the objects represented by the words or signs. It is the composition of the mediating response which is the meaning of the sign.

The essence of Osgood's theory is that a part of the response to the *significate,* or the object, is transferred to the sign representing the significate. As Fodor (1965) has pointed out, such a theory is no different, in principle, from the direct conditioning model which Osgood rejected as inadequate. Traditional forms of the direct conditioning model relate meaning directly to the responses elicited to the significate while the mediation model suggests that meaning is covertly mediated by a representational response which is some proper part of the whole set of responses to the significate. If the mediating response is a proper part of the responses to the significate, then the same one-to-one relationship between word meaning and significate remains as in the case of direct conditioning. If the latter is the case, then little advance has been made in our understanding of meaning through the mediation model by Osgood's own criteria. As Fodor notes, the conditioning and mediational models seem inadequate because words, or other linguistic responses, do not appear to be primarily dependent on specifiable external stimuli; many linguistic utterances are functionally equivalent despite the fact that their mode of acquisition is surely quite different; and there appears to be no apparent relation between the process of acquisition and the strength of the linguistic response acquired.

Osgood (1966), of course, disagrees with Fodor's analysis, arguing that the stimulus consequences ($s_m$) of the meaning response ($r_m$) lead to the acquisition of new responses to the sign which are entirely independent of the responses to the significate itself. Herein lies the difference between single-stage conditioning models and the mediation model. There will, of course, never be a resolution to the issue which would allow these two protagonists to agree since Osgood is arguing within the paradigmatic view of behavioristic psychology while Fodor

**Figure 5-1**

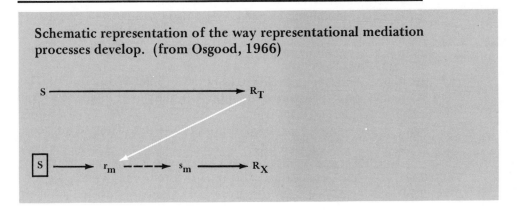

Schematic representation of the way representational mediation processes develop.  (from Osgood, 1966)

is arguing within the paradigm of the mentalistic, rationalistic, psycho-linguistics which Osgood rejects.

## SEMANTIC FEATURE THEORY

An approach to the problems of semantics was, however, slow to come from those who were critical of behaviorism. Even the linguists had not provided many clues. Chomsky had not discussed semantics in his first book (Chomsky, 1957) and, as noted in Chapter 1, when he expanded his position (Chomsky, 1965) the semantic component of his theory led to considerable controversy among linguists. One approach to semantics was suggested by Katz and Fodor (1963), who contributed an outline of a semantic theory based upon feature analyses, a theory which Katz (1972) more fully developed. Gradually psychologists have begun to make tentative use of some of those theoretical ideas.

   Clifton (1967) and McNeill (Miller & McNeill, 1967), for example, used the feature theory of semantics to account for the results of word association tests and the developmental changes observed in word association responses. The basic idea was that if the meaning of words is composed of bundles of features then, within the context of the usual word association test, people are likely to respond to the stimulus word with an associate which has many features in common with that word. Thus, associates tend to be opposites, superordinates, parts of wholes, and other words differing by only one or two features from the stimulus word. In the case of children's word associations, it had been observed that there is a shift in responding from so-called syntagmatic to paradigmatic responses as children grow older (Palermo, 1963). It was assumed by Clifton and McNeill that children have fewer features associated with any particular word and that features related to syntactic structure would be acquired before those associated with semantic structure. Therefore, syntactically related words, i.e., syntagmatic responses (e.g., deep-hole), would be more likely in young children while semantically related words, i.e., paradigmatic responses (e.g., deep-shallow), would be more likely from older children and adults. The normative data (Palermo & Jenkins, 1964) supported these theoretical arguments. McNeill (1966) bolstered this explanation by presenting some experimental data demonstrating the syntagmatic-paradigmatic shift as a function of amount of training with artificially created words.

Further research within the feature theory framework grew out of some experiments on memory for sentences. Both Sachs (1967) and Fillenbaum (1966) had reported that recall of sentences seemed to reflect memory for the semantic message of the sentence and a loss of syntactic structure and specific lexical items. As we noted in the previous chapter, Sachs' data indicated that people listening to connected discourse tend to remember the meaning of sentences but to forget rather rapidly the form of the sentence. Fillenbaum found that memory for specific words was poor when equivalent substitutes were used in a recognition test. People are likely to say that they recognize "The door is not open" as a sentence they have been exposed to when the sentence actually presented was "The door is closed." These lexical changes were more likely to be accepted in the case of contradictories such as *open* and *close* than in the case of contraries such as *hot* and *cold* where the meaning of *not cold* does not necessarily mean *hot*.

## FEATURE THEORY AND MARKEDNESS

Clark and Clark (1968) suggested that the results of sentence memory experiments and the errors which occur in them may be conceived in terms of the feature theory of meaning. They argued that the concept of *markedness* is an important variable in these experiments. They suggested that the unmarked form of word pairs is semantically and syntactically simpler than the marked form. For instance, the unmarked singular is simpler than the marked plural and the unmarked comparative adjective (e.g., *long*) is simpler than its marked counterpart (e.g., *short*). The assumptions of their theory are that when people listen to sentences they extract semantic distinctions or features to remember. Memory failures involve loss of semantic feature distinctions which are assumed to be more likely for marked than unmarked lexical items. Further, they assume that recall consists of attempting to reconstruct sentences from the semantic distinctions or features that can be remembered.

Clark and Clark report an experiment in which three types of markedness were manipulated: the temporal order of events ($S_1$ before $S_2$), the order of mention of those events, and the main-subordinate relation of the two described events. In all three cases, sentences in which the unmarked form occurred were better recalled than the respective marked-form sentences regardless of their transformational complexity. When errors were made, they tended to take the form of changes from marked to unmarked forms, i.e., single features were lost from the more complex and specific marked forms, reducing them to the less complex and more general unmarked forms. Similar results were obtained by Clark and Stafford (1969), who presented sentences in which the verb was in the past or present, progressive or nonprogressive, and perfect or nonperfect forms. Recall resulted in errors which were biased toward the unmarked nonperfect, and nonprogressive forms of the verb. These changes were interpreted as having occurred because of the loss of one semantic feature, resulting in a semantic simplification of the verb form. There were also a large number of shifts to the marked past tense which were not in accord with the feature theory, but which were attributed to changes in time relations from presentation of the sentences to recall test.

A further experiment by Clark and Card (1969) extended the theory to memory for sentences involving comparative adjectives, such as in sentences of the type, "A is happier than B," "A is narrower than B," and so on. The results indicated that recall was better for sentences with the unmarked adjectives and that errors tended to change marked adjectives to their unmarked counterparts. The data were interpreted as further support for the theory that the meanings of words are composed of semantic features and those words which are more complex by virtue of having more features tend to be recalled with some features missing. Marked forms are recalled as the simpler unmarked form more frequently than the reverse because the marked form has one additional feature. Notice that in all three of these experiments, the sentences were presented in isolation with no context, a point which will be relevant to a discussion later in the chapter.

Clark (1969) elaborated this theoretical approach to meaning and extended it to the more general process of reasoning. He argued that reasoning is accomplished primarily through very general linguistic processes. Three principles are advanced by Clark to account for so-called two- and three-term series reasoning problems. The first principle concerns the primacy of functional relations in sentences. Clark argues that in processing a sentence, a person stores the primitive conceptual relations out of which the sentence is constructed, i.e., the subject-of, predicate-of, direct-object-of, and main-verb-of the sentence. Other aspects of the sentence are secondary to these so-called functional relations.

The second principle is an elaborated version of lexical marking which states that the senses of unmarked adjectives are less complex than their marked opposites. The unmarked forms such as "good" or "long" are considered less complex on the basis of the fact that they can be neutralized in certain contexts. A question such as "How long is the table?" makes no assumptions about whether the table is long or short. The question is neutral with respect to length. The question "How short is the table?" is not neutral because it presupposes that the table is short and the question is about just how short it is. In addition, the unmarked form is the one which is nominalized to refer to the entire dimension, i.e., the *goodness* and the *length* dimensions. The fact that unmarked adjectives are the more general, having two senses (nominal and contrastive), while the marked adjectives have only the contrastive sense, makes the latter more complex in the sense of being a special case of the former. The marked form is less general, requiring at least one more feature than the unmarked form to specify its meaning.

Third, the principle of congruence specifies that in answering a question a person's search for the answer seeks information from previous knowledge which is congruent at the level of functional relations with the information asked for in the question. The person either must find congruent information or reformulate the question so that it is possible to find it.

Clark presents experimental data to demonstrate that the functional relations of sentences are more available than comparative relations, that unmarked comparatives are more available than marked comparatives, and that questions which are congruent with the base string of the propositions giving the information are more easily answered than those which are not. In solving a three-term series problem such as *If John is better than Pete, and Pete is better than Dick, then who is the best?* it is predicted that the correct answer will be much more rapid, or available, than for the problem *If John is not as good as Pete, and John is not as bad as Dick, then who is worst?* The prediction for these most extreme cases is based on the fact that in the first case the primacy of the functional relations, the lexical markings, and the congruence relations are all arranged to allow fast processing while in the latter case they are not. The power of the theoretical analysis is revealed in the correct predictions made for the intermediate cases as well. Thus, the analysis of the processes involved in understanding sentences involved in reasoning problems of this sort seems to be the primary variable in accounting for the difficulty of the problems themselves, although Huttenlocher and Higgins (1971) have provided data supporting the hypothesis that spatial imagery is also important to the solution of such problems. As we shall see later in the chapter, there are other theoretical accounts of these experiments.

# METHODOLOGICAL ISSUES

Before proceeding with the discussion of additional research stimulated by feature theory, an important methodological point should be made. If one plans to study problems of semantics, then one must be certain that the experimental demands made on the subject require that the linguistic material be processed in terms of the meaning of that material. Most readers of this volume are aware that one can read or listen to some language material and not know at the end the meaning of what has been read or heard. You have to process the material at some semantic level to be able to recall it. Bobrow and Bower (1969) were among the first to look at this problem. They found, for example, that if a person is presented with two nouns and asked to generate a sentence linking them, subsequent recall of the second noun, given the first, is far better than if the nouns are presented in a sensible sentence which the experimenter presents. Similarly, if the task is to disambiguate a sentence as opposed to locating spelling errors in the same sentence, recall of the semantic content of the sentence is far better. Bobrow (1970) took another approach to make the same point. He presented sentences and later requested recall of the object noun in the sentence given the subject noun. The subject and object nouns were repeated twice during the presentation sentences. The words themselves were ambiguous so that the repetitions of the words were contained in sentences which used the same meaning twice or each of the two ambiguous meanings once. For example, the word *bark* was used either in two sentences with the same meaning, such as a reference to the noise of some animal, or it was used in one sentence with the animal noise meaning and in another sentence to refer to the covering of a tree. At recall, the object nouns were more frequently remembered when the same meaning had been repeated than when the two different semantic readings of the same word were used. This was a clever demonstration that the semantic processing of one meaning has little effect on the semantic processing of the other meaning of the same phonological form, at least when the sentences are unrelated.

Similar findings have been reported by Hyde and Jenkins (1973) in a series of experiments dealing with processing lists of words. When subjects are asked to remember a list of words, they must process them in terms of their meaning or recall will be poor. For example, a person who is asked to rate words as to pleasantness or frequency of usage must process them semantically to make the judgment. If, on the other hand, the individual is asked to indicate the part of speech of the word or something about the letters in the word, semantic processing is not required. Hyde and Jenkins found that people asked to do the first two tasks remembered as many words as those specifically asked to remember the words while those who performed the second two tasks remembered significantly less. In short, memory for words requires processing of meaning, and without such processing, the words cannot be recalled although other characteristics of the materials presented may be recalled.

## LEXICAL MEANING RELATIONS

A number of researchers investigating the meaning of language have taken as their starting point the assumption that the meaning of a lexical item is, or is a function of, the meaning relations or associations that exist between that item and other items in the same domain. This assumption is clear, for example, in Deese's (1965) efforts to approach the problem of meaning by analyzing word association data with factor analytic techniques. By determining the network or distribution of associative connections of one word to others and the clusters of associative relations into which words enter, one can, it was argued, describe the associative meaning of those words which was assumed to describe the associative concept named by the word.

Miller (1967, 1969) chose another way to approach the same problem. His procedure was to select a set of words and ask subjects to sort them into clusters. An individual might be given forty-eight common nouns, for example, and asked to sort them into categories by judging the similarity of their meanings. The number of categories was not specified. The sortings of the judges were pooled and the assumption was made that the number of judges who sorted two words into the same category was a measure of the proximity of the two items. By determining the group of words as pairs with other words, a hierarchical clustering organization was determined through mergers of larger and larger groups of words. The hierarchy which emerged was taken to be the structure underlying our system of verbal concepts. Miller (1969) suggests that the technique has plausibility because the clusters which emerge are readily interpreted in terms of abstract concepts that appear to incorporate the important components, or features, of the definitions of the items included, while the features which are excluded in order to achieve the clusters are not so essential. For example, humans cluster together at a low level, cluster with plants at a higher level, and with nonliving objects at a still higher level. The assumption is made that the low level clusters have many features in common and more features are ignored in order to achieve the higher level clusters. It is suggested that the clusters might be used to identify semantic markers or features which are inherent to the lexical items. Furthermore, Miller argues that the features derive from the presuppositions and assertions contained in the definitions of the words. For example, *cook, doctor,* and *umpire,* which presuppose "person," were clustered together by most judges. Fewer people included in that cluster *mother* and *knight,* presumably because they presuppose not only what the other words presuppose but some additional presuppositions as well. One must ignore more presuppositions and/or assertions to include more words in a category and the hierarchical clustering structure reflects the generality or lack of presuppositions and/or assertions which are attended to in sorting the words. In this sense, the procedure produces linguistically relevant structures as well as plausible structures. Other than a study done by Anglin (1970) with children, which we shall mention in the next chapter, little has been done with Miller's technique to fulfill his expectation that it would provide a useful test for semantic hypotheses.

Fillenbaum and Rapoport (1971) have also made the meaning relation between words their empirical starting point. Their extensive research program was designed to characterize the semantic structure of the subjective lexicon of nine diverse semantic domains ranging from pronouns and kinship terms, to verbs of judging, and evaluative adjectives. They used a multiple technique approach, making use of linear graph methods, multidimensional scaling, and the cluster analysis used by Miller. The idea was to try to avoid imposing a structure on the semantic fields by the techniques used. They assumed that if similar results were obtained by different techniques, more confidence could be placed in the results. People were presented, for example, with fifteen emotion words and asked to construct labeled trees based on similarity in meaning, or to construct complete undirected graphs connecting the words, or to rank order 105 pairs of emotion words in terms of similarity of meaning, or to rate the 105 pairs with regard to dissimilarity on a scale from 1–19. The data were then analyzed in terms of the meaning relations which emerged from the graph constructions, cluster analyses, multidimensional scaling, and other measures and techniques which Fillenbaum and Rapoport varied depending on the characteristics of the semantic domain being investigated.

The results of these procedures yielded very plausible results, in Miller's terms, for the color names, kinship terms, and pronouns. This lends credence to the analyses of the other domains. The methodological variations revealed that some semantic domains were organized dimensionally, some hierarchically, and some seemed to be mixtures of both types of organization. In short, it appears that people organize different domains in terms of different principles. The analyses presented of the various domains are of interest in illustrating the manner in which people do seem to conceptualize these semantic areas or spaces and interrelate the exemplars within them. As the authors conclude, these data on the subjective lexicon do not provide a theory of semantic performance but they do provide some constraints on semantic theorizing. Those who construct such theories must be able to relate them, at some level, to the organization of the subjective lexicon.

## COMPUTER-BASED SEMANTIC MODELS

Still another approach based on the same basic set of assumptions has been advanced by Quillian (1967) and followed up by Collins and Quillian (1969). Quillian's theory is based on a computer memory model in which words are stored with a configuration of pointers to other words and that configuration of pointers is taken to be the meaning of the word. The configuration for any particular word will be a part of a hierarchically arranged superset, with a particular word having a pointer to its category name which in turn may be a component of a higher category (e.g., a canary is a bird, a bird is an animal, and so on). In addition, words will have pointers to properties. The properties will be specific to the word and will not be identified if they are more general and, therefore, properties of the concept name. "Canary," for example, will have property pointers to "yellow" and "singing," which are specific to canaries, but no pointers to "wings" because this would be a pointer property of "bird" which is a superordinate of "canary." In essence, the reduction in redundancy achieved in this conception of the hierarchical structure of properties is similar to Miller's conception of presuppositions and assertions he postulates to account for the hierarchically related clusters in his analysis of word relations.

It follows from Quillian's model of semantic organization that when a person is asked to verify a statement about a canary it should take less time to verify the statement if the relevant material required is located close to the level at which the semantic hierarchy is entered. For example, if one is asked about a superset or a property of canaries, it should be possible to retrieve the information stored with the pointers of "canary" more rapidly than that stored with the pointers of "animal." Thus, one should verify that a canary is yellow faster than that a canary has skin, which is a property, and therefore associated with the pointer, of animals. Collins and Quillian (1969) tested this deduction from the model and found that for both superset category levels in the hierarchy and for properties associated with each superset level, the closer the category level and associated properties to the word being tested the faster the reaction time in verifying the truth of the statement. If the lower category relationship to the superset is primed by a context-setting prior sentence, then the reaction time for a property associated with the higher superset category can be reduced (Collins & Quillian, 1970a). For example, if "A canary can fly" is preceded by the sentence "A canary is a bird," then the verification time of the former sentence is reduced as if the contextually preceding sentence had made the superset property of birds (i.e., flying) as available as the properties of canary. Finally, Collins and Quillian (1970b) have shown that category size does not seem to affect the time taken to make these decisions. Normative frequency with which people associate a property with its category is, however, decisive in determining reaction time (Conrad, 1972), suggesting a weakness in establishing the position of properties in the superordinate hierarchy of categories on logical grounds rather than empirical ones.

Winograd (1972) has at this time carried the computer modeling approach the furthest. He has described a computer system for understanding English which takes into account not only semantics but syntax, inference, and the context in which the statements are made. While the system seems quite satisfactory for interacting with a computer over a limited semantic domain, the validity of the analogy to the human has not been tested, nor is it clear how the complex proposal can stimulate research on the part of others without the same computer facilities and programming capabilities. The Winograd monograph should be consulted, however, by those interested in such an approach because it is a particularly complete description and because many other attempts to use computers for language analyses are discussed. Furthermore, the computer simulation approach (more than any other) forces the consideration of a detailed analysis of what precisely must be considered in a model of language comprehension.

The general approach taken by Collins and Quillian has also been used by Rumelhart, Lindsay, and Norman (1972) and, with some modifications in assumptions, by Meyer (1970). In all these theories, the computer model is basic to the models developed and has led the researchers involved to assume logical relations among the categories and properties of the categories. For example, it is assumed that in order to save memory space, there is an hierarchical category structure and that properties are not repeated at all levels but are logically arranged to prevent redundancy, an assumption we have just noted does not always hold up under empirical test (Conrad, 1972). This approach has, therefore, made strong assumptions about semantic structures while the approaches taken by Miller (1969) and Fillenbaum and Rapoport (1971), for example, have tried to see empirically what semantic structures emerge when a person is given the opportunity to categorize or indicate similarities among lexical items.

Rips, Shoben, and Smith (1973) have tried to demonstrate the value of using the latter approach with the former. Rather than approach the problem in terms of subsets in which a person must traverse routes among levels of subsets in order to recover semantic information related to a particular word, Rips et al. have argued for semantic distance as the explanatory concept accounting for the results of the earlier studies. They were particularly concerned that a theory built on logical structures does not take account of within-set as well as between-set semantic distances. When they obtained experimental results which did not support the subset logical relations presumed by the earlier models, they asked people to rate the semantic relatedness of the words used. The ratings indicated that despite the logical relations assumed by the other models, the semantic distances among members of subsets and between subset members and superset members varied considerably. In short, people are not as logical in organizing semantic relations as the models had assumed. Furthermore, the semantic distance revealed that the subset effect observed in the earlier studies only obtained when the rated semantic distance between any distance and its immediate superordinate was less than between that instance and its higher level superordinate in the superset structure. Semantic distance also predicted the variations in within-set reaction times. The results of this research take us right back to an analysis of semantics in terms of the relations among members of the subjective lexicon or a feature comparison model (Smith, Shoben, & Rips, 1974; Rips, 1975).

The focus of the work discussed up to this point has been on the description of the meaning of words. Osgood has assumed that the meaning of words derives from the learning of representational mediating responses and Clark has assumed that the meaning of words is composed of bundles of features. Deese, Miller, Fillenbaum and Rapoport, Collins and Quillian and others have, if not explicitly, seemed to assume that the study of networks of related words will somehow allow the important features of words to emerge or be induced. The general orientation of these approaches is more or less explicitly directed to determining the elements of which meaning is composed. The researchers involved make the assumption, drawn from linguistic theory (Katz, 1972), that meanings are bundles of features and, in one way or another, research must be directed toward discovering what those features are. Presumably the features are the universal abstract elements which form the basis of the semantic system of all languages.

## SEMANTICS AND KNOWLEDGE

A number of researchers, however, have taken a somewhat different orientation toward the problem of meaning. These psycholinguists have more or less explicitly assumed that language is little more than a tool for the exchange of knowledge between speaker and listener. As such, the meanings of words are in some sense dependent on the conceptual system of the speaker and listener and the context in which they are uttered. An utterance contains a message and that message is determined by the knowledge of the speaker and the contextual situation in which the utterance is made. Meanings of words, therefore, are less specific than is implied by a bundle of features. Meanings are instead constructed for linguistic utterances by the speaker-listener dyad within the particular context of use. In this sense, words in isolation have little meaning. Only when words can be set in some context relevant to the knowledge system of the user in a particular context, linguistic and nonlinguistic, is it possible to construct meanings for individual words.

Perfetti (1972) has placed the issues in the context of a distinction between semantic conceptions of syntactic relations and the semantic structure of lexical meanings. As he notes, in his review of what he calls psychosemantics, psycholinguists have not looked extensively at semantic conceptions of syntactic relations, i.e., the case relations which Fillmore (1968) discusses or the ideas advanced by the generative semanticists as represented, for example, by McCawley (1968). Instead the focus has been on the semantic features of lexical meaning as Katz (1972) has conceptualized them. Such an analysis of meaning loses much of its impact, as Perfetti points out, as soon as the broader conceptions of meaning in terms of syntactic relations and, of course, extra-linguistic context are considered.

Olson (1970) moved in this direction when he proposed that a theory of semantics is dependent on the speaker's knowledge of intended referents. He argued that most theories of meaning are not adequate in the sense that they do not specify the relations between perceived referents, in context, and the nature of the utterance. Semantic decisions are not based on semantic features which define words, but, rather, on the speaker's knowledge of perceived and intended referents. Ambiguity results not from the use of words with different dictionary readings, for example, but from failure to specify the intended referent from the several alternatives available within the context at hand. Olson proposes that words do not name things but, instead, words designate or specify an intended referent relative to a set of alternative referents from which it must be differentiated. The meaning of an utterance is dependent on the context of alternatives. Since a message is created to distinguish among alternatives, an utterance does not exhaust the potential features of a perceived referent but only those necessary to differentiate the one in question. The extent of elaboration necessary to differentiate alternatives among which the listener must choose is all that is required. Olson provides a paradigmatic case to illustrate his point. Given a white circle in the context of a black circle, one need say no more than "the white one" to identify the referent. But in the context of a white square, a black circle, and a black square it is necessary to say, "the round white one." Olson is, therefore, offering a cognitive theory of semantics in the sense that word choice is determined by the knowledge of the speaker, including his or her knowledge about the listener, and the perceived context in which the speaker is differentiating an intended referent from a set of perceived alternatives. Ford and Olson (1975) have provided data to support this general theoretical position by showing that when children are presented with the paradigmatic case described above they do seem to use language in the manner described.

## MEMORY AND MEANING

It appears that as one delves further and further into the problem of meaning, the scope of the problem becomes larger and larger. Some present-day psychologists seem to be coming to this conclusion although this position has an earlier history in psychology. Bartlett (1932), for example, in evaluating an extensive series of his own experiments on memory found himself faced with the problem of meaning. His thoughts in this connection have had a marked influence on present-day thinking about the processes of remembering and on the nature of the problem of meaning. Bartlett came to the conclusion that remembering is a constructive process in the sense that when a person is given a story to remember and later is asked to recall that story, the process of recall seems to be one of building or rebuilding the schema which is that story for the person doing the remembering. There are no traces, bundles of features, or small units strung together as a story. But, rather, there is "something of the nature of attitude" (Bartlett, 1932, p. 207). Bartlett meant by this that the person recalling from memory is not building up details into a total story. Instead, the person seems to begin with an impression of the whole story which is used to reconstruct the details that fit the whole story or justify the impression of the story and, thus, create or construct the schema which is the story for that person. Remembering, to use Bartlett's words again, ". . . is an imaginative reconstruction, or construction, built out of the relation of our attitude towards a whole active mass of organized past reactions or experience, and to a little outstanding detail which commonly appears in image or language form" (p. 213). In that statement lies the heart of the memory problem. One needs to account for the fact that both the general idea of a story and some specific details seem to be recalled and used as the basis for creating the total recall as a set of specifics tied together by a theme and woven into a cohesive fabric created upon demand.

But, as Bartlett viewed it, memory is only one aspect of the cognitive processes stretching from perception to thinking, all of which are an "effort after meaning," i.e., an attempt to connect something that is given with something other than itself. While wary of getting into a discussion of what meaning is, and its place in a theory of knowledge, Bartlett did reject Watson's notion that meaning is no more than the observable actions of the organism and Titchener's notion that meaning is the organization or perception of psychological materials given by context, i.e., meaning is context. Bartlett suggests that remembering, like perceiving, imaging, thinking, and reasoning, is an effort after meaning, while meaning is the reactive significance of the cognitive processing which leads to an awareness of the material being processed. Meaning is not context, rather, it is found in context. Meaning is not actions, but it does involve activity, cognitive activity of the kinds indicated. Meaning thus emerges, Bartlett suggests, from a cognitively active organism's efforts to fit the material within the context of the moment into the knowledge system of the organism so that some conscious awareness of the material is possible. The concept of a cognitively active organism operating in contexts against a background of knowledge is the idea which has influenced many psychologists working on similar problems today.

## WHOLISTIC SEMANTIC IDEAS

Recent attempts to approach the problem of meaning within the general context of Bartlett's ideas have been made by Bransford and Franks (1971) and Cofer (1973). Noting that most previous work on memory had been conducted with single words in isolation and presented as lists, Bransford and Franks felt that a more insightful approach to meaning in its relation to memory would be made through the study of wholistic semantic ideas. Furthermore, they pointed out that such wholistic semantic ideas, or abstract schemata in Bartlett's terms, are not necessarily expressed in single sentences but are often constructed through the integration of information expressed in several sentences which may not necessarily be experienced consecutively in time.

The initial research of these two investigators was an effort to study the acquisition of intersentential information and its integration into a single wholistic semantic idea as revealed in memory for sentential material. The technique consisted of presenting people with related information in short sentences and measuring recognition recall of those sentences and others that contained similar material. For example, they began with the integrated semantic idea expressed in the sentence, "The ants in the kitchen ate the sweet jelly which was on the table." That sentence expresses four basic parts of the integrated idea:

1. The ants were in the kitchen.
2. The jelly was on the table.
3. The jelly was sweet.
4. The ants ate the jelly.

Those four sentences express the four ideas of the complex sentence one at a time. The same ideas could also be expressed two at a time, as in:

1. The ants in the kitchen ate the jelly.
2. The ants ate the sweet jelly.
3. The sweet jelly was on the table.
4. The ants ate the jelly which was on the table.

And, of course, the same ideas could be expressed three at a time, as in:

1. The ants ate the sweet jelly which was on the table.
2. The ants in the kitchen ate the jelly which was on the table.
3. The ants in the kitchen ate the sweet jelly.

Note that the syntactic form of the sentences changes in the various sets of sentences.

The initial study consisted of presenting people with twenty-four sentences, six from each of four idea sets such as the one about the ants. The six sentences included two with one idea, two with two ideas, and two with three ideas. The complete four-idea sentence was never presented during acquisition. A check on comprehension was made after each sentence. Following acquisition, a recognition reten-tion test was given in which a set of sentences was presented and the task was to indicate those which had been heard before. The recog-nition set contained some of the old one-, two-, and three-idea sen-tences, some new one-, two-, and three-idea sentences, the four-idea sentence, and some noncase control sentences which combined ideas across the four different idea sets. In addition to indicating whether each sentence was new or old, the subjects were asked to indicate their confidence in the judgment they had made on a five-point rating scale.

The results were dramatic in revealing that people were most confident that they had heard the sentence which integrated the four ideas in each set and which they had never heard at all. They were less confident of the three-idea sentences, still less confident of the two-idea sentences, and least confident about the one-idea sentences. There was little evidence that the old sentences were any better recog-nized than the new ones and, finally, the noncase sentences were easily identified as not having been presented. In short, the data were inter-preted as strong support for the hypothesis that people integrate information presented in individual sentences to construct wholistic semantic ideas. The individual sentences, or component ideas, lost their identity as they were incorporated into the wholistic representation of the semantic events. But, as Bransford and Franks note, what was actually acquired during the task, the nature of the semantic precision involved, and the limits on the general phenomenon of linguistic abstraction are not clarified by this single set of experiments. Obviously, as Bartlett before them had noted, while integration takes place in the construction of the wholistic structure, specifics are also a part of the process and can be recalled as such. The task of accounting for these phenomena must take both into consideration.

One step in this direction was taken by Bransford, Barclay, and Franks (1972) in a set of experiments which looked at some aspects of the abstract semantic information individuals obtain as a result of linguistic input. They argued that the interpretive approach to semantics advocated by Katz (1972), for example, and assumed in much research discussed thus far in this chapter, is not a sufficient characterization of the meaning of a sentence. Interpretive semanticists propose that the deep structure of a sentence is the input to the semantic component of the grammar and that the latter gives the sentence ". . . a full analysis of its cognitive meaning" (Katz & Postal, 1964, p. 12). In contrast to this view, Bransford et al. take the position that sentences are forms of information which people use to construct semantic descriptions of situations. Furthermore, the constructed descriptions of the situations contain more information than the sentences themselves. If that assumption is correct, then it follows that a purely linguistic and interpretive analysis will not adequately characterize the information or meaning available to, or constructed by, the listener.

Bransford et al. tested their hypothesis by presenting a set of sentences to subjects with instructions indicating that they would be asked questions about the sentences later. The presentation and test sentences dealt with simple spatial relations of the following types:

Presentation:
  Three turtles rested *beside* a floating log, and a fish swam beneath *them*.
or
  Three turtles rested *on* a floating log, and a fish swam beneath *them*.
Test:
  Three turtles rested *beside/on* a floating log, and a fish swam beneath *it*.

Note that the deep structure of the presentation sentences differs only with respect to the lexical items *on* or *beside*. Semantically, however, there is an important difference because in the case of the *on* sentence, although not stated in the sentence and therefore not a part of the deep structure to be interpreted, is the information that the fish swam under the log as well as under the turtles. We obtain this information because our general cognitive knowledge of spatial relations in the world allows us to know that if the turtles were on the log and the fish swam under the turtles, then the fish must of necessity have swum under the log as well. The latter relationship, of course, does not necessarily hold for the *beside* presentation sentence. The experiment, therefore, consisted of determining whether people would falsely recognize the test sentence after hearing the *on* sentence as opposed to the *beside* sentence. Again confidence ratings were obtained as well as yes/no recognition decisions. The results were clear in demonstrating that people did gain the additional information which was not actually presented and, thus, accepted the *it* test sentence as one they had heard when preceded by the *on* sentence but rejected it when preceded by the *beside* sentence. In short, recognition was primarily a function of the complete semantic descriptions constructed by the person rather than a function of just that information specified by the deep structure of the sentence per se. A sentence is not just a perceptual object, it is also a source of information which the listener assimilates to existing cognitive knowledge.

Bransford et al., in attempting to account for semantic constructions which they feel cannot be satisfactorily dealt with within the interpretive semantic theory, make a number of points worth considering. First, they do not wish to argue that the constructions involve making the information concrete as, for example, in an image. Imagery was used by subjects in their experiments, but these researchers consider that people use linguistic information in conjunction with previous knowledge they have in order to construct semantic descriptions. The image may sometimes play a part in the process, but it is only a part and it is used only in some situations. The fact that an image is formed does not, of course, account for the meaning of a sentence because, just as in the case of a sentence, the image itself must be interpreted even when it is created as a part of the process of comprehending. To make the point empirically clear, Franks and Bransford (1972) demonstrated that the same results obtained when the content of the sentences is abstract rather than concrete.

Second, Bransford et al. note that the meaning is not in the sentence but in the people who hear it. The linguistic input is but a cue used to recreate and modify information the listener already has of the world. The meaning, i.e., what is comprehended and remembered, depends on the listener's general knowledge. Finally, they note that while there is no denying the psychological reality of a linguistic representation at some level in memory, they do wish to deny that specifying this representation is sufficient to characterize the information available to the listener.

Barclay (1973) followed up the previous study with another within the same general framework but directed toward comparing the constructive theoretical model and the deep structure analysis with specific reference to Clark's theory that the meaning of a sentence consists of a complex of semantic features. Noting that Clark and Card (1969), in their study of comparative sentences, argue that memory involves the retention of sets of features and that some semantic distinctions such as functional relations and unmarked adjectives should be retained longer than others, Barclay designed his experiments to contrast the analytic interpretive process theory of Clark with the assimilation or constructive theory. As Barclay points out, the former theory assumes that sentences are treated as objects and analyzed independently of other sentences in terms of the feature elements of the words. The latter theory, however, assumes that " . . . semantic representations derive from the interplay of sentential information, the context of knowledge to which that information is assimilated, task demands, and the assimilative processes themselves, including integrative and logical operations" (p. 232).

The experiments consisted of memory for comparative sentences like those examined by Clark and Card (1969). For example, people were presented with sentences such as:

(a) The cowboy is taller than the salesman.
(b) The salesman is shorter than the fireman.
(c) The fireman is taller than the cowboy.

They were told that the experimenter was concerned with the communicative properties of sentences, but nothing about a subsequent test of memory. Ten sentences involving relative heights of five people were presented in such a way that the five people could be ordered with respect to each other. The memory test presented (1) old sentences; (2) sentences with subject and object of an old sentence reversed so that a false relationship among the heights of the persons resulted; (3) sentences with the comparative term reversed (false); (4) sentences which were new but equivalent to the old sentences in terms of the height relationships, such as, "The cowboy is shorter than the fireman," rather than sentence (c) above; (5) sentences which were consistent with the ordering established by the old sentences but which had never been presented (true); and (6) sentences which were new and false.

According to Clark's theory, recall of the six different kinds of sentences should be ordered from best to worst as follows: old, relation reversal, true new sentence, equivalent, subject-object reversal, and false new sentence. Assimilation theory, however, predicts that all true sentences would be regarded as old and all false sentences as new. The results strongly favored the latter theory. All the true sentences were about equally often designated as old and all the false statements about equally often designated as new. The interpretive theory relying on semantic features received little support except when the subjects were asked to memorize the sentences as opposed to understanding the relations among the people. Under the memory instructions, the sentences were presumably treated as objects to remember and under those conditions the order of error probabilities was as predicted by the interpretive theory. There was also a tendency for the unmarked forms to occur more frequently than the marked forms when a recall measure was used.

In another study using similar material, Barclay and Reid (1974) found evidence using recall measures which indicated that presented sentences and inferences about relations among the people referred to in the presented sentences could not be distinguished. Even when the presented sentences were well learned, inferential sentences were not distinguished from presented sentences.

Brewer and Lichtenstein (1974), in a direct test of memory for sentences using marked and unmarked adjectives, found that errors in recall were meaning preserving, i.e., *unfair* was changed to *not fair* rather than to *fair*. No evidence could be adduced for the semantic feature hypothesis that unmarked adjectives are better recalled than marked adjectives.

Harris and Brewer (1973) made a similar analysis of the Clark and Stafford (1973) study of verb tenses. While Harris and Brewer were able to replicate the tense-shifting phenomenon demonstrated by Clark and Stafford, they did not agree with the theoretical account which was based on loss of features to explain the tense shifts that occurred. In particular, the relatively frequent occurrence in both studies of the shifts to past tense, presumably a marked form, seemed problematic for Clark's theory. An alternative theory was offered, based on the linguistic consideration that tense is one of the *deictic aspects* of language. Deictic aspects indicate the spatiotemporal (space/time) nature of utterances in the context within which they occur and, therefore, they are easily lost to memory when sentences are presented in isolation but not when the same sentences occur in a relevant context. In the Clark and Stafford study, according to Harris and Brewer, the tenses had very little meaning because there was no context. Since meaningless material is difficult to remember, tense shifts occurred.

Harris and Brewer tested their hypothesis by presenting groups of twelve sentences to people and asking them to recall the sentences given the initial noun phrase as a cue. Six different verb tenses were used. Half the sentences included a temporal adverb appropriate to the verb tense (e.g., tomorrow), and half an adverb of the nontemporal sort (e.g., certainly). The results indicated that with only the addition of that single temporal adverb as context, the tense shift phenomenon was significantly decreased relative to the control sentences with non-temporal adverbs.

The extensive set of experiments by Barclay and the studies by Brewer and his colleagues suggest that the problem of meaning will require a much more complicated theory than the one proposed of the interpretive semantic theory as developed in terms of feature bundles or complexes. As Barclay points out, the intuitive appeal of feature theory is weakened when one considers the set of related sentences people are required to remember in these experiments and the precision with which they seem to keep all the semantic relations clear. Furthermore, there is nearly no evidence in these studies that errors of remembering the opposite prevailed. And yet, according to feature theory, single features are relatively easily lost, making it highly likely that sets of similar sentences would be confused and opposites often mistakenly remembered. Feature theory does seem to account for the data in the restricted context of treating sentences as objects to remember in a situation where one sentence is unrelated to the next and, therefore, relatively meaningless. When the same sentences are embedded in a meaningful context which allows them to be integrated with other information, intrusion of inferences is more frequent and not perceived as different from the actually perceived sentences. The type of inference made is determined by the use being made of the sentential information in the particular context at hand. Sentence comprehension or meaning within assimilation or constructive theory thus becomes a part of the larger problem of knowledge acquisition.

## MEANING AND PROSE

As indicated earlier, memory for linguistic materials reveals recall of specifics as well as the integration which takes place in the construction of wholistic ideas. Brockway, Chmielewski, and Cofer (1974) have reported an extensive set of experiments directed at the conditions which foster accuracy for specifics on the one hand and for productive construction on the other. They presented people with short passages and then asked them to identify by recognition those sentences which had or had not been in the passage. The subjects were also asked to recall the passage and to construct sentences germane to it. The results indicated that recognition of sentences which were logical inferences of the passage content was about the same as that for "old" sentences which actually occurred in the passage. Other related sentences and new sentences were not accepted as having been in the passage. Free recall was relatively poor, but old sentences and logical inferences occurred relatively frequently in the generated sentence recall.

Next, Brockway et al. asked another set of subjects to scale the relation of the free-recall and generated sentences to the passages used in the previous experiment. They found that the free-recall sentences, as might be expected, were rated as more closely related to the passage than were the generated sentences. In essence, the instructions to recall led to a greater accuracy set and, therefore, revealed less of the people's knowledge of the paragraph than did the generated-sentence instructions which, while less accurate in detail, revealed that more was known about the passage than the recall sentences alone indicated, i.e., relaxing the accuracy set allowed more knowledge to be revealed.

In another experiment, these authors asked a number of subjects to read the same passage and then to indicate in a recognition test which sentences had been in the passage. The sentences were those on which scale values had been obtained so that they ranged from "old" sentences to those rated as new or totally unconnected to the passage. Recognition tests were given immediately after the passage, twenty-four hours later, or seven days later. Finally, instructions for different groups indicated that recognition should be confined to sentences which actually appeared in the passage, or could be inferred from the passage, or were compatible with the ideas of the passage.

The results indicated that relaxing the accuracy set in the instructions to include inferred or compatible sentences produced an increased rate of acceptance in the recognition test for sentences with middle scale values but had no effect on those with very high or very low scale values. In other words, these subjects knew more about the stories than the old sentences alone allowed them to express, but they also knew what was unrelated to the passage. The time of the recognition test had a similar but less marked effect. Long delays did not affect performance on the old sentences nor on the unrelated sentences.

In summary, this set of experiments demonstrates that the effects of reading a prose passage, and probably any verbal or nonverbal experience (e.g., Franks & Bransford, 1971; Knutson, 1973), go beyond what is ordinarily measured in recall or recognition tests. Such experiences engage some structure or concepts and concept relations, i.e., knowledge structures, to allow people to gain more or produce more than was actually in the experience itself. There is, of course, still an open question relating to the nature of the interface between the material in the experience and the knowledge structure of the person engaged in the experience.

## CONTEXT AND MEANING

Before giving consideration to aspects of the larger issue of knowledge, there is some additional research that further demonstrates the complexity of the problem with which we are dealing. Discussion of the previous research has continually referred to the context of prior knowledge as an important determinant of linguistic meaning. Several studies have been directed at examining this issue. Dooling and Lachman (1971), for example, have shown the context effect in a set of experiments which compared recall of a paragraph about a particular metaphorically described topic relative to recall of a random ordering of the words in the passage. The important finding of the study was that the passage was better recalled when a title was given to it prior to recall than when no title was given. The title provided a context which allowed the passage to be related to prior knowledge and thus gave meaning to a series of perfectly grammatical sentences which seemed to have little relation to each other without the context of the title. Bransford and Johnson (1972) elaborated on this theme by using a pictorial context and titles for nonmetaphoric passages and measuring recall of ideas in the passages presented. To obtain an idea of how a passage can have little meaning despite the fact that it is composed of sentences which follow all the rules of English grammar, read the following paragraph taken from Bransford and Johnson.

> If the balloons popped, the sound wouldn't be able to carry since everything would be too far away from the correct floor. A closed window would also prevent the sound from carrying, since most buildings tend to be well insulated. Since the whole operation depends on a steady flow of electricity, a break in the middle of the wire would also cause problems. Of course, the fellow could shout, but the human voice is not loud enough to carry that far. An additional problem is that a string could break in the instrument. Then there would be no accompaniment to the message. It is clear that the best situation would involve less distance. Then there would be fewer potential problems. With face-to-face contact, the least number of things could go wrong.

As you can see the paragraph does not make very much sense. It has little meaning despite your efforts to create some sort of context in which it would have meaning. But turn the page and look at the

**Figure 5-2**

**Picture used to provide context for balloon passage. (Taken from Bransford and Johnson, 1972.)**

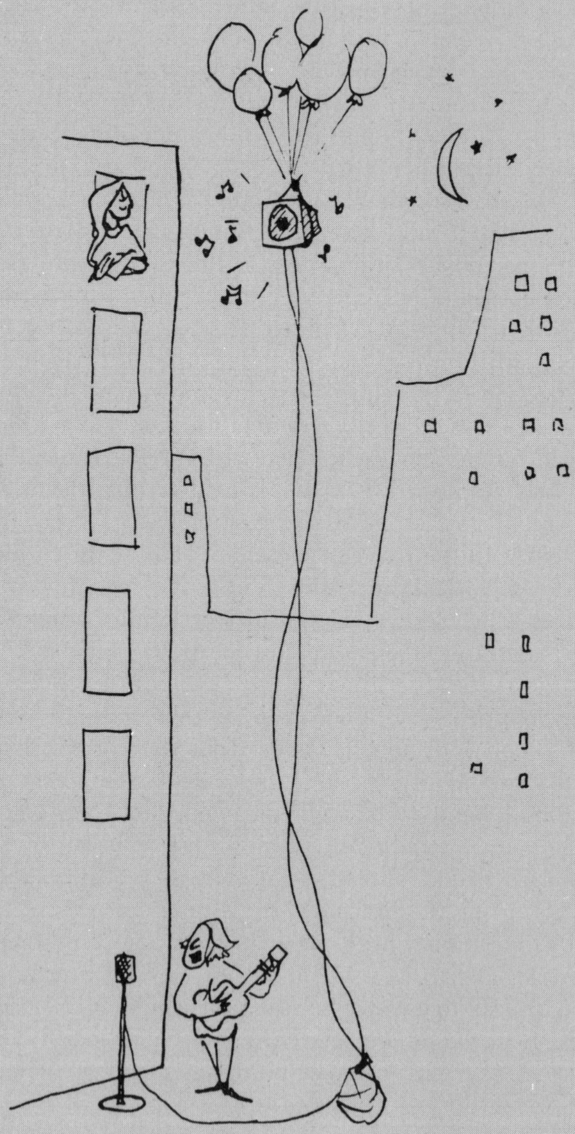

picture. The paragraph still does not make much sense, but if you go back and read the paragraph again, having looked at the picture, you will find that it is suddenly very meaningful. In essence, you have just participated in one of the Bransford and Johnson experiments. They asked people to listen to that paragraph, rate it for comprehensibility, and then recall as much of it as they could. One group heard it after seeing the picture for 30 seconds, one group saw the picture after hearing the passage, one group heard the passage without context, another heard it twice without context, and finally, another group saw all the same objects in another picture but with the objects arranged in a different relationship to each other. Only the group with the appropriate context rated the paragraph as high on comprehensibility, and that group was also able to recall at least twice as much as any of the other groups. None of the other groups differed in ratings or recall from each other. Similar results were obtained when people were given nonmetaphorically constructed passages about washing clothes and flying kites with and without a title indicating the context of the paragraph.

Barclay, Bransford, Franks, McCarrell, and Nitsch (1974) showed the context effect for both words and sentences by demonstrating that cues for recall are effective only if they are contextually relevant to the material to be recalled. For example, if you are to recall the word *piano* sometime after hearing the sentence, "The man lifted the piano," an effective cue would be "something heavy" and not "something with a nice sound," but the latter cue is more effective for recalling *piano* when it has been presented in the sentence, "The man tuned the piano."

These data, along with those of Dooling and Lachman, are interpreted by Bransford and Johnson to be strong evidence for the contention that an activated semantic context is essential to the comprehension of linguistic input. The semantic context must be activated during the ongoing process of comprehension to be effective, as demonstrated by those who, like you, received the picture or topic title after the passage. Notice also that the context, i.e., prior knowledge of the person, gives the passage its particular meaning but that a different context could have given the same passage a different meaning (Bransford & McCarrell, 1974), and that any number of different messages could have been developed for the same pictorial context. The latter point makes it clear that information about the topic is not essential. The picture did not give the story a topic—only a context in which a myriad of topics could be developed. Note also that people with different prior knowledge activated during comprehension will construct different kinds of meanings for the same linguistic input. The latter point may be seen most clearly from developmental comparisons, a point which Piaget has argued for many years, but it should also be clear that it is not limited to developmental comparisons (Barclay et al., 1974). (We shall, however, consider developmental aspects of semantics in Chapter 7.) Finally, it should be noted in connection with these experiments that the results of recall for the subjects who had an appropriate context and those who did not parallel the results of the experiments discussed earlier (e.g., Hyde & Jenkins, 1973) which showed differences in recall as a function of whether words were being semantically processed or processed at some other level.

Bransford and McCarrell (1974) and Franks (1974) have summarized the research they have done (along with that of others from this general theoretical point of view) and tried to show what it means to comprehend, i.e., construct the meaning of linguistic input and how that meaning fits into the broader context of knowledge of those who are trying to comprehend. They emphasize that knowledge is not simply copies from sensory input, but, rather, the objects which are the cause of the sensory input, whether they are words, or pictures, or any other form of sensory input, must be represented in terms of their relations to other objects. A person must, in turn, learn how to evaluate similarities and differences among objects and how objects are related one to another. Such knowledge is not automatically given by sensory input. It is constructed  and assimilated to a larger whole, the person's knowledge system. In other words, an object gains meaning as it is related to what we already know. As we modify what we know, we also give new meaning to that sensory input. For example, casting your eye to the sky at night allows you to perceive a complex of shining points in the blackness. You see those same shining points in a different way when you learn about constellations. In the same sense, many people find baseball dull until they acquire a knowledge of the subtleties of the game and only then do they begin to perceive more going on in the game, i.e., more meaning to the game, than they saw before when they looked at the same events. Consider, for example, observing a man dressed in a cap, a shirt with "Rose" printed on the back, knickers, and a pair of spiked shoes running from one square pillow to another in the middle of an open field surrounded by cheering people. Ask yourself what meaning that would have for someone who is not a baseball fan and has no idea what a baseball game is—to say nothing of who Pete Rose is or the Cincinnati Reds are. It would be as meaningless as my understanding of cricket. The Bransford and McCarrell chapter provides a host of such examples and reemphasizes the nature of the relationship between the meaning of events perceived, the context in which they occur, and the knowledge system into which it is being incorporated. Franks (1974), in turn, discusses the nature of tacit knowledge structures, the knowledge we have available to us which allows us to generate particular derivations from underlying knowledge structures.

## PARADOXES, PHILOSOPHY, AND THEORY

Now, if you have been thinking about the arguments of Bransford and his colleagues, you may have become concerned about a paradoxical problem which is inherent to the position they take. The paradox (really two) is this: you cannot come to know, gain the meaning of, or learn anything new unless you already know it and yet you cannot know anything unless you have already learned it. As Weimer (1973, 1974) points out, this is the paradox Plato presented in the *Meno* quite some time ago. The paradox arises and must be dealt with now because the Aristotelian philosophical position of nominalism and associationism which have long dominated the thinking of psychologists are being questioned and rejected by some in favor of the Platonic doctrine of forms and the doctrine of anamnesis. According to Weimer's interpretation, Plato's theory of knowledge assumes that the mind is primarily acquainted with abstract concepts which are the essences, or forms, of things. We are acquainted with concrete particulars only in a derivative manner. Thus, the appearances of our experience, the particulars, are known because we know the reality of the abstract concepts of which those particulars are exemplars. Note that it is the forms, the abstract entities, which are considered the reality and not the material world of which we may be aware.

Plato's theory assumes that the human being, as a function of being human, already knows everything there is to know. The human being already has the forms or essences and must only relate appearances in the material world to the abstract entities already known. If the abstract forms are known, then learning (of particulars) is not important for everything is already known. Plato's doctrine of anamnesis assumes that there is no learning from particular experiences but only recollection of the forms already known and related to the material world through that recollection. Remembering or recollection becomes the important factor and learning unimportant.

Such a conception of humanity and the nature of the psychological problems for investigation is, of course, radical for it turns around all the issues considered of importance for so many years. Most psychologists, and philosophers as well, have accepted the Aristotelian position of nominalism which assumes no abstract entities, and associationism which assumes that knowledge is built, acquired, or learned through the principles of similarity, contrast, and contiguity.

But notice that while the Platonic conception of human knowledge is incompatible with most contemporary thought and the traditional paradigm of the psychology of learning, it is quite compatible with the position Bransford and his colleagues have taken and, in fact, it resolves the paradoxes with which they are faced. That being the case, it may be worthwhile to examine the notions of the abstract as primary in conceptualization and recollection as the relational tie between instance and concept to see if the Platonic position can be given adequate contemporary formulation.

Weimer points out that there are a number of reasons for the abandonment of nominalism and for acceptance of the conceptual primacy of the abstract. First, facts which are the foundation of both knowledge and science in the Aristotelian tradition are relative rather than absolute. Facts cannot be the basis from which an empirical system is built (by association) because it takes an active cognitive process to construct facts out of the experience or sense data of the scientist. One must have knowledge of the general abstract categories to perceive the specific facts. One needs a theoretical orientation, as noted in the introductory chapter, in order to know what the facts are. The same sensory data may be interpreted in quite different ways, depending on the view of the world we hold as we look at them. As Weimer puts it, "Observation is not merely focusing one's attention on the data, but rather assimilation of data into the conceptual scheme of the observer" (p. 20).

If we are assimilating data to a conceptual system, or tacit knowledge relations in Franks' terms, then any particular instance of a concept cannot be known as an instance of the concept unless we already "know" the concept so that we can recognize the instance as belonging to the concept. Thus, in order to classify, we must have an abstract system of categories which allows us to proceed with the process of classification. We need a theory of kinds of things so that we can categorize things into kinds. Once again we see that the process of abstraction is primary. This is really not very surprising when we consider our theories of the world, be they scientific or otherwise, for we conceptualize the world in terms of ideals rather than in terms of concrete particulars. We talk of straight lines and spheres, for example, but we never experience such things. We conceptualize idealized forms of these concepts and categorize actual nonidealized experiences in terms of our idealized concepts.

Weimer goes on to note that Hayek (1952) makes the point that we do not sense an object or event at all unless we have some sort of classification for the object or event. That classification exists in the functioning of the nervous system. That system is one of abstract rules of action which are a result of our physiological structure as evolutionarily developed. Those abstract rules thus give a physiological and an evolutionary basis for the mind and at the same time a basis for the doctrine of anamnesis. The doctrine of anamnesis is, in modern-day dress, removed from the human soul as Plato had argued and given a basis in the physiological structure which has developed during human evolution and passed from generation to generation through the genetic structure.

As Weimer points out, such an argument fits nicely with the philosophical position of structural realism where a distinction is made between phenomenal experience, which is knowledge with which we are directly acquainted, and knowledge by description, which is knowledge about things or events that cannot be directly experienced. We know of our headache by direct acquaintance, but we know that people's headaches are caused by lack of sleep by description. Scientific knowledge is, of course, knowledge by description and consists of the structured characteristics of the world. Thus, the observation of objects and events which is basic to science, as to everyday living, in this view, is a matter of determining the structural relations that our sense impressions have to the external objects which are their causes. Science is not a determination of the intrinsic properties of the objects in the real world.

It was clear in the previous chapters that we had accepted the Platonic notion of forms as soon as we had accepted the idea of deep structure as basic to language. Deep structures are not manifest, they are abstract, as are transformational rules. Clearly our knowledge of the rules of language is abstract and has no empirically observable basis. Somehow the importance of this obvious departure from the assumptions of the Aristotelian tradition has not been realized clearly by many researchers dealing with syntactic problems. But the weight of the rejection of those assumptions can not be entirely ignored in an examination of the semantic component of language. If we accept this orientation to our subject matter, we must first recognize that the primary object of our scientific endeavor is abstract, and then we can look more carefully to the conception of abstract entities in the biological system of the human organism and establish how that set of abstract entities is brought into play as we interact with our environment. We shall return to this issue again in the last chapter.

## SUMMARY

In this chapter we began with the behavioristically oriented approach to meaning which seemed so reasonable to linguist and psychologist alike for many years. We found, however, as we began to scratch its surface, that the problem of meaning seemed to mushroom. We began with simple reactions to objects as constituting the essence of meaning and then we were led to mediating responses, associations, semantic fields, bundles of features, unmanifest implications in meanings, contextual effects and, finally, found the whole knowledge system had to be discussed in order to make sense out of meaning. In an important sense, we moved from an analysis of the external characteristics of human behavior and the structure of a communication system called language which humans seem to use in meaningful ways, to an analysis of the internal nature of humans and how we use language meaningfully as a part of a larger system of knowledge. We found that we were forced to consider the biological nature of the organism, the perceptual system, and the nature of the knowledge of the organism in order to come to grips with even the simplest cases of meaning. As a result, we were finally forced to reconsider our basic orientation toward the investigation of the phenomenon of meaning. At that point, we found ourselves considering the philosophical problems relating to the nature of man which Plato and Aristotle resolved in different ways so long ago.

## REFERENCES

Anglin, J. M. *The growth of word meaning.* Cambridge, Mass.: M.I.T. Press, 1970.

Barclay, J. R. The role of comprehension in remembering sentences. *Cognitive Psychology,* 1973, *4,* 229–54.

Barclay, J. R., Bransford, J. D., Franks, J. J., McCarrell, N. S., & Nitsch, K. Comprehension and semantic flexibility. *Journal of Verbal Learning and Verbal Behavior,* 1974, *13,* 471–81.

Barclay, J. R., & Reid, M. Characteristics of memory representations of sentence sets describing linear arrays. *Journal of Verbal Learning and Verbal Behavior,* 1974, *13,* 133–37.

Bartlett, F. C. *Remembering: A study in experimental and social psychology.* Cambridge, England: Cambridge University Press, 1932.

Bloomfield, L. *Language.* New York: Henry Holt, 1933.

Blumenthal, A. L. *Language and psychology.* New York: Wiley, 1970.

Bobrow, S. A. Memory for words in sentences. *Journal of Verbal Learning and Verbal Behavior,* 1970, *9,* 363–72.

Bobrow, S. A., & Bower, G. H. Comprehension and recall of sentences. *Journal of Experimental Psychology,* 1969, *80,* 445–61.

Bransford, J. D., Barclay, J. R., & Franks, J. J. Sentence memory: A constructive versus interpretive approach. *Cognitive Psychology,* 1972, *3,* 193–209.

Bransford, J. D., & Franks, J. J. The abstraction of linguistic ideas. *Cognitive Psychology,* 1971, *2,* 331–50.

Bransford, J. D., & Johnson, M. K. Contextual prerequisites for understanding: Some investigations of comprehension and recall. *Journal of Verbal Learning and Verbal Behavior,* 1972, *11,* 717–26.

Bransford, J. D., & McCarrell, N. S. A sketch of a cognitive approach to comprehension: Some thoughts about understanding what it means to comprehend. In W. B. Weimer & D. S. Palermo (Eds.), *Cognition and the symbolic processes.* Hillsdale, N.J.: Lawrence Erlbaum Associates, 1975. Pp. 189–230.

Brewer, W. F., & Lichtenstein, E. H. Memory for marked semantic features versus memory for meaning. *Journal of Verbal Learning and Verbal Behavior,* 1974, *13,* 172–80.

Brockway, J., Chmielewski, D., & Cofer, C. N. Remembering prose: Productivity and accuracy constraints in recognition memory. *Journal of Verbal Learning and Verbal Behavior,* 1974, *13,* 194–208.

Chomsky, N. *Syntactic Structures.* The Hague: Mouton, 1957.

Chomsky, N. *Aspects of a theory of syntax.* Cambridge, Mass.: M.I.T. Press, 1965.

Clark, H. H. Linguistic processes in deductive reasoning. *Psychological Review,* 1969, *76,* 387–404.

Clark, H. H., & Card, S. K. Role of semantics in remembering comparative sentences. *Journal of Experimental Psychology,* 1969, *82,* 545–53.

Clark, H. H., & Clark, E. V. Semantic distinctions and memory for complex sentences. *Quarterly Journal of Experimental Psychology,* 1968, *20,* 129–38.

Clark, H. H., & Stafford, R. A. Memory for semantic features in the verb. *Journal of Experimental Psychology,* 1969, *80,* 326–34.

Clifton, C., Jr. The implications of grammar for word associations. In K. Salzinger & S. Salzinger (Eds.), *Research in verbal behavior and some neurophysiological implications.* New York: Academic Press, 1967. Pp. 221–37.

Cofer, C. N. Constructive processes in memory. *American Scientist,* 1973, *61,* 537–43.

Collins, A. M., & Quillian, M. R. Retrieval time from semantic/memory. *Journal of Verbal Learning and Verbal Behavior,* 1969, *8,* 240–47.

Collins, A. M., & Quillian, M. R. In A. F. Sanders (Ed.), *Attention and performance III.* Amsterdam: North Holland, 1970a. Pp. 304–14.

Collins, A. M., & Quillian, M. R. Does category size affect categorization time? *Journal of Verbal Learning and Verbal Behavior,* 1970b, *9,* 432–38.

Conrad, C. Cognitive economy in semantic memory. *Journal of Experimental Psychology,* 1972, *92,* 149–54.

Deese, J. *The structure of associations in language and thought.* Baltimore: The Johns Hopkins Press, 1965.

Dooling, D. J., & Lachman, R. Effects of comprehension on retention of prose. *Journal of Experimental Psychology,* 1971, *88,* 216–22.

Fillenbaum, S. Memory for gist: Some relevant variables. *Language and Speech,* 1966, *9,* 217–27.

Fillenbaum, S., & Rapoport, A. *Structures in the subjective lexicon.* New York: Academic Press, 1971.

Fillmore, C. J. The case for case. In E. Back & R. T. Harms (Eds.), *Universals in linguistic theory.* New York: Holt, Rinehart & Winston, 1968.

Fodor, J. A. Could meaning be an $r_m$? *Journal of Verbal Learning and Verbal Behavior,* 1965, *4,* 73–81.

Ford, W., & Olson, D. The elaboration of the noun phrase in children's description of objects. *Journal of Experimental Child Psychology,* 1975, *19,* 371–82.

Franks, J. J. Toward understanding understanding. In W. B. Weimer & D. S. Palermo (Eds.), *Cognition and the symbolic processes.* Hillsdale, N.J.: Lawrence Erlbaum Associates, 1975. Pp. 231–62.

Franks, J. J., & Bransford, J. D. Abstraction of visual patterns. *Journal of Experimental Psychology,* 1971, *90,* 65–74.

Franks, J. J., & Bransford, J. D. The acquisition of abstract ideas. *Journal of Verbal Learning and Verbal Behavior,* 1972, *11,* 311–15.

Harris, R. J., & Brewer, W. F. Deixis in memory for verb tense. *Journal of Verbal Learning and Verbal Behavior,* 1973, *12,* 590–97.

Hayek, F. A. *The sensory order.* London: Routledge, 1952. Reprinted by University of Chicago Press, 1963.

Huttenlocher, J., & Higgins, E. T. Adjectives, comparatives, and syllogisms. *Psychological Review*, 1971, *78*, 487–504.

Hyde, T. S., & Jenkins, J. J. Recall of words as a function of semantic, graphic, and syntactic orienting tasks. *Journal of Verbal Learning and Verbal Behavior*, 1973, *12*, 471–80.

Katz, J. J. *Semantic theory*. New York: Harper & Row, 1972.

Katz, J. J., & Fodor, J. A. The structure of a semantic theory. *Language*, 1963, *39*, 170–210.

Knutson, A. The abstraction and integration of visual events. Unpublished master's thesis, The Pennsylvania State University, 1973.

McCawley, J. D. The role of semantics in grammar. In E. Bach & R. T. Harms (Eds.), *Universals in linguistic theory*. New York: Holt, Rinehart, & Winston, 1968.

McNeill, D. A study of word association. *Journal of Verbal Learning and Verbal Behavior*, 1966, *5*, 548–57.

Meyer, D. E. On the representation and retrieval of stored semantic information. *Cognitive Psychology*, 1970, *1*, 242–300.

Miller, G. A. Psycholinguistic approaches to the study of communication. In D. L. Aim (Ed.), *Journeys in science*. Albuquerque: The University of New Mexico Press, 1967. Pp. 22–73.

Miller, G. A. A psychological method to investigate verbal concepts. *Journal of Mathematical Psychology*, 1969, *6*, 169–91.

Miller, G. A., & McNeill, D. Psycholinguistics. In G. Lindzey & E. Aronson (Eds.), *Handbook of social psychology* (rev. ed.). Reading, Mass.: Addison-Wesley, 1967.

Mowrer, O. H. The autism theory of speech development and some clinical applications. *Journal of Speech and Hearing Disorders*, 1952, *17*, 263–68.

Mowrer, O. H. The psychologist looks at language. *American Psychologist*, 1954, *9*, 660–94.

Olson, D. R. Language and thought: Aspects of a theory of semantics. *Psychological Review*, 1970, *77*, 257–73.

Olson, D. R., & Filby, N. On the comprehension of active and passive sentences. *Cognitive Psychology*, 1972, *3*, 361–81.

Osgood, C. E. The nature and measurement of meaning. *Psychological Bulletin*, 1952, *49*, 197–237.

Osgood, C. E. Meaning cannot be $r_m$? *Journal of Verbal Learning and Verbal Behavior*, 1966, *5*, 402–7.

Osgood, C. E. *Interpersonal verbs and interpersonal behavior*. Technical Report No. 64, Institute of Communications Research, Urbana, University of Illinois, 1968.

Osgood, C. E. Where do sentences come from? In D. D. Steinberg & L. A. Jakobovits (Eds.), *Semantics*. Cambridge, England: Cambridge University Press, 1971. Pp. 497–529.

Osgood, C. E., Suci, G. J., & Tannenbaum, P. H. *The measurement of meaning*. Urbana, Ill.: University of Illinois Press, 1957.

Palermo, D. S. Word associations and children's verbal behavior. In L. P. Lipsitt & C. C. Spiker (Eds.), *Advances in child development and behavior* (Vol. 1). New York: Academic Press, 1963.

Palermo, D. S., & Jenkins, J. J. Word association norms: Grade school through college. Minneapolis, Minn.: University of Minnesota Press, 1964.

Perfetti. C. A. Psychosemantics: Some cognitive aspects of structural meanings. *Psychological Bulletin*, 1972, *78*, 241–59.

Quillian, M. R. Word concepts: A theory and simulation of some basic semantic capabilities. *Behavioral Science*, 1967, *12*, 410–30.

Rips, L. J. Quantification and semantic memory. *Cognitive Psychology,*
    1975, *7,* 307–40.

Rips, L. J., Shoben, E. J., & Smith, E. E. Semantic distance and the verification of
    semantic relations. *Journal of Verbal Learning and Verbal Behavior,*
    1973, *12,* 1–20.

Rumelhart, D. E., Lindsay, P. H., & Norman, D. A. A process model for long-term
    memory. In E. Tulving & W. Donaldson (Eds.), *Organization of memory.*
    New York: Academic Press, 1972. Pp. 198–248.

Sachs, J. S. Recognition memory for syntactic and semantic aspects of connected
    discourse. *Perception and Psychophysics,* 1967, *2,* 437–42.

Smith, E. E., Rips, L. J., & Shoben, E. J. Semantic memory and psychological
    memory: A featural model for semantic decisions, *Psychological Review,*
    1974, *81,* 214–41.

Snider, J. G., & Osgood, C. E. *Semantic differential technique: A sourcebook.*
    Chicago: Aldine, 1969.

Weimer, W. B. Psycholinguistics and Plato's paradoxes of the *Meno.*
    *American Psychologist,* 1973, *28,* 15–33.

Weimer, W. B. Overview of a cognitive conspiracy: Reflections on the volume.
    In W. B. Weimer & D. S. Palermo (Eds.), *Cognition and the symbolic
    processes.* Hillsdale, N.J.: Lawrence Erlbaum Associates, 1974. Pp. 415–42.

Winograd, T. Understanding natural language. *Cognitive Psychology,*
    1972, *3,* 1–191.

# Language Acquisition: Morphophonemics and Syntax

CHAPTER **6**

Perhaps one way we can summarize the contents of this book is by looking at the process of language acquisition. Children, after all, are linguists and psycholinguists combined as they proceed to acquire language. All normal children, in a matter of a few years, are capable of acquiring all of the necessary knowledge about language, all the rules of phonology, syntax, and semantics which are followed by speakers of their own language. They do so in a small portion of their lifetimes while linguists and psycholinguists, with all their knowledge of language accumulated in the centuries they have devoted to studying language, have not been able to solve the puzzle of what the rules are nor how they are related to language use.

Consider the enormity of the problem for the child. Suppose for a moment that you were placed in an environment in which no one understood your language and you did not understand theirs. Under these circumstances, there would be a number of things you would notice when the people around you spoke to you. First, it would seem that everyone was speaking very rapidly. You would also notice that the sounds of their language were rather strange. You would find that you could not discriminate the beginnings and endings of words within sentences. In fact, you would not even be able to tell where sentences began and ended except, of course, when the sentence initiated or ended what they were saying. Finally, you would have no idea of the meaning of what was being said. Some of you may have had some of these experiences when visiting another country.

As a function of knowing a language yourself, you would obviously know that the strange noises the other people uttered were speech, and in that stream of speech there would be words and sentences which have meaning. But think now of the baby who, during the period from six months of age to three or four years of age, manages to acquire the basic elements of language without even knowing that the sounds people make at various times are language, that language is composed of phonemes, that strings of phonemes make words, and that strings of words are put together in certain ways to construct sentences. How is it possible for a baby, without language and, presumably, without any knowledge that languages even exist, to acquire such a complex system as we have indicated that language is in the preceding chapters?

## ACQUISITION OF THE SOUND SYSTEM

To begin, the child must be able to recognize the acoustic characteristics of speech relative to those sounds which are not speech. As we noted in Chapter 3, that seems to be a distinction which is built into the psychological structure of the organism (Molfese, Freeman, & Palermo, 1975). The differential reactivity of the left and the right hemispheres to speech and nonspeech stimuli is apparent in the first week of life. Furthermore, the infant in the first month or so of life is sensitive to phonologically important variations in speech sounds and insensitive to variations in speech stimuli which are phonologically irrelevant (e.g., Eimas, Siqueland, Juzczyk, & Vigorito, 1971; Eimas, 1974; Trehub, 1973). In short, it appears that the infant already knows which sounds are speech sounds and which are not. The infant also already knows which acoustic variations in those speech sounds are relevant to language distinctions and which are not. In terms of the acoustic and phonological systems of language, infants appear to have the forms, the abstract entities, which allow them to classify sounds into categories of language and nonlanguage and within the language category they seem to know the variations which are language relevant.

Once language begins, assuming Jakobson's theory is correct (Jakobson, 1968), the child begins to classify sounds productively as well as perceptually. As we noted in Chapter 2, the biological system is apparently modified to allow speech production as well as perception. As the child grows, the vocal tract changes shape in a manner which makes it possible for speech sounds to be created (Lieberman, 1973). Although the evidence to support Jakobson's theory is not yet large, the creation of those sounds appears to follow a pattern of development based on feature distinctions which the biological system becomes capable of producing. Children ignore both the differences in fundamental frequency among the voices of people and the differences between their own voices and the voices of others. They ignore differences in speed of speech production and differences in intensity and voice quality. On the other hand, they attend to differences in manner and place of articulation both in what others produce and in their own productivity. In other words, at least within the speech mode, children categorize speech sounds in terms of distinctive features both receptively and productively. Furthermore, that categorization is different in kind from the graduated discriminations made in the nonspeech mode. One speech sound does not gradually merge into another as with the perceptual characteristics of nonspeech sounds. Rather, speech sounds are categorically perceived. While categorical perception appears to be present naturally long before production, we find that categorical production seems to develop more slowly. The productive categories emerge as more and more features are used to articulate the sounds (Menyuk, 1971) and, in turn, form the language-relevant phonological categories based on the feature distinctions.

## Morphophonemic Rules

Let us turn now from the acquisition of the specific features that comprise the sounds of the language we discussed in Chapter 3 to the rules the child is learning with respect to combinations of sounds. We have noted in Chapter 3 the difficulties children have with consonant blends, but there are other kinds of phonological rules which have been investigated. For example, Messer (1967) presented three- and four-year-old children with pairs of nonsense words, one of which followed the structural rules of English syllables (e.g., /frul/) and one of which did not (e.g., /nrul/). The children were asked to pronounce both and to tell which one sounded most like a word. The children indicated their knowledge of the phonological rules of English by selecting the words that followed the rules. In addition, it was noted that articulation errors occurred more frequently with the words that did not follow the rules. Changes in the sounds which occurred when errors were made usually involved only one distinctive feature difference (e.g., /škib/ to /skib/). Not only can children select those nonsense words which are most similar to their own language, but they do not have any difficulty learning to respond to words that follow other rules. Menyuk (1968) demonstrated this in a study which required children in kindergarten through second grade to learn to respond by identifying objects given names which either followed or did not follow English phonological rules. The rate of learning was no different at any age for the two types of names, although the children made more errors when they were required to articulate the names that did not follow the rules. Although it was not reported in the original article, Menyuk later indicated (1971) that the errors were minimally different from the correct articulation in terms of distinctive features, as was the case in the Messer study. The data of these two studies give additional support to the psychological reality of the distinctive features.

While these two studies indicate that children are aware of sequential phonological rules at an early age, of somewhat more interest, perhaps, are the studies which have examined the acquisition of specific *morphophonemic sequencing rules*. Research in this area was begun by Berko (1958), who was primarily interested in the acquisition of the morphological rules associated with the formation of plurals, possessives, and third person singular of verbs, and the inflections for the past tense of regular verbs. Since all the sounds used in producing these inflections were within the articulatory abilities of the children, the question of concern was whether the children had acquired the phonological rules that determine the particular inflectional ending for each phonological context, i.e., the three allomorphs for past tense (/t/, /d/, /əd/) and the three allomorphs for pluralization (/s/, /z/, /əz/).

Berko's procedure involved presenting children aged between four and eight years with pictures which were referred to with non-sense or real English names and then eliciting the appropriate names with an inflection. For example, she presented a child with a picture of two animals and said, "This is a lun. Now there is another one. There are two of them. There are two _____." The child filled in the blank, in this case with "luns," using the /z/ phoneme if a correct response was given.

In general, the results indicate that children show continued improvement in various aspects of phonological development in the areas measured throughout the age range from four to seven. Pluralization of the nonsense words was generally 70 percent correct or better for all ages when the /s/ and /z/ allomorphs were required but less than 40 percent correct when the /əz/ allomorph was correct. Similarly, when the /əz/ inflection was required in forming the third person singular of a verb or the possessive form of a noun, performance was poor. This was true despite the fact that 99 percent of the older children correctly inflected *glass* for the plural form. In the case of past tense inflection, performance ranged from approximately 50 to 85 percent correct when the /t/ or /d/ inflection was called for but less than 35 percent correct at all ages when the /əd/ inflection was correct, although the verb *melt* was correctly inflected by better than 70 percent of all children.

It would appear that with both pluralization and past tense inflection rules, the child at this age has collapsed the three rules involved into two, at least insofar as the productive extension of the rules is concerned. The child is able to extend the /s/ and /z/ plural allomorphs and the /t/ and /d/ past tense allomorphs to new forms, but fails to use the /əz/ and the /əd/ allomorphs. Another interpretation is that the child has three rules in each case, but for nouns ending in a sibilant or verbs ending in /t/ or /d/, pluralization and past tense respectively are formed by a zero allomorph, that is, the inflection is not overtly marked. Alternatively, Berko favors the argument that there is only one rule in each case, a rule that a final sibilant makes a word plural and a rule that /d/ added to a verb makes it past tense and, under certain conditions, the /d/ becomes a /t/ automatically.

One further point with respect to this study pertains to the finding that the plural of some of the nonsense nouns, for example *heaf,* and the past tense of some of the nonsense verbs, for example *gling,* were treated as irregular forms by a significant number of adults who offered the plural form *heaves* (42 percent) and the past form *glung* or *glang* (75 percent), which the children very seldom produced. This finding suggests that children learn some irregular forms by rote and later acquire an alternative rule which is based on a few irregular words in the language and may be extended to new words with a similar overall phonological form to the irregular words already known. The fact that the /əz/ plural for *glass* was correctly used by 99 percent of the older children but not generalized to new words suggests that rote learning may be a general initial strategy in language acquisition, at least of this aspect of language, and only when the memory load or some other factor makes rote learning unmanageable does the use of more general rules come into play. Moskowitz (1973) has made a similar argument with respect to individual phonemes, but MacWhinney's research (1975) with acquisition of pluralization by Hungarian children suggests that rote memorization is of minimal importance.

In discussing some aspects of her data, Berko suggests that children may generalize responses on the basis of feature similarity rather than sound similarity. This point was cleverly investigated by Anisfeld in a series of three studies which examined some aspects of the development of phonological rules in young children and avoided some of the methodological difficulties of the Berko study (Natalicio & Natalicio, 1969).

In the first of this series, Anisfeld and Tucker (1967) provided a number of interesting insights to the development of pluralization rules. An initial experiment with six-year-old children established not only that children of this age have difficulty with the pluralization rule in which /əz/ is used, but they are aware of both the concept of plurality and the phonological problems involved with words ending in sounds which require the /əz/ plural form. These aspects of the child's conceptual as well as linguistic processes are revealed by the finding that the children tended to use numbers in their responses when they were not sure of the correct pluralization rule, usually when /əz/ was required. Thus, for example, when told that an object in a picture was a *tek* and asked what was shown in a picture of several of these objects, the child would respond *teks*. If the name was *nis,* however, the children were much more likely to respond with the number of *nisses* and an erroneous pluralization of *nis* (e.g., three *nis*). Thus the children responded as if they knew that their pluralization of *nis* might not convey the semantic concept and therefore preceded the word by the appropriate number to achieve the same effect.

A second study indicated that five-year-old children seem to have a concept that the plural form of a word is the singular form with something appended. When given a choice of two artificial words, neither of which was an English plural form of a singular artificial word, the children strongly preferred the pluralization achieved by some phonemic addition to the singular form, as compared to no addition, or a singular form changed in another manner. It would seem that children of this age have the concepts of one and more than one, the ability to recognize when they do not know how to pluralize a word correctly, and the concept that pluralization demands some sort of phonological addition to the word to make it plural although they may not know what that addition should be. Finally, the authors attempted to determine, using the Berko type of methodology, both the recognitory and productive capacities of the child at approximately six years of age for the specific English pluralization rules. The results confirmed the difficulty that children at this age have with the productive use of the /əz/ inflection and the relative lack of difficulty with the /s/ and /z/ inflections.

A study by Anisfeld, Barlow, and Frail (1968) delves specifically into the child's generalization of phonological rules in relation to the distinctive features of the sounds. Children six to nine years of age were presented with consonant-vowel-consonant (CVC) nonsense words ending in /l/, /r/, or /n/ presented as a singular name and asked to choose which of a pair of plural alternatives they preferred. The plural alternatives were formed by adding to the singular form one of the following sounds /p/, /b/, /m/, /f/, /v/, /k/, /g/, /t/, /d/, /n/, or /ch/.

Note that the rule in English phonology calls for the /z/ ending in every case so that the results were tabulated in terms of the distinctive features the chosen consonants had in common with the correct /z/ plural form. Obviously, a random distribution of choices would be expected if the generalization of phonological rules played no part in affecting the choice of responses. It was found that [+ continuant] (/f/ and /v/) and [+ strident] (/f/, /v/, and /ch/) sounds were significantly preferred by the first and second graders, although not by the younger six-year-old children. Further, the older groups tended to select the artificial plural marker with the fewest feature differences compared to the /z/. The authors argue that the features of [+ continuant] and [+ strident] are more important than the features

[+ diffuse], [− grave], [+ voice], and [− nasal] which also characterize /z/, because it is the two features [+ continuant] and [+ strident] which distinguish the plural marked /z/ from more consonants than any of the other features. The additional fact that voicing was not an important distinguishing feature was interpreted by the authors to indicate that pluralization rules are not formulated in terms of the voiced /z/ and voiceless /s/. Rather, a more general rule which states that an inflectional suffix has the same sign on voicing as the preceding sound pertains to all suffixes and therefore is not an important feature distinction in a particular instance such as pluralization. In other words, there are two levels of rules: those which generally apply across all situations and those which are specific to a particular context. Berko made the same point in her study.

A study by Anisfeld and Gordon (1968) more thoroughly examined the problem of inflectional rules. In this case, a large number of consonantal endings was used and the inflection of synthetic verbs for past tense was investigated. The use of the past tense test was added for two reasons: first, to demonstrate that the findings of this and the previous study were not due merely to particular sound preferences regardless of the task and, second, to show that the voicing feature is a part of a more general voicing-assimilation rule applicable to inflections in general rather than pluralization in particular.

The results showed that adults restricted their choices when possible to sounds which were [+ strident] (ch and j), [+ continuant] (th), or both (f, v, and sh). The first- and fourth-grade children showed preferences only for /sh/, and /ch/ and /j/. The latter make up the subclass of sounds which along with /s/ and /z/ are the functionally significant sounds in English pluralization in that when they occur at the end of a word, they all take the /əz/ form for pluralization. The children's rules thus seem more restrictive than those of the adults. Although they showed some tendency to prefer the /f/, /v/, and /th/ found acceptable by the adults, their preferences for all sounds were less strong than those of the adults in all cases. That the children's phonological rules do not seem as well developed nor as complete as those of the adults was also reflected by the fact that the adults favored /m/ and /n/ endings often used in irregular forms of pluralization (e.g., men) in English while the children showed no such preferences.

In the case of the past tense choices, the children showed significant preferences for /ch/ and /j/. The authors attribute this result to the fact that there are no other sounds relevant to past tense as there are in the case of pluralization. The authors argue that the /ch/ and /j/ sounds contain within them the regular past tense markers /t/ and /d/, that is, in the articulation of /ch/ and /j/, the /t/ and /d/ sounds are a part of the more complex /ch/ and /j/ respectively.

In addition, the children showed a significant rejection of the /s/ and /z/ sounds which are relevant to the pluralization inflection and, thus, in grammatical opposition to the past tense inflection.

In contrast to the efforts of Anisfeld to determine the phonological rules for appending a sound in the form of an inflection to an already complete word, Bruce (1964) looked at the child's ability to analyze the component sounds comprising a word unit. He presented children from five- to seven-and-one-half years of age (5 to 9 years mental age) a series of words and asked them to delete one sound from the word and pronounce the word with the sound deleted. All the deletions resulted in other real English words; for example, the word *stand* was presented and the child was asked to delete the "t" and articulate the remainder, in this case, *sand*.

Only children with a mental age of seven or higher evidenced any success at all with this task, and after age seven marked increases in success occurred so that children with mental ages of nine seemed to have little difficulty with the phonological analysis and elision required. The strategies employed in the task by the children at various ages is perhaps more revealing of the phonological development indicated by this task. Up to about mental age 6, the children were not able to separate sound from word. They could produce isolated sounds and words, but were unable to take from a word one of its component sounds regardless of whether that sound was at the beginning, middle, or end of a word. At mental age 6, the children began to be able to form new words but the relation of the words they formed and the satisfactory solution of the task was often remote. For example, when presented with *monkey* and asked to delete the *k* sound, one child responded with *kent*. Some children substituted one sound for another in the word, although not necessarily for the sound they had been asked to delete, e.g., *land* was given as a response to delete the *n* in *hand*. While the child of six has begun to get the idea of sounds within words, it appears that they are merely substituting word units for other word units as yet. Substitution responses of this sort decrease with mental age. The last stage prior to correct performance is characterized by elision, but errors of over-deletion or incorrect deletion are prominent, and deletion from the middle of a word is particularly likely to lead to error.

Because the children in the Bruce study had so much difficulty abstracting a phoneme from a word, a question arises about the size of the phonological unit for the early grade-school child. A study by Huttenlocher (1964) indicates that children at the preschool level cannot parse common phrases into word units, suggesting that the units may in some cases be even larger than the word at earlier age levels. Recognizing this problem and the implications it has for teaching a child to read, Zhurova (1973) made a specific effort to teach children between the ages of three and seven to isolate phonemes from words. Despite careful efforts in a gamelike situation and considerable coaching on the part of the experimenter, it proved very difficult for children in this age range to isolate the first or last consonant, for example, from a word. The youngest children did not have much success, but the older children were able to isolate some of the sounds when the experimenter carefully separated and produced the sound first and the child repeated it.

## Identifying Sound Units

These data, along with those from a study by Bryant and Anisfeld (1969) which show that children six years old have difficulty parsing the singular form from a plural form, suggest that children take a holistic approach to words as sound units. It may be that at earlier ages children treat whole sentences or phrases as undivided units, and as they acquire more language, they parse the larger units into smaller parts. In the age range from about five to about eight, at least, it would appear that the word, or syllable, is the sound unit children deal with because they lack the analytic abilities required to isolate and manipulate phonemic units within words. Savin and Bever (1970) have presented data to indicate that adults identify the syllable unit prior to the phonemic unit in some circumstances. Foss and Swinney (1973), in addition to replicating the Savin and Bever results, have shown that words may be identified before syllables.

Clearly the child must perceive the incoming signal at all levels—auditory, phonetic, and phonological—as well as identify the lexical, syntactic, and semantic characteristics of that signal. The young child, however, may not make identifications of the smaller units since he or she is seldom required to do so. As a result, processing of the linguistic units is in terms of the larger chunk. The elements of the larger chunks may not be identified or abstracted until the need arises as, for example, in the case of reading when phonemic distinctions are taught. The plausibility of this hypothesis is supported by the study of McNeill and Lindig (1973), who showed that the identification of elements in sentences is a function of both context and the strategies used in searching for the unit to be identified. In other words, children do not develop strategies for identifying phonemic elements, for example, until those elements are necessary for their own communication purposes. In short, children may not attend initially to the lower levels, or smaller units, but are concerned primarily with the total syntactic or semantic unit of the utterance. It may be that young children learning the phonological system are learning words as phonemic units which express semantic concepts. When they learn inflections, they may not be learning phonological rules for converting singular forms to plural forms, for example, but rather new words that express different semantic concepts. Only later do they recognize the relation between singular and plural words in terms of phonemic similarities and differences. Children may have developed a complex system of phonological rules by the time they are six or seven years old, but they may not have abstracted the phoneme from that system of rules and mastered the complex relationship which the phoneme has to the acoustic stimuli and to articulatory movements. While Templin's (1957) work suggests that by the age of eight years children can correctly articulate all the sounds and nearly all of the most complex sound combinations of English, only a good deal more research will establish whether at that age they have also mastered the phonological system of rules which the adult native speaker seems to possess.

Our analysis of the phonological system from speech sound perception in infancy to the rules for combining phonemes into the production of words seems to reflect a process of categorization and a process of categorical integration. The child appears fully capable from birth of making categorical differentiations in terms of language-relevant dimensions. The child also appears, perhaps as a function of physiological modifications which occur with maturation, to make categorizations of language sounds on the basis of an abstract set of features which are associated with place and manner of articulation and acoustic cues. Finally, we have noted in this section that the child gradually acquires a set of rules which allow the combination of categorized sounds into the blends of those categories which we know as syllables, words, and sentences.

The idea that the abstract forms, the essences of language sounds, are given in the human organism seems relatively clear from the data summarized above. The assertion that those forms exist in the biological nature of the child allows us to consider the doctrine of *anamnesis* (recollection) tenable as well. The sound system as conceptualized within the distinctive feature theory can easily be conceived within this framework. The information we have on phonemic acquisition can also be conceived within this framework but alternative interpretations are also more easily contrived. Certainly the sounds used in creating words and sentences are exemplars of an abstract system which we know for our language. Just as in the case of the exemplars of straight lines and spheres, those sounds differ from exemplar to exemplar, and only within the framework of knowing the abstract idealized forms can we know the language sound system. In short, it is relatively easy to conceptualize the sound system of language within the framework of the doctrine of forms. In addition, one can conceptualize the early acquisition of sounds as language develops in the child within the framework of the doctrine of anamnesis. But as language takes form it is more difficult, at least on the basis of the way the problems have been investigated, to have the same kind of confidence in the latter doctrine. It does, however, allow us a new perspective on the issues involved to at least give both doctrines some consideration. Most investigators have, of course, designed their research from the more traditional paradigmatic view.

## SYNTACTIC DEVELOPMENT

Let's turn our attention now to a consideration of the syntactic development of the child's language system. The syntax of adult language, of course, refers to the grammatical structure of sentences. When we consider the development of the child's sentences, we are immediately faced with the controversial question as to when syntactic development begins. Is it possible to argue that syntax begins at the one-word stage or must we have at least two-word utterances, as most people in the field have suggested? Let's begin by a consideration of the first word and move on from there.

### The One-Word Stage

It is difficult to establish the age at which the child utters its first word. The difficulty reflects an inability of the observer to comprehend the phonemic system of the child, a failure to recognize the referent the child may have in mind for the first word, and the unreliability of parental observers who are inclined to give their children credit for more than a trained observer might. Nevertheless, most observers are agreed that the first birthday, or just before, is about the time that most children utter their first word (McCarthy, 1954). Usually, the first words are reduplicated syllables which seem to grow out of sounds heard in the babbling stage. These syllables (e.g., *papa, mama, dada, bye-bye*), are classified as words because they are used consistently in particular contexts. The initial word signals the beginning of a period of about six months during which children gradually build a lexicon or vocabulary of about 200 to 300 words by the time they reach eighteen to twenty-four months, according to one estimate (Smith, 1926), although the range of individual differences may be very large.

The controversy mentioned above revolves about the interpretation to be placed on the child's use of the one-word utterance. Although the words are used singly, the child appears to be trying to convey more than a single word idea. It is difficult, however, to know what the child means except in the context of the utterance. Thus, the utterance /papa/ may be interpreted as meaning "Where is papa?"

"Come here, papa!" "Here comes papa," or any number of other meanings.

Perhaps the most widely accepted interpretation of the one-word stage is that while the child is able to produce only one word at a time, each word is used to mean a whole sentence. The child is, therefore, frequently described as being in the *holophrastic stage* when one word is a sentence. Such an interpretation suggests that the meaning of a sentence is in the word and that the child merely lacks the syntactic capability of filling in the rest of the words to make a complete, unambiguous sentence. Since it has been observed that children use their limited vocabularies in a variety of referential situations, it also means that several sentences may be contained in the meaning of a single word as used at this age. This holophrastic point of view was suggested, according to Greenfield and Smith (1976), by the early studies of Preyer (1890), Stern and Stern (1907), Bloch (1921), and Buhler (1926), and has been carried over into the current literature (e.g., McNeill, 1971).

Not much attention has been focused on the one-word stage in current research, but two recent volumes, one by Bloom (1973) and another by Greenfield and Smith (1976) have thrown new light on the one-word stage and the holophrastic interpretation. Greenfield and Smith have suggested that in the discussions of previous research there has been a failure to distinguish between the referential meaning of a word and the combinatorial meaning as it is used in sentential and extrasentential contexts. The error results from the assumption that the single words have nothing to combine with since there are no other words in the sentence. Thus, the child has given no evidence of syntactic knowledge since syntax involves the grammatical relations among words. But, as Greenfield and Smith point out, children do have the possibility of combining words with the extralinguistic context and herein lies the syntactic or, more important, the semantic use of single words by the child. The referential meaning of the words does not change on this view, only the combinatorial meaning as the child uses the word in various situations or contexts. They quote Guillaume (1927) as expressing essentially their position: "The child does not invent grammatical categories; he finds these tools already made, but he must learn the use of them by the direct relation of the sentence to the concrete situation" (Guillaume, 1927, p. 25). The child has the grammatical categories as given and needs only to determine how the words of the categories are used referentially with respect to the nonverbal context.

Greenfield and Smith use the case grammar of Fillmore (1968) as a framework for looking at the manner in which a child uses single-word utterances in combination with the context of the situation to communicate the semantic ideas inherent to the various cases. The basic assumption is that syntactic development begins at the one-word stage, not at the two-word stage when word combinations are manifest. The basic structural aspects of language begin ι .th the combination of words with nonverbal context. The child learns how to express the structural relations, already known, through language by observing those relations in a referential context and noting how they are related to the language.

Greenfield and Smith carefully observed the contextual use of single words by two children as they passed through the one-word stage. They kept diaries of the children's speech and the context in which the words were uttered from about seven months of age to about twenty-two months of age—from the beginning of the one-word stage to a period when longer utterances predominated. Further formal sessions were also included to check on observer reliability. The utterances were classified according to semantic function, i.e., the relationship between two elements in an event. While the child may only use one word which pertains to agent, action, object, location, and so on, the semantic relation was considered the important factor in the communicative function of the language the child was using in the context of the word uttered.

The results were impressive in showing how the same word may be used by the child in many different case relations in many different situations. Further, there were limits on the cases which the children expressed. Not all cases were present at the beginning and there was a relatively clear developmental order in the appearance of the various cases. Thus, the child begins with what are called pure performatives, such as "bye-bye" in the context of waving, then it develops vocatives, where it seems to be calling for "mama," for example, and progresses to object of demand; negative or affirmative; action of agent; object of direct action; action or state; locative; agent of action; and modification. As can be seen from this incomplete list, the child's single words become used for more and more conceptually complex relations and show a regular progression which can be conceived as leading naturally to the appearance of such relations in more complex linguistic utterances represented by two or more words.

The study of Bloom (1973) was conceived within a somewhat different theoretical framework, but her report of one child's development through the single-word stage plus supplementary data from three other children fortifies the general conclusions of Greenfield and Smith. Children do not use one word as a sentence, but the one-word stage is a period of acquiring strategies which lead naturally into the development of linguistic syntax. Evidence was found to suggest that while only one word was being used the children were talking about people doing things, objects being acted upon, objects located in space, existence, disappearance, nonexistence, and recurrence, much as Greenfield and Smith reported. In addition, Bloom's results clearly indicate that the use of the single words reflected the cognitive development of the child during the period from nine to twenty-two months of age. Bloom tends to be cautious in her interpretations, noting that the interpretive problems are much more severe in the one-word stage than in later development when cross-validating and linguistic evidence may be obtained to support interpretations given to any particular linguistic usage by the child.

The single word does seem to express semantic ideas and, in that sense, is an attempt to communicate in the manner of a sentence. On the other hand, it is the situational context which is used to support the message rather than words, a technique we adults often employ in our own language use. Surely more attention will be directed to this early language period since these studies have proven so informative and the relation between the beginnings of language use and cognitive development seem so obviously important. A more recent analysis of the holophrastic period (Dore, 1975) suggests new directions for research in this area focusing on the single word utterance as a speech act with a referential function and an intentional or pre-illocutionary force conveyed by intonational contours.

## The Two-Word Stage

We must step back conceptually a moment as we consider the study of the beginnings of word combination because the research on language acquisition within the recent psycholinguistic paradigm began with what was considered, at that time, the beginnings of syntactic development—the two-word utterance. When this research began, the investigators involved were just beginning to think in terms of transformational grammar and they were essentially exploring a new area with minimal theoretical guidance. We will consider that work in terms of the development of ideas about how to deal with the data and what those data might be interpreted to mean.

**Pivot and telegraphese descriptions.**   The first research to examine the child's two-word utterances was reported by Braine (1963a; 1963b) and shortly thereafter very similar data were reported by Miller and Ervin (1964) and by Brown and his students (Brown & Fraser, 1964; Brown, Fraser, & Bellugi, 1964). In each case, the authors were reporting the characteristics of a corpus of two-word utterances collected from a small group of between two and five children. While the size of the samples was rather small, the similarities among the reports were striking. All three groups of researchers reported that the utterances, despite the lack of grammatical completeness, seemed to express a complete idea or thought within the context in which they were uttered. It was usually not difficult to understand or interpret what the child meant. "Milk allgone," for example, does not resemble very closely anything an adult would say, but in context it is reasonable to give it a meaning without difficulty. Second, there was a similar patterning of responses which was noted by all three research groups. Third, the length of the child's utterances was restricted to one or two words, regardless of the length of the utterances directed toward the child. Often the child tended to contract what the adult said by repeating the one or two most important words in the adult sentence. The adult, in turn, tended to expand the utterances of the child to full sentences. Finally, there were no indications of morphophonemic inflectional rules for tense or pluralization, for example, in the child's utterances. In short, there appeared to be a rudimentary, or telegraphic, system used by these children in their constructions and the question for the researchers revolved about how to characterize that system.

All three investigators reported that the two-word utterance, which usually begins to occur when the child is between the ages of eighteen and twenty-four months, seems to involve more than random juxtaposing of words that the child has heard. There is an apparent system to the constructions which accounts for about 70 percent of the utterances heard. The system seemed in these early analyses to consist of using one word in a single position, and a large group of words in the other position. The children were heard in various appropriate situations to say, for example, "There bird," "There boat," "There kitty," "There mummy," and so on. On other appropriate occasions the children might be heard to say, "Bird allgone," "Eyebrow allgone," "Kitty allgone," "Reel allgone," and so on. In all the children observed, there was a small group of words which occurred fairly consistently in the first position, another, smaller group of words which occurred fairly consistently in the second position, and a very large group of words which occurred in either first or second position. The grammar of this stage in the child's language development seemed to be characterized as:

$$S \rightarrow \begin{Bmatrix} (P_1) + O \\ \\ O + (P_2) \end{Bmatrix}$$

That is, the sentence (S) is rewritten as a pivot word $(P_1)$ plus open class word (O) or open class word plus pivot word $(P_2)$. The pivot words are marked by a subscript because the pivot words that occurred in the first position did not seem to occur in the second position. The open class words, on the other hand, appeared to be used in both positions. The pivot words are placed in parentheses in the grammar to indicate that they could be omitted and a one-word utterance of an open class word alone is possible. Pivot words, however, did not seem to occur alone.

In general, most of the first language constructions of the child seemed to be of the P-O or O-P form. When the child used single word utterances, the words tended to come from the open class. The characteristics of the pivot and open class words were hard to specify within the framework of the adult grammar. They were grouped in that manner because of their distributional characteristics in the child's speech. Most of the open class words, however, tended to be nouns and verbs. The pivot words, on the other hand, tended to be adjectives, adverbs, pronouns, verbs, and articles. The combinations of words suggested that these two-word utterances were the beginnings of constructions which are the adult equivalents of demonstrative constructions (e.g., "that truck"), noun phrases (e.g., "two men"), verb phrases (e.g., "see boy"), and complete sentences. The children showed evidence of being able to conceptualize the relations expressed by the adult but the ability to produce a linguistically complete expression of those relations was only beginning to evolve (Brown & Bellugi, 1964).

Although the child's language consisted primarily of P-O and O-P types of constructions initially, there were exceptions for all the children studied. Some two-word utterances did not appear to fit any identifiable pattern and some utterances were several words long. In the latter case, each child seemed to have a few longer utterances which could be run off as units in appropriate situations.

The P-O type grammatical description was a start but not, however, a very helpful one. The problem is that it is based solely upon a distributional analysis of the surface structures used by the child. There is no way to map this system into adult grammar, as Braine and others found once they tried to account for longer utterances as the child's language continued to develop. The P-O grammar described some of the surface regularities in language use but had little usefulness beyond that since it failed to characterize the functional relations among the words and the semantic representations of the utterances.

The observation that when the pivot words were classified by the adult system of parts of speech, there appeared to be some syntactic relationships in skeletal form, led McNeill (Miller & McNeill, 1968) to analyze the relation between deep structure relations which the child might be trying to express and the two-word utterances which actually occurred. He argued that the telegraphic speech of the child at this stage appears to conform to one or another basic grammatical relation. Specifically, he suggested that the four relations P + N, N + N, V + N, and N + V reflected modifier plus head noun; modifier plus head noun or subject plus predicate; main verb plus object; and subject plus predicate, respectively. McNeill made a similar analysis of three-word utterances where eight combinations of the elements P, N, and V expressed possible grammatical relations relative to a linguistic syntactic analysis of language. Of the nine possible combinations of P, N, and V in two-word utterances and the twenty-seven possible combinations of the words in the three-word utterances, only the four and eight combinations respectively reflected direct manifestations of deep structure grammatical relations, according to McNeill. He examined all the two- and three-word utterances of Adam, one of the children in Brown's study, to determine whether any of these grammatical relations were represented in the child's utterances. Not only were all of the grammatical relations represented, but no other combinations were found. In short, McNeill argued that the child knows the basic, or deep structure, grammatical relations and expresses those relations in the two-word utterances. Since the child already knows the deep structure relations, McNeill argued that language acquisition consists of acquiring the stock of transformations which allow such relations to be manifest in many different surface forms (McNeill, 1966). The importance of McNeill's analysis, however, was in showing that one could go beyond the description of the distributional characteristics of the two-word utterances in terms of the P-O description and demonstrate a grammatical system in the child's utterances which makes contact with the adult system of syntax toward which the child is presumably moving in its language development.

**Semantic considerations.**    McNeill had, however, missed an important aspect of the data. As Bloom (1970) pointed out in her analysis of the language development of three children, the same two-word utterance could reflect more than one syntactic relation, depending on the context in which it was uttered. Without taking into consideration the context, it is impossible to disambiguate most two-word utterances. Bloom provides some very good examples. One of the children she studied said, "Mommy sock" in two different contexts: one when she picked up her mother's sock, suggesting that the utterance was expressing a genitive relation, while the second utterance occurred in the context of mommy putting the sock on the child, suggesting an agent-object relation with the verb absent from the surface form. While this example is particularly clear in demonstrating the point, it is equally obvious that an utterance such as "This cleaning" is also ambiguous without some particular context to allow the listener to determine the meaning the child might be trying to convey with the two words.

The point of Bloom's extensive analysis of the two-word utterances of the three children she studied is that it is necessary to interpret what the child says within the linguistic and extra-linguistic context in which it is said, a point which, of course, allowed the examination of single-word utterances as we have already noted. More important in the long run, perhaps, this study began a shift in conceptualization of language acquisition from a focus on syntax to a consideration of semantics. Previous studies had placed major emphasis on the acquisition of syntactic structures while Bloom's study, although analyzed in terms of the underlying syntactic structures, made it clear that syntactic analysis of sentences in isolation is not possible with two-word utterances (any more than, as we noted in the previous chapter, it is possible with the syntactically complete sentences of adults). In addition, Bloom makes the point that different children appear to use different strategies for acquiring even the early two-word structures they produce. While all the children seem to construct utterances which may be easily related to the adult model, some children seem to focus their attention on verb-object relations and others on subject-object relations or subject-verb strings. Some focus on one syntactic frame and make substantive substitutions within that frame while others show more variation in the frames used. In short, there seems to be more than one strategic route to the end result. Finally, Bloom emphasizes the interrelationships among the linguistic and nonlinguistic experiences of the child and the cognitive-perceptual development of the child. Language acquisition cannot be studied as an isolated form of mental or behavioral activity. One must view language acquisition within the broader context of the child's overall developmental level.

Nelson (1973) has also emphasized the individual differences in language acquisition in reporting her year-long longitudinal study of eighteen children who were ten to fifteen months of age when the study was initiated. The children in her study fell into two groups—those who seemed to use language to talk about objects around them and those who used language to talk about themselves and other people. Nelson suggests that language had a referential function for the former group and an expressive function for the latter group. The early words of the expressive group consisted of specific names of people and social comments directed at people (e.g., *go away, I want it*), and these children acquired two-word phrases much earlier than the referential children. The referential children's vocabulary grew faster than the expressive children and consisted more of object names and referred to more actions. These individual differences were shown to interact with parental use of language as well as with the strategies which the children used to acquire the language.

Bowerman (1973) reports a study similar in many ways to that of Bloom except that it examines the language acquisition of two

Finnish children. She compared the acquisition of that language with English, Samoan, Japanese, and Luo (a language spoken along the upper Nile River). As with the earlier studies, an effort was made to write a grammar for the Finnish children at the beginning and the end of the two-word stage. Bowerman, as had Bloom and others (e.g., Bar-Adon, 1971), found the pivot grammar inadequate. Bowerman also concluded that the transformational grammar was too powerful as a representation of the underlying structure of the children's utterances. Certain semantic functions of sentences and their constituents appear to be understood by children at this stage but other semantic functions of the same constituents are not understood. The child, for example, seems to conceptualize the abstract notion of agent but not the broader and more abstract notion of syntactic subject of a sentence. In an effort to determine whether the child's linguistic knowledge might be better represented in terms of semantic concepts, Bowerman also examined the utterances of her children within the framework of Fillmore's case grammar. The case grammar appeared to provide a more satisfactory account of the data but it was not entirely satisfactory either. Some cases were not used by the child, and others, like the syntactic categories of transformational grammar, appeared to be less general or abstract for the child than for the adult. In short, Bowerman found that the available linguistic theories appear to be too abstract and powerful to be applicable to the conceptual framework within which the child, at the two-word level, is using language. Clearly there is a distinction between deep structure and surface structure evidenced in the child's utterances, but constituent structures are not well defined by the child, hierarchical relationships are not clearly developed, and semantic considerations may be more important than syntactic structures initially. Only later do syntactic concepts develop. Bowerman's study moves the focus of attention even further than Bloom's toward semantics and deemphasizes the acquisition of syntax.

**Brown's analyses of the two-word stage.**    An overview of all these developments, plus additional data and a detailed analysis of the earliest developmental stages of language acquisition have been provided by Brown (1973), who has done more than any other single person in this field to advance our knowledge of the child's acquisition of its native language. In his book dealing with the early stages of language acquisition of Adam, Eve, and Sarah, the three children he and his students have studied extensively, Brown also brings together all the available data from other studies in an effort to present a coherent picture of the two-word stage of development. It should be noted here that children do not, of course, move neatly from one-, then two-, and subsequently to three-word utterances. Rather, there is a progression from shorter to longer utterances and the two-word stage is defined in terms of the period when the child first puts two words together and progresses until the mean length of utterance is longer than two words. Brown has found that mean length of utterance (MLU), rather than chronological age, provides a very good rough indication of language development, at least to the point where the child is using constructions four or five morphemes in length. He has divided the early developmental period into five stages defined in terms of a combination of MLU and maximum length of utterance. Stage I is the period when MLU is 1.75 and the upper bound of the longest utterance is five, in Stage II the MLU is 2.25 and the upper bound is seven, and Stage III is defined by an MLU of 2.75 and an upper bound of nine. Roughly speaking, the first two stages might be considered as the two-word stage. Figure 6–1 shows the relation between MLU and age for the three children studied extensively by Brown.

Brown characterizes these stages in terms of a number of dimensions. As we have noted, early speech (Stage I) tends to be telegraphic in nature, that is, the function words tend to be omitted and the constructions consist primarily of content words. This picturesque description, which Brown introduced early in his research, he would now like to discard because it is both imprecise and inaccurate as we shall see when we look at the analyses of his data. The early two-word utterances, for example, are not entirely devoid of function words. Those function words which do appear, however, are some of the most frequent in the language, are more salient in sentences, enter into semantic relations (e.g., recurrence, location, possession, agent-action, action-object), and are words which can be expressed in relation to other words in combinatorially simple ways. Thus, the child does use function words such as *more, here, my, I,* and *it,* but is less likely to use *the, of, and,* and *with,* for example.

The two-word utterances do suggest that the child attends to and makes use of word order. Children do not, despite their apparent lack of concern about being misunderstood, randomly juxtapose words. But rather, the use of word order seems, along with other evidence, to indicate semantic intentions on the part of the child and a use of word order to communicate semantic relations. There appear to be a rather small number of semantic relations which children express during Stage I. These include at least the relations of agent and action, agent and object, action and locative, entity and locative, possessor and possession, entity and attributive, and demonstrative and entity. While other semantic relations (about seven) have been found in some children's utterances, nearly all the above relations have been represented in the speech of nearly all children studied in both English and other languages. The relations expressed in three- or four-word utterances at this stage seem to consist of concatenations of words in which

**Figure 6-1**

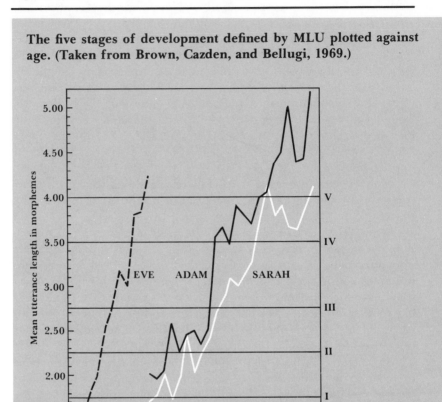

The five stages of development defined by MLU plotted against age. (Taken from Brown, Cazden, and Bellugi, 1969.)

two or more two-word utterances with some parts deleted are put together (e.g., "John hit" and "hit ball" are succeeded by "John hit ball"), or expansion of a noun phrase which is nominative, attributive or possessive, as in "Hit John ball."

Stage I appears to be a period in language development when the child is acquiring the means to express semantic relations and the increase in MLU reflects the child's increased capability to express nomination, recurrence, and nonexistence as operations of reference and to enter these referents into semantic relations of a rather limited kind. Finally, we see evidence of an increase in sentence complexity associated with combining simple relations in more complex forms. The latter increase in complexity seems to require a preliminary establishment of the simpler forms by themselves, followed by an increase in conceptual knowledge which allows the combination of the simpler forms into a more complex form as in the examples noted above.

In relating these developmental findings in language development to the general cognitive development of the child, Brown notes that the beginning of two-word utterances occurs at about eighteen months of age, which coincides with the culmination of the sensorimotor period of development within the Piagetian theoretical framework (Piaget, 1936; 1937; 1945). The semantic relations expressed by the child in its early utterances appear to be those which are available to the child in terms of cognitive functioning at this developmental point, just as described by Piaget. This same point has been made by Slobin (1973) and expanded and refined by Edwards (1973). At this stage, the child expresses action schemas involving agents and objects, statements about recurrence, nonexistence, location, possession, and other relations which are just those meanings universally acquired during this period in life. Language is thus formed on this cognitive substructure, reflects it, and subsequently interacts with it in a manner which aids in the subsequent development of both. One aspect of that development, Brown notes, is the somewhat egocentric assumption of children that, if they speak, they will be understood. That assumption is likely to be correct when they are in their own family environments but it is unwarranted as they move into a larger world. Less understanding people, however, force a shift in strategy which leads the child in Stage I from considering sentence constituents optional to a recognition that it is necessary to include them and to a concern with grammatical morphemic issues which are used but optional in Stage II.

Stage II, although reflecting sentences of only 2.25 MLU, is marked by the appearance of function words and inflections. The child begins to include a few spatial prepositions, articles, copular verbs, plural and possessive inflections on nouns; and progressive, past, and third person present indicative inflections on verbs, in addition to the pronouns, demonstratives, and prolocatives of Stage I language. In short, Brown describes the effect of these advances in grammatical constructions as the "modulation of meaning." In essence, he is suggesting that the child begins to introduce quality or precision of meaning into its utterances as opposed to the calling out of undifferentiated semantic ideas of the preceding stage. For example, the sentences "A boy hit ball" and "The boy hit ball" are modulated in meaning by designating a nonspecific as opposed to a specific boy.

The acquisition of grammatical morphemes, as Brown calls these small words and inflections, occurs in a very orderly manner. In an examination of fourteen specific instances which occurred with high frequency in the early stages, Brown found that inflection for present progressive was the first to be acquired followed in order by *in* and *on*, plural inflection, past irregular verb inflection, possessive inflection, uncontractible copula, articles, past regular verb inflection, third person regular verb, third person irregular, uncontractible auxiliary, contractible copula, and contractible auxiliary. The three children of Brown's study plus those of other studies (e.g., de Villiers & de Villiers, 1973a) show an amazing regularity in the order of acquisition of these various forms and a strong relation between order of acquisition and MLU. In general, it will be noted that the order of acquisition seems to be related to the relative complexity of grammatical and/or semantic concepts involved. The order is, incidentally, unrelated to the frequency of parental usage in language directed to the child. It should also be noted that while these forms begin to appear in Stage II, full control over their use does not occur for most of them until well after Stage II, and for some, is still not achieved by Stage V when MLU equals 4.00. There does not seem to be an insightful use of the various forms but, rather, the proportion of correct use gradually increases for each over time. Finally, these grammatical morphemes do seem to modulate meaning by adding number, tense, aspect, specificity and nonspecificity, containment, and support to the nouns, verbs, and relations expressed by these words in Stage I.

Brown summarizes his extensive analysis of Stages I and II with a number of points. He argues that language development is probably invariant across children and across languages, although the rate of development may vary widely from child to child as a function of the general intelligence of the child. The order of development appears to be a function of cumulative semantic and grammatical complexity (Brown & Hanlon, 1970). Thus, we find in the language acquisition data support for a modified form of the derivational theory of complexity (DTC), which we noted in Chapter 4 has received little support elsewhere. We have already noted that McNeill (1966) advanced a form of the DTC hypothesis when he argued that the early utterances of the child are a relatively direct function of deep structure and the acquisition process is one of acquiring transformations, i.e., developing derivational complexity. Brown does not embrace that version of the hypothesis, but reformulates the hypothesis so that complexity is not defined in terms of the number of transformations but in terms of the acquisition of construction types. The test of increased complexity, therefore, becomes one of identifying components, semantic and syntactic, in children's utterances and noting the manner in which those components are combined to form more and more complex utterances. Progress toward greater complexity is equated with the addition of components to previously used units. Thus, given the use of $x$ and $y$ as components, an indication of additional complexity may be assumed in a construction $x + y$ and, in turn, additional complexity is assumed when a third component, $z$, is added to the

$x + y$ construction. The components are not necessarily cast in the precise formal manner sought by the linguist. As Brown points out, the development of language seems to follow such a combinatorial progression and those interested in that process must begin to examine it without waiting for the linguists to work out the details of the formal system.

Finally, Brown suggests that the frequency of linguistic forms in adult usage, perceptual saliency of those forms, and reward and punishment for producing various forms seem to be of relatively minor consequence to the acquisition process. They are not irrelevant variables, perhaps, but little strong evidence for their importance has been found when people have looked at them. We are left, he suggests, with respect to the latter considerations, with little understanding of why the child's language improves. There is little obvious reason why a child who manages to communicate despite incomplete and incorrect forms of language by adult standards, and who is not taught the grammatical structure by reward and/or punishment (Brown & Hanlon, 1970), proceeds from one-, two-, or three-word utterances to the complex adult grammar.

## Steps in Achieving the Target Syntactic Forms

The studies of syntactic development discussed up to this point have been based on the research strategy of inducing generalizations about syntactic development from a corpus of utterances obtained at regular intervals as the child develops. The corpus is examined at each succeeding point in time to establish the regularities in the forms produced. Another methodological approach to the same problem has been to start with the target syntactic forms used by adults and examine the stages the child goes through to reach those forms and the ages at which they are achieved. One of the earliest attempts to approach syntactic development in this manner was an extensive study by Menyuk (1969). She obtained large samples of children's language in response to a projective test, conversations with adults and peers in semistructured situations, and spontaneous speech. The children were in nursery school, kindergarten, and first grade, ranging in age from two years, ten months, to seven years, one month.

The analyses performed by Menyuk are based on an examination of the rules followed by the children in their sentence constructions relative to those used in the adult model language. She wrote grammars that described the children's utterances and examined them to determine how the child's grammar is restricted in comparison to that of the adult speaker. In general, the results appear to parallel those of Berko (1958) in the sense that the children's syntactic constructions, like their morphological constructions, tend to exhibit simplified versions of the adult rules: where the adult may make several distinctions in the formulation of an utterance, the child makes only a few, with many omissions, redundancies, and substitutions apparent in the constructions. The general results, however, were interpreted by Menyuk to indicate that the three-year-old child uses almost all the basic syntactic structures employed by adults. Menyuk argued that most aspects of the grammar have been acquired by the time the child is five years old; and improvement is very slow thereafter, although increasingly elaborated structures are used as the child gets older. The child appears to proceed from the most general rules to increasingly differentiated rules. Menyuk noted that the frequency of errors on particular types of constructions seems to follow a fluctuating course rather than a smooth growth curve to complete mastery of the grammar. The fluctuations, or oscillations, are caused by the use of increasingly complex rules in the grammar. The addition of new rules adds new errors which are subsequently corrected before more complex rules are added to cause new errors.

The tendency for errors to occur in cyclical wave fashion is apparent at the morphophonemic level in the case of pluralization and past tense inflections, as observed by Ervin (1964) in the English language and reported by Slobin (1966a) for Russian. In the case of past tense inflections, for example, the child begins using verbs with no inflection for tense. The first indication of inflection for past tense occurs with irregular verbs such as *came, broke, ran,* and *did,* while verbs which take the regular past inflection such as *kicked, rubbed,* and *seated* are not inflected. Subsequently, the rule for regular inflection is acquired and the child correctly inflects the regular verbs but overgeneralizes the rule to the previously correctly inflected irregular verbs. At that time, the child begins to produce such past forms as *comed, breaked, runned,* and *doed* where the correct forms had been used earlier. Often the latter errors may be observed to occur occasionally even in the grade-school years. Similar behaviors have been observed in laboratory tasks when some analogous rules with exceptions are acquired by college students (Palermo & Eberhart, 1968; Smith, 1973). These latter experiments suggest that the frequency and type of error made when rules with exceptions are acquired relate to the number of irregular forms, the frequency with which the irregular forms occur relative to the regular forms, and the types of rules involved (Palermo & Parrish, 1971; Smith, 1973).

**Negatives.** Study of the emergence of adult syntactic structures reveals the same ebb and flow of errors as is evidenced in analyses of the early negative and interrogative structures of the child (Bellugi, 1965; Brown, 1968; Klima & Bellugi, 1966). In these studies, the general strategy, as in the Menyuk studies, was to try to characterize the rules of the adult forms and then to observe how the child begins to construct such forms and eventually progresses to the final adult forms. For example, Klima and Bellugi report a set of rules for negation in adult English which accounts for the use of negatives with auxiliary verbs, negative imperatives, and negation with indefinite forms. Their rules deal with negation in sentences such as:

| | |
|---|---|
| The baby can stand up. | The baby can't stand up. |
| They are coming here. | They aren't coming here. |
| I have done it. | I haven't done it. |
| You have some milk. | You haven't any milk. |
| I want something. | I don't want anything. |
| | Don't trip over that. |
| | Don't be late, will you? |

These forms of the negative do not exhaust the types of negative structures used in English, but the rules that allow the generation of these forms will account for all the negative constructions which appear in the early speech of children and they are complicated enough to illustrate the difficulties children have with the construction of negative syntactic forms. Furthermore, those constructions directed toward children by adults do not involve the more complex negative structures.

Initially, the child negates by using the single negative form, "no." At the two-word stage, the child merely appends the negative morpheme to the beginning or end of the word or phrase being negated, as in such utterances as:

No wash.
No more.
Not fit.
Wear mitten no.

The child appears to be directing attention to some aspect of the environment and negating it, i.e., the syntactic form is concatenation of the affirmative and the negative. The child at this point does not give any evidence of comprehending negatives which are any more complicated. Unless the adult puts the negative element outside the sentence directed toward the child as in, "No, I am not sure," the child gives no indication of understanding negation, according to Klima and Bellugi (1966).

In Stage II, the child moves the negative element within the sentence and begins to use a variety of negative forms, all of which appear at about the same time. While the new constructions do not always resemble those of adults, even those which do cannot be interpreted to reflect adult competence. For example, children at this stage use "can't" and "don't" in constructions such as "I can't see you," and "I don't want it," but they never use the auxiliary verbs alone. Although the children seem to comprehend negatives contracted with auxiliaries in sentences adults use, it would appear at this stage that the contraction is incorporated in the child's system as a negative verb rather than an auxiliary plus a negative element, as in the adult system. Other forms of negation include the negative element within the sentence but not connected to an auxiliary, negative imperatives, and a form of question negative, as in the following examples:

That no fish school.
That not milk.
Don't leave me.
Why not me sleeping?

Stage III is marked by advances in the use of auxiliaries and questions which are reflected in negative constructions. Not only does the child begin to use some of the auxiliaries by themselves in affirmative sentences, but all auxiliaries used can now be combined with negatives although the contexts in which they occur vary. For example, *be* is restricted to predicate and progressive forms and occurs optionally while *can* and *do* are used only with nonprogressive main verbs. Another peculiarity of Stage III is caused by the first use of indefinite determiners and pronouns which lead to syntactic errors not seen before, as evidenced in the last two examples of the types of negative constructions typical of Stage III:

I don't want cover on it.
He is not a girl.
I not crying.
Why the kitty can't stand up?
I didn't see something.
He won't have some.

Before the latter type of construction assumes the adult form, the child shifts to the use of negative indefinites in negated sentences which leads to utterances such as:

He can't have nothing.
Nobody won't recognize us.

One child even produced a triple negative:

I can't do nothing with no string.

As we noted earlier, the child may be seen to gain control of some structures only to lose them again as the total syntactic development progresses to include more and more complex forms which require adjustments in the rules that had worked satisfactorily in earlier simpler forms. In short, there is an interaction among rules such that expansions in syntax involve the acquisition of new rules which supersede the scope of portions of old rules and lead to errors which persist until the child is able to differentiate the boundaries of the old rules relative to the new ones.

Before leaving the topic of negation, we should note that there are semantic considerations to take into account when examining the development of the syntax of negation. McNeill and McNeill (1968) noted this when studying a child's acquisition of Japanese where various semantically different forms of negation such as nonexistence, rejection, and denial are morphologically marked in that language. While marking of such negative forms does not occur in English, Bloom (1970) observed that the acquisition of negatives, when viewed in terms of the context of use, reflects an ordering of the appearance of these semantic forms of the negative. Children begin by negating existence as in the case of the child saying "No more milk" only after the milk is gone as opposed to refusing more milk, for example. Next to be observed is the use of negatives to denote rejection as when the child rejects something that is present. At least one of the children Bloom studied marked these forms differently by saying "no more _____" in the case of nonexistence and just "no" in the case of rejection. Another child distinguished between rejection of an event in which the child was the actor-agent and one in which someone else was actor-agent. The latter occurred developmentally later and was initially expressed in a syntactically less mature manner. McNeill and McNeill had made the same observation about their Japanese child. The third form, denial, was the last to be observed in expressions such as, "I not tired," and "That not blue one." While these three semantic distinctions occurred primarily in what would be the first two or three stages of Klima and Bellugi's analyses, it is clear that semantic considerations provide a much richer understanding of the language acquisition process than does the description of the syntactic forms alone.

Comprehension and production of negatives also vary as a function of the context in which they occur and the cognitive development of the child. Donaldson (1970), for example, found that even when children are as old as five or six years, they cannot, when presented with a yellow circle, construct a sentence which states that "This circle is not green," even when the experimenter presents the first four words. The child has no problem completing the same sentence with the negative deleted. As Donaldson implies in discussing these results, the child must decenter attention from the perceptual attributes of the object presented and complete the sentence with an attribute of some other object. As we shall note in discussing passive sentences, such a task may require the cognitive abilities which appear at about age seven and are associated with concrete operations in Piagetian terminology. However, de Villiers and Flusberg (1975) have shown that with a little training, two-, three-, and four-year-olds can perform the Donaldson task. As in earlier studies with adults by Wason (e.g., 1965), reaction time was related to the plausibility of the negatives and the confusability between the items in the array presented to the child. For example, with an array of seven cars and a baby's bottle, positive statements made by the experimenter such as, "This is a \_\_\_\_\_," when pointing to one of the items were completed faster by the child than negative statements such as, "This is not a \_\_\_\_\_." Negatives such as, "This is not a \_\_\_\_\_" were completed faster when they were plausible, i.e., the experimenter pointed to the bottle, than when they were implausible, i.e., the experimenter pointed to a car in the array. Finally, it was easier to complete the negatives when dissimilar items such as cars and a bottle were used than when similar items (e.g., horses and cows) were used. In summary, the cognitive factors noted by Donaldson are surely important to comprehension and production of negatives in various tasks, but the de Villiers and Flusberg study moderates their importance in light of the performance differences which may be affected by contextual modifications.

**Interrogatives.**    Analyses of interrogative forms have been reported for Stages I, II, and III by Brown (1968) and Klima and Bellugi (1966). Although there have been suggestions that precursors of the interrogative structure are evidenced in the rising intonational contour associated with yes/no questions heard in the babbling period and at the one-word stage (Menyuk, 1974), the evidence for speculation about interrogative syntactic forms at these early developmental periods is rather limited. Neither Weir (1966) nor Miller and Ervin (1964) found any evidence of consistent prosody patterns in the early utterances of the children they studied. Greenfield and Smith (1976) report very few questions in the one-word stage and Bloom (1973) argues that there is no evidence for such structures at the one-word stage. Beginning with the two-word stage, however, evidence for interrogative structures is much clearer.

Questions develop right alongside of negatives, and knowing the sequential development of the negative forms gives us some hints as to how question structures are acquired. The child is acquiring the syntactic system as a whole. Thus, while negatives begin with an appendaged negative element, questions begin with a superimposed rising intonation or an appendaged question marker as in "See hold?" and "Where Daddy going?" In Stage II, when negative auxiliaries appear, they may be seen in questions as well (e.g., "You can't fix it?" and "Why not he eat?"). Brown (1968) has argued, however, that children's questions in Stages I and II are only routines, or memorized units, because most of them are repetitions of the same question ("What dat?") and little evidence is given that the child comprehends questions from others, i.e., irrelevant answers are given to most questions.

Stage III, however, reflects a significant advance in the production of interrogative structures both in terms of the number and the types of questions asked. Appropriate answers to questions indicate an advance in comprehension as well. The appearance of auxiliaries at Stage III is an essential ingredient to the syntactic structure of the interrogative form, for it is the transposing of the auxiliary to the front of the subject noun phrase in both yes/no and Wh-questions which is crucial to the question structure. In the case of yes/no questions, rising intonation is also an interrogative signal, while in the case of Wh-questions, the Wh word itself is a signal of interrogation in addition to the auxiliary inversion. In any case, at Stage III the child appropriately transposes the auxiliary in yes/no questions (e.g., "Does lions walk?" and "Will you help me?") but does not do so with Wh-questions (e.g., "What John will read?" and "What that is?"). The latter development must await a subsequent stage.

Ervin-Tripp's (1970) analyses of question-answer exchanges between adult and child suggest that yes/no questions are the easiest for children to comprehend. There is a definite developmental trend in the ability to deal with the various Wh-questions, indicating that some Wh-questions are much easier than others. She found, based on children's appropriate responses to questions asked about a story, that the developmental order of correct responding to various Wh-questions was *what, where, what-do, whose, who, why, where-from, how,* and *when.* Aside from the complexity of the syntactic markers necessary to correctly respond to these various Wh-questions, the order of acquisition would appear to roughly relate to the cognitive complexity of the questions. The questions acquired earliest relate to objects and events which are here and now and to which one can point, while the last to be acquired appear to be more abstract and remote in location and time.

**Passives.**   The other major syntactic form that has received a good deal of attention is the passive construction. Since the passive is not a frequently used sentence structure even by adults, research on this topic has focused primarily on comprehension of passives and experimental efforts to induce children to use passives. Slobin (1966), for example, presented subjects between the ages of six and twenty with sentences paired with pictures. The task was to indicate whether the picture correctly depicted the semantic content of the sentence. In general, passive sentences were more difficult than simple, active, affirmative, declarative sentences unless the subject and object of the sentence were not reversible, in which case there was no problem with the passive. Thus, "The cat was chased by the dog" was more difficult than "The dog chased the cat," but "The girl is watering the flowers" was not easier than "The flowers are being watered by the girl." It would appear from Slobin's data that six-year-olds had no difficulty with passive sentence comprehension but they were more affected by the reversible passives than adults. It seems that part of the difficulty with passive sentences, particularly for the young child, lies in keeping track of which noun is the subject and which is the object of the sentence. In sentences such as, "The flowers are being watered by the girl," there is no problem because the child's prior knowledge of the world makes it clear that flowers cannot water girls but cats can chase dogs as readily as the reverse, which makes the reversible sentence more difficult to decode.

Hayhurst (1967) demonstrated that when the actor is omitted in a passive sentence, as in "The cat was chased," then passives are easier for children to comprehend. The Hayhurst study, however, makes it clear that even with training in constructing passive sentences, production of passives is not easy and certainly not a natural syntactic form for children of five, six, or even nine years of age.

Turner and Rommetveit (1967a) provide support for Slobin's hypothesis that children have difficulty with the passive because they confuse the subject and object of the sentence. In a developmental study of active and passive sentence imitation, comprehension, and production, they found that 95 percent of the errors made in the various tasks involved inversion of the subject and object nouns. Most of the errors occurred on the reversible sentences, although a surprisingly large percentage (33 percent) occurred on the nonreversible sentences, suggesting that even with semantic support, children in the age range from four to nine continue to have difficulty with comprehension and production of passive sentences. Not until the age of eight was there evidence that performance was better than 60 percent correct on either comprehension or production tests involving passives. In another study, the same authors (Turner & Rommetveit, 1967b) attempted to induce children of the same age to use passive sentences with little more success than Hayhurst had in her study.

Most of the studies mentioned above were conducted with the implicit assumption that passives are more difficult than other constructions because they are derivationally more complex than other structures. The results were surprising, however, in indicating that the derivationally simpler negative sentence was found to be more difficult to verify than the passive (Slobin, 1966), the nonreversible passive sentence was as easy to comprehend as an active sentence (Slobin, 1966), the derivationally more complex truncated passive was as easy to comprehend as an active sentence, and the truncated passive was also easier to comprehend than the full passive (Hayhurst, 1967). These results were a part of the accumulated evidence which led to Fodor and Garrett's paper (1966) pointing out the theoretical simplicity and inadequacy of the derivational theory of complexity, although they did not speak directly to the acquisition problem.

In a broader analysis of the processes of the acquisition of linguistic structures, Bever (1970) was one of the first to argue that children are not innately given deep structures as McNeill (1971), for example, had argued. More radical for the time, however, was Bever's suggestion that children may not acquire deep structures initially as a part of the acquisition of various sentence structures. Indeed, Bever argued that children use a number of strategies for decoding the utterances of others as well as in constructing their own utterances. Some of the strategies are semantic in nature. A person listening to a sentence may, for example, group phrases within a sentence by their likely semantic organization in addition to processing syntactic information. Thus, it is the knowledge of the semantic properties of individual words and groups of words which, for example, allows the rapid processing of nonreversible passive sentences as opposed to reversible passives, where semantic constraints are not available. In short, sentences are processed by making use of all the surface structure cues available to the child, a point which had been made earlier by Fodor and Garrett (1966) about adult performance. Bever suggested that in addition to such semantic strategies used by adults, the young child may use a variety of other strategies in acquiring a knowledge of the structure of language. As with many hypotheses which the child uses to process the variety of morphophonemic and syntactic forms we have discussed already, the strategies that are used at any particular stage work most of the time, but they must be discarded as inefficient when the child's level of language advances further.

Bever suggests that one of the helpful early strategies used by the child is that any noun-verb-noun (N-V-N) sequence within the surface structure is interpreted as an actor-action-object syntactic unit. Such a strategy, of course, usually works because most sentences are of the simple active form which is constructed with that particular ordering. If one uses that strategy with a passive sentence, however, errors of interpretation should result which reverse the relationship between actor and object, especially in reversible sentences where there are no semantic constraints to block that strategy. Bever's research with children in the two- to four-year age range indicates that the youngest children respond randomly to passive sentences and then adopt the N-V-N strategy of analyzing surface structure resulting in a systematic decrease in performance on passives before correct comprehension appears after four years of age. The child's knowledge of the world increases, however, and by about age four, semantic constraints begin to affect the child's interpretation of sentences by blocking some, for example, nonreversible passives, interpretation of which had previously been based on the order strategy alone. The results of Bever's research have not been consistently replicated (e.g., de Villiers and de Villiers, 1973b; Maratsos, 1974), nor have his interpretations been completely accepted. In addition, other cues such as stress patterns in the sentence are surely used by the child (Hornby, 1971). Thus, the interpretation of passive sentences at four or five years of age may not always be correct, but it does seem clear that the children are basing their interpretations on perceptual strategies related to the sequential arrangement of the sentence elements, their knowledge of the world, and their cognitive developmental level.

The latter factors have been focused on by Beilin and his associates (Beilin, 1975). A careful review of the literature led Beilin to conclude that the comprehension and production of passive sentences is subject to a variety of strategies on the part of the child which gradually lead to complete ability to handle the various forms of this syntactic structure. Full competence with passives, however, is not reached until at least the age of seven, when the child has reached the cognitive developmental stage of concrete operations as defined by Piagetian theory. Beilin's research suggests, for example, that until the child is capable of reversibility, decentration, and the associated logical functions of the concrete operations period, full grasp of passives and their relation to other linguistic structures is not achieved. Prior to age seven, the child can, of course, use some passive forms correctly, both in terms of comprehension and production. Furthermore, children prior to the age of seven show some evidence of knowing the equivalence of the active and passive forms. In recall of passive sentences, young children make errors which convert passive sentences to active ones while at the same time they preserve the meaning relations of the two. Not until age seven, however, were the children in Beilin's studies able to make the judgment that a passive sentence has the same meaning as its active equivalent. Beilin's research has demonstrated that the appearance of the latter ability is correlated with the appearance of concrete logical operations. While a causative relation between cognitive development and language competence has not been established by Beilin's studies, this research is one more step in the direction of establishing that language is acquired within the context of a supporting cognitive structure.

## Syntactic Development after Age Five

The syntactic forms of the studies discussed up to this point have been those involving gross sentential differences. The conclusions based on at least the early research suggest that by four or five years of age, the child has succeeded in mastering the exceedingly complex structure of his or her native language. While the four- or five-year-old child can carry on a most intelligent and syntactically correct conversation for the most part, it has become fairly clear in the research we have already discussed, as well as in some to follow, that considerable development in syntax and other aspects of language occurs after age five (Palermo & Molfese, 1972). A study by C. Chomsky (1969) opened the investigation of some of the more subtle aspects of syntactic development which seem not to be fully mastered until long after age five.

Chomsky (1969) studied aspects of comprehension as a function of sentence complexity, selectional restrictions, and subcategorization restrictions. She was concerned with the developmental control over deep structure-surface structure relations when particular lexical items do not conform to rules that frequently relate surface structure to deep structure. She focused her attention on the lexical items *ask, tell,* and *promise;* the formation of pronouns (pronominalization); and the syntactic comprehension of sentences in which the surface structure subject is not the deep structure subject. Her subjects ranged in age from five to ten years of age. A Piagetian interviewing method with structured tasks and specified initial questions was used with subsequent open questioning to evaluate the child's comprehension of the language-task relations.

In the case of *promise*, the so-called minimal distance principle applicable to most verbs is violated. In sentences which conform to the minimal distance principle, the noun phrase that immediately precedes an infinitive complement verb is the subject of that verb. Thus, in "John wanted Bill to leave," it is Bill who does the leaving, but in "John promised Bill to leave," it is John who does the leaving. The former sentence conforms to the minimal distance principle and the latter does not.

Chomsky's results indicate that while even the youngest children in this age range seem to know the meaning of the word *promise* when asked, they do not correctly comprehend sentences involving both *promise* and the minimal distance principle until they are about eight years old. They seemed to show a systematic developmental trend in gaining control over this rule, beginning with a stage in which they applied the minimal distance principle to all cases across the board. Next, as the children began to recognize exceptions to the rule, they made errors with sentences that followed the minimal distance principle as well as those that did not. In the third stage, the children finally straightened out the cases to which the minimal distance principle applied, but continued to mix their responses to the exceptions so that sometimes they treated *promise* appropriately and sometimes overgeneralized the principle. Only at the fourth stage was errorless performance achieved in all cases. While there was a good deal of variability with respect to the ages of the children who achieved each stage, the sequence of achieving the stages was orderly.

Similar results were found when *ask* and *tell* were used in another experimental task in which *ask* was used both as a command and a question. *Tell* consistently follows the minimal distance principle, while *ask* is inconsistent and does not follow the rule when used in the command or request form (e.g., Ask/tell Laura what to feed the doll). Development of the correct interpretation of *ask* in the command form was correlated with the development of *promise,* and similar stages of confusion with *tell* were apparent. Comprehension of *promise,* which consistently violates the minimal distance principle, always preceded the comprehension of *ask,* which is inconsistent with respect to this rule. Kessel (1970) also investigated the *ask-tell* relationships with a group of children in the same age range and found essentially the same results, including the invariant sequence in the acquisition of *ask* and *tell.*

Chomsky's (1969) examination of the comprehension of sentences, in which the surface structure subject is not the deep structure subject, made use of the responses of children to the sentence "Is this doll easy to see or hard to see?" in the context of a blindfolded doll. Her results indicated that five-year-old children tend to interpret the sentence to mean that the doll is hard to see, that is, that *doll* is the deep structure object of the sentence rather than the subject of the infinitive. By nine years of age, no child incorrectly interpreted the question.

Both Kessel (1970) and Cromer (1970) improved on Chomsky's methodology and found similar results. Cromer examined the comprehension of sentences in which the nouns and verbs were held constant, but adjectives, such as *eager* and *easy* determined the relation of the deep and surface structure objects. His subjects used hand puppets to act out the sentences uttered by the experimenter (e.g., "The wolf is happy to bite" versus "The wolf is tasty to bite"). Cromer used four adjectives that unambiguously required the noun to be interpreted as the subject of the sentence, four adjectives that unambiguously required the noun to be interpreted as the object of the infinitive verb, and four adjectives that rendered the sentences ambiguous (e.g., "The wolf is nice to bite"). The results indicated that children of mental age up to 5 years, 7 months, tend to interpret all sentences as if the noun were the subject of the sentence; between 5 years, 9 months, and 6 years, 6 months, the children were in a transition stage in which the first type of sentence is correctly interpreted but there are both correct and incorrect interpretations of the second type of sentence; and children over mental age 6 years, 8 months, interpret both sentence types correctly. Cromer also found that all but two of the youngest children had no difficulty comprehending passives, indicating that these children knew that what appears to be the surface subject in sentences need not necessarily be the deep structure subject. Finally, he presented the children two nonsense words in sentence frames which required them to be differentiated with respect to what was to be taken as the deep structure subject, and then tested for comprehension of the two nonsense words. Children in the first stage failed to make the differentiation; some of the children in the transition stage correctly interpreted the two new words, but most of them did not; and, finally, those children who were in the third stage correctly interpreted the two new nonsense words on the basis of hearing them used in only one repeated sentence. In summary, these stages, in which syntactic relations among components of sentences are dependent on particular lexical items within the sentences, are not fully mastered until middle childhood, although children are capable of comprehending and producing some of these syntactic forms earlier. Analysis of structures which may be problematic, and careful observation of children's performance with those structures, can provide a comprehensive picture of the child's developing knowledge of the rules of language.

Finally, Chomsky found that children learned the nonidentity restriction for pronominalization between five and six years of age, while seven year olds were able to handle, in addition, the identity case. Thus, the younger children were able to comprehend sentences such as, "He knew that John was going to win the race," in which *he* and *John* refer to two different persons. Not until the children were older, however, did the identity situation, as in "John knew that he was going to win the race"—where *John* and *he* refer to the same person—no longer present any difficulties. Chomsky predicted the order of correct comprehension, based on the argument that the second form required a more complex set of rules because of the ambiguity involved. The matter is more complicated than ambiguity alone, however, since semantic, pragmatic (Garvey, Caramazza, & Yates, 1975), and stress variables (Maratsos, 1973) influence the interpretation of the pronoun referent as well. It is clear, from what little we know, that pronouns appear at Stage I in Brown's system when *I, you, my,* and *it* are observed, but full command of pronouns in their simplest syntactic uses to replace nouns or noun phrases takes several months (Huxley, 1970), and the anaphoric use of *it* to refer to a preceding word or group of words is problematic until at least age six (Chipman & deDardel, 1974). Full comprehension of the syntactic relations determined by relative pronouns may not occur until early adolescence (c.f., Palermo & Molfese, 1972). It is unlikely that our understanding of the syntactic problems associated with pronouns will be clarified in the near future.

## Some Conclusions about Syntactic Development

Although some research has been reported which examines the development of other syntactic forms, the various studies we have examined are enough to allow us to draw a number of conclusions about syntactic development. First, children build a syntactic system of rules very gradually. Initially, they rely heavily on the nonlinguistic environmental context in which the words are uttered but, as they acquire the capability of producing larger utterances, they can also be more precise in their linguistic specification of the message and therefore rely less on unverbalized contextual factors. In short, the children themselves become more and more able to specify the context linguistically. Second, children appear to formulate broad hypotheses about the relations between the *form* of the message and the *content* of the message. The earliest hypotheses are too broad and need continual revision to achieve the greater and greater precision required by an expanding knowledge system and associated lexicon. Third, children build on an expanding cognitive structure a linguistic system which allows the expression of that cognitive structure and, at the same time, facilitates the further development of the cognitive structure. Finally, in each syntactic area we have explored, the research probing has inevitably led to semantic issues.

Slobin (1973) has attempted to formalize some of the particulars of the development of grammar which are more generally presented above. Specifically, Slobin has tried to cast the language acquisition process within the framework of a set of operating principles or strategies which children, regardless of the language being acquired, use to construct the structure, i.e., grammar, of their language. Slobin advances seven such operating principles, along with a number of what he calls universals which specify developmental predictions about the form acquisition will take. For example, the first operating principle attributed to children is that they pay attention to the ends of words. The universal which follows from this principle is that children will, for any given semantic notion (e.g., locatives) acquire the grammatical realization of that notion earlier if it is in the form of a suffix or postposition than in the form of a prefix or preposition. This operating principle and associated universal allows the prediction, for example, that English-speaking children will acquire the plural and past tense inflection forms which are marked at the ends of words earlier than the definite and indefinite article forms which precede words.

Slobin's other operating principles indicate that the child recognizes that phonological forms of words can be systematically modified and that the order of words and morphemes is important. The child avoids interruptions or rearrangements of linguistic units, and exceptions to rules. Finally, the child operates as if the marking of underlying semantic relations should be clear and overt, and grammatical markers should make semantic sense. Slobin indicates that a variety of evidence gleaned from reports of forty different languages provides empirical support, indicating that children do seem to follow these operating principles and the associated universals as they acquire language.

While Slobin's principles are focused primarily on the acquisition of syntax, he has made it clear that the process of syntax acquisition is clearly based on the cognitive developmental level of the child as well as semantic considerations. The child is assumed to have certain semantic intentions or ideas to communicate, and those semantic intentions depend on the current cognitive developmental state of the individual. Given the semantic intentions, it is Slobin's claim that the child seeks syntactic means for expressing those intentions by attending to the utterances of other persons who are expressing the meanings the child has in mind. This general contention is the same as that expressed by Macnamara (1972) in discussing the cognitive basis of infant language acquisition. The child's cognitive structure allows the assimilation of linguistic and nonlinguistic material which takes on meaning in terms of that cognitive structure. The child seeks from the linguistic material ways to express meanings by means of the linguistic form. The search is guided by the strategies or operating principles which are used to direct attention and formulate the rules of linguistic expression and, in turn, lead to accommodation of structures at both the linguistic and cognitive levels. In short, children actively process the input in terms of their individual cognitive level of development and achieve cognitive advances through accommodation of new meanings to old structures. The influence of Piagetian theory is clear in Slobin's analysis of the processes of grammar acquisition, as we have noted it in the theorizing of other persons whose work we have discussed.

## Imitation and Syntactic Development

Slobin's analysis of the acquisition of syntax leads us naturally into a consideration of semantics, but we need to tie down two other points before we turn from syntax to the research which has focused on semantic development. Both points are related to Slobin's thesis. One has to do with the issue of whether comprehension precedes production, which might be inferred from Slobin's arguments, and the other relates to whether children's acquisition of language involves imitation of what those around the child say.

Let's consider the latter issue first. It was assumed initially that children could not possibly acquire language by imitation because their early utterances reveal marked deviations from the utterances of adult native speakers of the language. Who, after all, has ever heard an adult say anything resembling, "Allgone outside"? That argument seemed reasonable until it was recognized that no one had listened to what parents say to their children. In effect, it was not known what the input was and, therefore, whether children do or do not imitate the speech of others. It is obvious that children attend to some of the speech around them since they always acquire the same language as those in their environment. The question is, do they imitate the language they hear?

When researchers began to look systematically at the language environment of the child, the first obvious observation was that the language directed toward children by adults consists of sentences which are well formed, shorter, and of simpler construction than those sentences directed toward other adults (Phillips, 1973). Furthermore, adults adjust the complexity of their language to the level of the child's language. As the child's language advances, the adult's language increases in complexity (Moerk, 1974). This adult adjustment seems to hold regardless of whether or not the adult is the parent of the child or what the particular language, culture, or socioeconomic level of the persons involved happens to be (Slobin, 1975; Snow, 1972; Snow, Arlman-Rupp, Hassing, Jobse, Joosten, & Vorster, 1976). Furthermore, it appears that there is not a great deal of difference between the speech of mother to child and the speech of child to child (Slobin, 1975). Finally, one observation Brown and his colleagues made early in their investigations (Brown & Bellugi, 1964) is that when a child produces an incomplete utterance, the adult is likely to expand that utterance into a full sentence for the child, providing an ideal opportunity for imitation if the child were so inclined.

Another aspect of adult speech directed toward children beginning to speak is a great deal of repetition (Friedlander, Jacobs, Davis, & Wetstone, 1972). The parent tends to say something to the child and repeat it several times although, as Snow (1972) notes, there is often a good deal of variation in the structure of the repetitions so that the semantic idea may be presented in a variety of structural forms rather than exact repetitions as, for example, "Give me the big doll. No the big one. I want the big doll. Where is the big one? I don't want the little doll. Show me the big doll."

In short, it would appear that the people around a child who is acquiring language are sensitive to the child's level of development and try to provide a linguistic environment which is ideally suited to language acquisition. Their articulation tends to be clearer, their speech tends to be slower, the sentences shorter and less complex, and the ideas are stated in several ways to achieve communication. Except for the latter characteristic, the language environment seems ideal for the child to adopt a strategy of imitating the language he or she hears, if that were an adaptive approach to acquiring language. The evidence, however, certainly would not force one to that conclusion. Ervin (1964) was one of the first to examine the relation between adult utterances and child efforts to imitate them. Her technique was to write a grammar for the child's spontaneous utterances and a grammar for the child's imitations. When she compared the two grammars, she concluded that there was not the slightest indication that the imitations were more advanced than the spontaneous utterances and, therefore, there was no evidence that imitation plays a part in grammatical development.

Slobin (1968), in a finer-grained analysis of exchanges between child and adult, looked at those situations in which the parent expanded an utterance of the child and the child then imitated the expansion. While such exchanges appear to be relatively infrequent, Slobin did find that in about one-half of such exchanges, the child's second utterance was more advanced than the first. He concluded that this particular type of exchange may be an excellent teaching situation for the child. The hypothesis that expansions of children's utterances provide an ideal context for language acquisition led to an experiment by Cazden (1965). She compared the advances in language development of children, whose utterances were systematically expanded by an adult, with those of a comparable group to whom the usual model of language use was presented in the form of natural, well-formed conversational sentences in response to the child's utterances. The advances in language development were no greater in the expansion group than in a control group which received no treatment. In contrast, the group for whom language was modeled in a normal conversational manner showed significant advances on the variety of language measures Cazden used. In short, responding to a child's utterance by simply demonstrating the right way to say what the child was trying to produce is not an effective way to teach language. Nelson, Carskaddon, and Bonvillian (1973), however, have shown that expansions do help when they are made a part of normal conversation. It would appear that the critical factor is the exchange of messages between child and adult, and that an adult model expanding the child's incomplete utterances should maintain a natural conversation in which the expansions—or any other attempts to improve the child's language—do not interfere with this exchange. K. Nelson (1973), incidentally, suggests that imitation is a language acquisition strategy which is used after children have begun to acquire their first words but it is a strategy used by less advanced talkers by the age of two years.

We have already noted that Brown has examined his data pertaining to the reward and punishment parents provide for correct and incorrect syntactic utterances of their children (Brown & Hanlon, 1970). Those analyses gave no support to the contention that parents teach syntax via reward and punishment. In fact, when parents do provide approval or disapproval, it is almost always related to the truth (semantics) or the phonological aspects of the utterance and almost never to the syntactic characteristics of what the child has said. It would appear from the evidence in observations of the natural course of language acquisition that imitation plays little significant role in the acquisition of language and that reward and punishment are seldom used to influence the course of syntactic development.

The issue is not closed, however, for Whitehurst and Vasta (1975), after reviewing the literature in the psycholinguistic, operant, and social learning areas, argue that previous considerations of the effects of imitation have used a too-restrictive definition of imitation. Furthermore, they argue that experimental rather than observational research techniques must be used to investigate the role of imitation in language acquisition. They propose that the child acquires language through "selective imitation" rather than through direct copying of adult speech. They suggest that the child imitates the structure, form, and/or function of the adult utterance rather than the exact words. Such imitation occurs when the adult models those structures and functions so that the child is given the opportunity to imitate the model selectively. The process requires that the child comprehend the utterances first; then imitate their structural characteristics but not necessarily their content; and finally, create novel utterances derived from the structures acquired from the model. While these authors minimize the importance of reinforcement in the productive phase of this developmental sequence, they do argue that reinforcement must be explicitly present during the comprehension phase which must precede production.

The nature of the abstracting processes which allow the child to identify structures in, and functions of, language is not made clear by these authors. However, a good deal of evidence has accumulated about the relation between the development of comprehension and production, to which we shall now turn. Unfortunately, the findings of research in this area do not provide strong support for the Whitehurst and Vasta theoretical position because, as we shall see, comprehension does not always precede production.

## The Relation between Comprehension and Production

Bloom (1974) has provided an excellent review of the literature and presentation of the issues involved in the comprehension-production question. Ignoring the research demonstrating that infants make phonological distinctions as a form of comprehension (Eimas et al., 1971) , we will focus here only on the problem of syntactic and semantic comprehension and production.

The early observations of the natural development of language led many researchers to the conclusion that children comprehend language before they produce it. Thus, the child in the holophrastic stage of production was assumed to comprehend utterances of others which were structurally more complex. It has often been reported that throughout early acquisition, children appear to understand commands, directions, and other statements given in complex syntactic forms relative to the child's own syntactic constructions. Bloom (1973) , for example, has reported such observations. But, as she later notes (Bloom, 1974), the question of language comprehension as opposed to contextual comprehension is more complex than may be possible to disentangle by observation in the natural situation. Adults speaking to children frequently repeat, as we noted earlier, but they also exaggerate the stress on important words and point or gesture to aid understanding of the message which the child may not be able to comprehend on the basis of language alone. In order to establish the independent role of language, it is necessary to establish conditions in which language is the only clue to the message.

Fraser, Bellugi, and Brown (1963) were the first to attempt a systematic examination of this problem. They devised an imitation, comprehension, and production test (ICP) which consisted of pairs of pictures which represented contrasts of various grammatical relationships. For example, they presented a pair of pictures in which one sheep was jumping a fence while another sheep was watching in one picture, and two sheep were jumping the fence in the other. In the comprehension test, children were asked to point to the picture which was appropriate to the statement, "The sheep is jumping the fence" or "The sheep are jumping the fence." The production task required each child to produce the sentence appropriate to each picture. The imitation task did not involve the pictures but only a repetition of the sentence uttered by the experimenter. Some of the other grammatical contrasts included mass versus count nouns (e.g., milk versus glass; you take *some* milk but *a* glass), affirmative versus negative statements, passive versus active sentences, and sentences including indirect objects and direct objects.

The results were clear in supporting the hypothesis that comprehension precedes spontaneous production for three-year-old children on all the grammatical forms tested. Imitative production, on the other hand, was more advanced than comprehension. In short, three-year-old children can produce sentences involving all the grammatical forms used if the only requirement is to imitate someone else; they have greater difficulty understanding the same utterances; and the most difficulty creating sentences which reflect the same syntactic forms. Lovell and Dixon (1967) and Nurss and Day (1971) found similar results with two- and four-year-old children.

The ICP procedure and results have been criticized, however, by Baird (1972) on statistical grounds and by Fernald (1972) on methodological grounds. Fernald pointed out that the scoring procedure used by Fraser et al. artificially inflated the number of errors on the production task compared to those on the comprehension task. In the latter task the child must point to one or the other picture and, therefore, chance performance would be 50 percent correct. In the production task there are more than two possible responses the child can make so that if the child were responding on a chance basis the average score would be something less than 50 percent correct. Fernald replicated the Fraser et al. procedure and found that production performance was as good as comprehension when the scoring bias was eliminated.

Keeney and Wolfe (1972) report a study of subject-verb agreement in which they observed that three- and four-year-old children spontaneously produced sentences which correctly followed the rules of agreement. They also correctly imitated sentences with subject-verb agreement and at the same time corrected any violations of the rule in the model sentence. But in three different tests of comprehension, the same children indicated only a slightly above-chance correct performance. Thus, the children had productive command over the syntactic rule of agreement but they showed little evidence that they comprehended the relation between verb number inflection and the meaning of singular or plural. Similarly, Chapman and Miller (1975) found that production performance preceded comprehension of subject-object structures at the two- to three-word stage of development. They found, however, that sentences with an animate subject and inanimate object were always comprehended correctly, suggesting that semantic strategies may play an important role in sentence interpretation. The use of stress may also help in the comprehension of some kinds of sentence structures (Maratsos, 1973), although not necessarily all sentence structures (Lahey, 1974). Comprehension is also influenced by contextual factors such as event probability (i.e., it is more likely that a man will swat a fly than that a fly will swat a man) as well as strategic factors such as those suggested by Bever (1970) in which all sentences are interpreted in the actor-action-object order (Strohner & Nelson, 1974).

The comprehension-production research seems to indicate that children may have little difficulty constructing sentences to convey the ideas they have in mind while at the same time they are incapable of consistently comprehending similar sentences when semantic or contextual factors and adopted strategies for interpreting sentences conflict with the syntactic structures used by a speaker to whom the child is listening. As Bloom (1974) concludes, it certainly seems to be true that there are times when production precedes comprehension as well as times when comprehension precedes production but it appears to be too early to draw firm conclusions about the general order of development in these two spheres of language acquisition. Surely the complex interaction of the four factors of comprehension, production, cognitive status of the developing child, and the context in which language is used will not allow a simple statement that comprehension precedes or follows production in the process of acquisition. The relative importance of each variable will differ in each situation and at different developmental levels.

## SUMMARY

We have seen in this chapter that the young child begins very early to use words to convey complex messages. When a single word is the productive limitation of the child, extra-linguistic context is used effectively to convey the message intended. In effect, the context is used by the child to expand the syntax of the message which the child is unable to produce linguistically. Gradually, the child adds to the linguistic portion of the message as syntactic and morphophonemic rules are acquired. Acquisition of those rules appears to reflect an interaction between the complexity of the rules per se and the complexity of the messages to be communicated. Syntactic and morphophonemic complexities are usually expressed initially in forms simpler than those used by adults. The child seems to formulate more and more complex hypotheses or strategies for coping with the problems of encoding and decoding messages. As for the complexity of the messages themselves, the research has led investigators away from language as such and into the broader realm of cognitive development. Not surprisingly, the nature of what children discuss is directly related to the level of their cognitive development as independently established in, for example, research related to Piagetian theory. More surprising, perhaps, there seems to be little relation between the acquisition process and what is ordinarily thought of as efforts to teach language. Although adults and children do adapt their language to the level of the child, there is little evidence that the child attempts to imitate the language of others. Rather, children formulate broad rules and the process of language acquisition appears to be a matter of refining those rules to the specifics of individual structures in the language. While the strategies used by individual children do vary, the formulation of those rules for comprehending and producing specific constructions is very regular both between children and across languages. Developmental psycholinguists have been driven at every turn, however, as have their counterparts who have focused on the psychology of language with adults, from the study of syntax to the study of semantics. The former cannot be understood independently of the latter. Thus, we turn in the last chapter of this text to the examination of semantic development.

# REFERENCES

Anisfeld, M., Barlow, J., & Frail, C. M. Distinctive features in the pluralization rules of English speakers. *Language and Speech*, 1968, *11*, 31–37.

Anisfeld, M., & Gordon, M. On the psychophonological structure of English inflectional rules. *Journal of Verbal Learning and Verbal Behavior*, 1968, *7*, 973–79.

Anisfeld, M., & Tucker, G. R. English pluralization rules of six-year-old children. *Child Development*, 1967, *38*, 1201–17.

Bar-Adon, A. Primary syntactic structures in Hebrew child language. In E. Bar-Adon & W. F. Leopold (Eds.), *Child language: A book of readings*. Englewood Cliffs, N.J.: Prentice-Hall, 1971. Pp. 433–73

Baird, R. On the role of chance in imitation-comprehension-production test results. *Journal of Verbal Learning and Verbal Behavior*, 1972, *11*, 474–77.

Beilin, H. *Studies in the cognitive basis of language development*. New York: Academic Press, 1975.

Bellugi, U. The development of interrogative structures in children's speech. In K. F. Riegel (Ed.), *The development of language functions*. Ann Arbor, Michigan: Center for Human Growth and Development, University of Michigan, Report No. 8, 1965.

Berko, J. The child's learning of English morphology. *Word*, 1958, *14*, 150–77.

Bever, T. G. The cognitive basis for linguistic structures. In J. R. Hayes (Ed.), *Cognition and the development of language*. New York: Wiley, 1970. Pp. 279–352.

Bloch, O. Les premiers stages du langage de l'enfant. *Journal de Psychologie*, 1921, *18*, 693–712.

Bloom, L. *Language development*. Cambridge, Mass.: M.I.T. Press, 1970.

Bloom, L. *One word at a time: The use of single word utterances before syntax*. The Hague: Mouton, 1973.

Bloom, L. Talking, understanding, and thinking. In R. L. Schiefelbusch & L. L. Loyd (Eds.), *Language perspectives: Acquisition, retardation, and intervention*. Baltimore, Maryland: University Park Press, 1974. Pp. 285–311.

Bowerman, M. *Early syntactic development: A cross-linguistic study with special reference to Finnish*. New York: Cambridge University Press, 1973.

Braine, M. D. S. On learning the grammatical order of words. *Psychological Review*, 1963a, *70*, 323–48.

Braine, M. D. S. The ontogeny of English phrase structure: The first phase. *Language*, 1963b, *39*, 1–13.

Brown, R. The development of Wh questions in child speech. *Journal of Verbal Learning and Verbal Behavior*, 1968, *7*, 279–90.

Brown, R. W. *A first language: The early stages*. Cambridge, Mass.: Harvard University Press, 1973.

Brown, R. W., & Bellugi, U. Three processes in the child's acquisition of syntax. *Harvard Educational Reveiw*, 1964, *34*, 133–51.

Brown, R., Cazden, C. B., & Bellugi, U. The child's grammar from I to III. In J. P. Hill (Ed.), *Minnesota symposium on child psychology* (Vol. 2). Minneapolis: University of Minnesota Press, 1969. Pp. 28–73.

Brown, R., & Fraser, C. The acquisition of syntax. In U. Bellugi & R. Brown (Eds.), *The acquisition of language.* Monograph of the Society for Research in Child Development, 1964, *29*, No. 1, 43–79.

Brown, R. W., Fraser, C., & Bellugi, U. Explorations in grammar evaluation. In U. Bellugi & R. W. Brown (Eds.), *The acquisition of language.* Monograph of the Society for Research in Child Development, 1964, *29*, No. 1, 79–92.

Brown, R. W., & Hanlon, C. Derivational complexity and order of acquisition in child speech. In J. R. Hayes (Ed.), *Cognition and the development of language.* New York: Wiley, 1970. Pp. 11–54.

Bruce, D. J. The analysis of word sounds by young children. *British Journal of Educational Psychology*, 1964, *34*, 158–69.

Bryant, B., & Anisfeld, M. Feedback versus no-feedback in testing children's knowledge of English pluralization rules. *Journal of Experimental Child Psychology*, 1969, *8*, 250–55.

Buhler, K. Les lois génerales d'évolution dans le langage de l'enfant. *Journal de Psychologie*, 1926, *23*, 597–607.

Cazden, C. B. Environmental assistance to the child's acquisition of grammar. Unpublished doctoral dissertation, Harvard University, 1965.

Chapman, R., & Miller, J. Word order in early two- and three-word utterances: Does production precede comprehension? Paper presented to the Fifth Annual Child Language Research Forum, Stanford University, April 7, 1973.

Chipman, H. H., & deDardel, C. Developmental study of the comprehension and production of the pronoun "It." *Journal of Psycholinguistic Research,* 1974, *3*, 91–99.

Chomsky, C. A. *The acquisition of syntax in children from 5 to 10.* Cambridge, Mass.: M.I.T. Press, 1969.

Cromer, R. F. 'Children are nice to understand': Surface structure clues for the recovery of deep structure. *British Journal of Psychology*, 1970, *61*, 397–408.

de Villiers, J. G., & de Villiers, P. A. A cross-sectional study of the acquisition of grammatical morphemes in child speech. *Journal of Psycholinguistic Research*, 1973a, *2*, 267–78.

de Villiers, J. B., & de Villiers, P. A. Development of the use of word order in comprehension. *Journal of Psycholinguistic Research*, 1973b, *2*, 331–41.

de Villiers, J. G., & Flusberg, H. B. T. Some facts one simply cannot deny. *Journal of Child Language*, 1975, *2*, 279–86.

Donaldson, M. Developmental aspects of performance with negatives. In G. B. Flores d'Arcais & W. J. N. Lavelt (Eds.), *Advances in psycholinguistics.* Amsterdam: North Holland Publishing Co., 1970.

Dore, J. Holophrases, speech acts, and language universals. *Journal of Child Language*, 1975, *2*, 21–40.

Edwards, D. Sensory-motor intelligence and semantic relations in early child grammar. *Cognition*, 1973, *2*, 395–434.

Eimas, P. D. Auditory and linguistic processing of cues for place of articulation by infants. *Perception and Psychophysics*, 1974, *16*, 513–21.

Eimas, P. D., Siqueland, E. R., Jusczyk, P., & Vigorito, J. M. Speech perception in infants. *Science*, 1971, *171*, 303–6.

Ervin, S. M. Imitation and structural change in children's language. In E. H. Lenneberg (Ed.), *New directions in the study of language.* Cambridge, Mass.: M.I.T. Press, 1964.

Ervin-Tripp, S. Discourse agreement: How children answer questions. In J. R. Hayes (Ed.), *Cognition and the development of language.* New York: Wiley, 1970. Pp. 79–108.

Fernald, C. D. Control of grammar in imitation, comprehension and production: Problems of replication. *Journal of Verbal Learning and Verbal Behavior,* 1972, *11,* 606–13.

Fillmore, C. The case for case. In E. Bach & R. T. Harms (Eds.), *Universals in linguistic theory.* New York: Holt, Rinehart & Winston, 1968.

Fodor, J., & Garrett, M. Some reflections on competence and performance. In J. Lyons & R. H. Wales (Eds.), *Psycholinguistic papers.* Edinburgh: Edinburgh University Press, 1966. Pp. 135–53.

Foss, D. J., & Swinney, D. A. On the psychological reality of the phoneme: Perception, identification, and consciousness. *Journal of Verbal Learning and Verbal Behavior,* 1973, *12,* 246–57.

Fraser, C., Bellugi, U., & Brown, R. W. Control of grammar in imitation, comprehension, and production. *Journal of Verbal Learning and Verbal Behavior,* 1963, *2,* 121–35.

Friedlander, B. Z., Jacobs, A. C., Davis, B. B., & Wetstone, H. S. Time-sampling analysis of infants' natural language environments in the home. *Child Development,* 1972, *43,* 730–40.

Garvey, C., Caramazza, A., & Yates, J. Factors influencing assignment of pronoun antecedents. *Cognition,* 1975, *3,* 227–43.

Greenfield, P. M., & Smith, J. H. *The structure of communication in early language development.* New York: Academic Press, 1976.

Guillaume, P. Les débuts de la phrase dans le langage de l'enfant. *Journal de Psychologie,* 1927, *24,* 1–25. Reprinted in C. A. Ferguson & D. I. Slobin (Eds.), *Studies of child language development.* New York: Holt, Rinehart & Winston, 1973. Pp. 522–41.

Hayhurst, H. Some errors of young children in producing passive sentences. *Journal of Verbal Learning and Verbal Behavior,* 1967, *6,* 634–40.

Hornby, P. A. Surface structure and the topic-comment distinction: A developmental study. *Child Development,* 1971, *42,* 1975–88.

Huttenlocher, J. Children's language: Word-phrase relationship. *Science,* 1964, *143,* 264–65.

Huxley, R. The development of the correct use of subject personal pronouns in two children. In G. B. Flores d'Arcais & W. J. M. Levelt (Eds.), *Advances in Psycholinguistics.* Amsterdam: North-Holland, 1970.

Jakobson, R. Child language aphasia and phonological universals. (Trans. by Allan R. Keiler.) The Hague: Mouton, 1968.

Keeney, T. J., & Wolfe, J. The acquisition of agreement in English. *Journal of Verbal Learning and Verbal Behavior,* 1972, *11,* 698–705.

Kessel, F. S. *The role of syntax in children's comprehension from ages six to twelve.* Monographs of the Society for Research in Child Development, 1970, *35,* No. 139.

Klima, E. S., & Bellugi, U. Syntactic regularities in the speech of children. In J. Lyons & R. J. Wales (Eds.), *Psycholinguistics papers.* Edinburgh: Edinburgh University Press, 1966.

Lahey, M. The use of prosody and syntactic markers in children's comprehension of spoken sentences. *Journal of Speech and Hearing Disorders,* 1974, *17,* 656–68.

Lieberman, P. On the evolution of language: A unified view. *Cognition,* 1973, *2,* 59–94.

Macnamara, J. Cognitive basis of language learning in infants. *Psychological Review,* 1972, *79,* 1–13.

MacWhinney, B. Rules, rote, and analogy in morphological formations by Hungarian children. *Journal of Child Language,* 1975, *2,* 65–78.

Maratsos, M. P. The effects of stress on the understanding of pronominal co-reference in children. *Journal of Psycholinguistic Research,* 1973, *2,* 1–8.

Maratsos, M. P. Children who get worse at understanding the passive: A replication of Bever. *Journal of Psycholinguistic Research,* 1974, *3,* 65–74.

McCarthy, D. Language development in children. In L. Carmichael (Ed.), *Manual of child psychology* (2nd ed.). New York: Wiley, 1954.

McNeill, D. The creation of language by children. In J. Lyons & R. J. Wales (Eds.), *Psycholinguistic papers.* Edinburgh: Edinburgh University Press, 1966.

McNeill, D. The capacity for grammatical development in children. In D. Slobin (Ed.), *The ontogenesis of grammar: Some facts and several theories.* New York: Academic Press, 1971. Pp. 17–40.

McNeill, D., & Lindig, K. The perceptual reality of phonemes, syllables, words, and sentences. *Journal of Verbal Learning and Verbal Behavior,* 1973, *12,* 419–30.

McNeill, D., & McNeill, N. B. What does a child mean when he says "no"? In E. M. Zale (Ed.), *Language and language behavior.* New York: Appleton-Century-Crofts, 1968. Pp. 51–62.

Menyuk, P. The role of distinctive features in children's acquisition of phonology. *Journal of Speech and Hearing Research,* 1968, *11,* 138–46.

Menyuk, P. *Sentences children use.* Cambridge, Mass.: M.I.T. Press, 1969.

Menyuk, P. *The acquisition and development of language.* Englewood Cliffs, N.J.: Prentice Hall, 1971.

Menyuk, P. Early development of receptive language: From babbling to words. in R. L. Schiefelbusch & L. L. Lloyd (Eds.), *Language perspectives—acquisition, retardation, and intervention.* Baltimore, Maryland: University Park Press, 1974. Pp. 213–35.

Messer, S. Implicit phonology in children. *Journal of Verbal Learning and Verbal Behavior,* 1967, *6,* 609–13.

Miller, G. A., & McNeill, D. Psycholinguistics. In G. Lindzey & E. Aronson (Eds.), *The handbook of social psychology* (2nd ed., Vol. 3). Reading, Mass.: Addison-Wesley, 1968.

Miller, W., & Ervin, S. M. The development of grammar in child language. In U. Bellugi & R. Brown (Eds.), *The acquisition of language.* Monograph of the Society for Research in Child Development, 1964, *29,* No. 1. Pp. 9–34.

Moerk, E. Changes in verbal child-mother interactions with increasing language skills of the child. *Journal of Psycholinguistic Research,* 1974, *3,* 101–16.

Molfese, D. L., Freeman, R. B., Jr., & Palermo, D. S. The ontogeny of brain lateralization for speech and nonspeech stimuli. *Brain and Language,* 1975, *2,* 356–68.

Moskowitz, A. I. The two-year-old stage in the acquisition of English phonology. In C. A. Ferguson & D. I. Slobin (Eds.), *Studies of child language development.* New York: Holt, Rinehart & Winston, 1973. Pp. 52–69.

Natalicio, D., & Natalicio, L. The child's learning of English morphology revisited. *Language Learning,* 1969, *19,* 205–15.

Nelson, K. *Structure and strategy in learning to talk.* Monographs of the Society for Research in Child Development, 1973, *38,* Nos. 1–2. Pp. 1–135.

Nelson, K. E., Carskaddon, G., & Bonvillian, J. D. Syntax acquisition: Impact of experimental variation in adult verbal interaction with the child. *Child Development,* 1973, *44,* 497–504.

Nurss, J. R., & Day, D. E. Imitation, comprehension and production of grammatical structures. *Journal of Verbal Learning and Verbal Behavior,* 1971, *10,* 68–74.

Palermo, D. S., & Eberhart, V. Lynn. On the learning of morphological rules: An experimental analogy. *Journal of Verbal Learning and Verbal Behavior,* 1968, *7,* 337–44.

Palermo, D. S., & Molfese, D. L. Language acquisition from age five onward. *Psychological Bulletin,* 1972, *78,* 409–28.

Palermo, D. S., & Parrish, M. Rule acquisition as a function of number and frequency of exemplar presentation. *Journal of Verbal Learning and Verbal Behavior,* 1971, 44–51.

Phillips, J. R. Syntax and vocabulary of mothers' speech to young children: Age and sex comparisons. *Child Development,* 1973, *44,* 182–85.

Piaget, J. *The origins of intelligence in children* (Margaret Cook, trans.). New York: International Universities Press, 1952 (original French ed., 1936).

Piaget, J. *The construction of reality in the child* (1st ed., 1937). New York: Basic Books, 1954.

Piaget, J. *Play, dreams and imitation in childhood* (1st ed., 1945). New York: Norton, 1962.

Preyer, W. *The mind of the child. Part 2. The development of the intellect* (H. W. Brown, trans.). New York: Appleton-Century-Crofts, 1890.

Savin, H. B., & Bever, T. G. The nonconceptual reality of the phoneme. *Journal of Verbal Learning and Verbal Behavior,* 1970, *9,* 295–302.

Slobin, D. T. The acquisition of Russian as a native language. In F. Smith & G. A. Miller (Eds.), *The genesis of language: A psycholinguistic approach.* Cambridge, Mass.: M.I.T. Press, 1966a.

Slobin, D. I. Grammatical transformations and sentence comprehension in childhood and adulthood. *Journal of Verbal Learning and Verbal Behavior,* 1966b, *5,* 219–27.

Slobin, D. I. Imitation and grammatical development in children. In N. S. Endler, L. R. Boulter, & H. Osser (Eds.), *Contemporary issues in developmental psychology.* New York: Holt, Rinehart & Winston, 1968. Pp. 437–43.

Slobin, D. I. Cognitive prerequisites for the development of grammar. In C. A. Ferguson & D. I. Slobin (Eds.), *Studies in child language development.* New York: Holt, Rinehart & Winston, 1973. Pp. 175–208.

Slobin, D. I. On the nature of talk to children. In E. H. Lenneberg & E. Lenneberg (Eds.), *Foundations of Language Development: A Multidisciplinary Approach* (Vol. 1). New York: Academic Press, 1975. Pp. 283–97.

Smith, K. H. Effects of experience on verbal reconstructive memory. *Journal of Experimental Psychology,* 1973, *97,* 119–39.

Smith, M. E. An investigation of the development of the sentence and the extent of vocabulary in young children. *University of Iowa Studies in Child Welfare,* 1926, *3,* No. 5.

Snow, C. E. Mothers' speech to children learning language. *Child Development,* 1972, *43,* 549–65.

Snow, C. E., Arlman-Rupp, A., Hassing, Y., Jobse, J., Joosten, J., & Vorster, J. Mothers' speech in three social classes. *Journal of Psycholinguistic Research,* 1976, *5,* 1–20.

Stern, C., & Stern, W. *Die Kindersprache.* Leipzig: Barth, 1907.

Strohner, H., & Nelson, K. E. The young child's development of sentence comprehension: Influence of event probability, nonverbal context, syntactic form, and strategies. *Child Development,* 1974, *45,* 567–76.

Templin, M. C. *Certain language skills in children: Their development and interrelationships.* Institute of Child Welfare Monographs. Serial No. 26. Minneapolis: University of Minnesota Press, 1957.

Trehub, S. E. Infants' sensitivity to vowel and tonal contrasts. *Developmental Psychology,* 1973, *9,* 91–96.

Turner, E. A., & Rommetveit, R. The acquisition of sentence voice and reversibility. *Child Development,* 1967a, *38,* 649–60.

Turner, E. A., & Rommetveit, R. Experimental manipulation of the production of active and passive voice in children. *Language and Speech,* 1967b, *10,* 169–80.

Wason, P. C. The contexts of plausible denial. *Journal of Verbal Learning and Verbal Behavior,* 1965, *4,* 7–11.

Weir, R. H. Some questions on the child's learning of phonology. In F. Smith & G. A. Miller (Eds.), The Genesis of Language: *A Psycholinguistic Approach.* Cambridge, Mass.: M.I.T. Press, 1966.

Whitehurst, G. J., & Vasta, R. Is language acquired through imitation? *Journal of Psycholinguistic Research,* 1975, *4,* 37–59.

Zhurova, L. Ye. The development of analysis of words into their sounds by preschool children. In C. A. Ferguson & D. I. Slobin (Eds.), *Studies of child language development.* New York: Holt, Rinehart & Winston, 1973. Pp. 141–54.

# Language
# Acquisition:
# Semantic
# Development

CHAPTER 7

We come, finally, to the heart of the language acquisition process: establishing the relation between meaning and the linguistic system being acquired. Probably we should say "meanings" rather than "meaning" since the meaning of a word or sentence within the system cannot be static because it will vary with the cognitive level of the child. In fact, the cognitive status of the child must be considered as part of the context within which utterances are produced and understood by that child. Note how complex the problem of understanding the acquisition of meaning becomes when we try to take into account cognitive development as well as the other contextual issues raised in Chapter 5. It is no wonder that psycholinguists have worked most frequently with the presumably less complex problems of phonology and syntax.

## THE ORIGINAL WORD GAME

Brown (1958a) took up a part of the problem of acquiring meaning under the title "The Original Word Game." The game requires a tutor who knows the language and a player who is learning. The tutor names things according to the custom of the community and the player forms hypotheses about what category is being named and then tests those hypotheses by naming some things which the tutor checks for accuracy. The feedback to the player eventually leads to a good fit between the names and the nonlinguistic categories named.

As Brown (1958b) has pointed out elsewhere, the referential aspect of meaning involved in the original word game is not a simple one because most objects have many names. He provides the example of an object which may be referred to as a dime, a coin, money, a metal object, a thing, or more particularly, a 1952 dime, and even a particular 1952 dime with certain scratches on it. Similarly, a dog may be referred to as Pretzel, dog, mixed breed, quadruped, animal, and so on. Consider, too, the man on the street who is referred to as Mr. Jones, man, and Daddy by various children.

When adults name objects for children, they tend to use the shortest, most frequently used name—but not always. Brown suggests that it is not the frequency-brevity principle which is important but, rather, the level of usual utility that determines which name the adult will give the child. Similarly, it is not a matter of concreteness versus abstractness that establishes the name used by the adult. Things are named so as to categorize them in a maximally useful manner. Thus, faced with a pineapple, the child is told it is a *pineapple,* not a *fruit,* while a beagle is referred to as a *dog,* not a *beagle,* nor a *mutt,* nor an *animal.* It appears that adults seldom use the most abstract category name. Sometimes they use concrete terms but most often they use terms at a middle level of abstraction. The natural selection of the middle level terms for use with children fits nicely with the recent research of Rosch, Mervis, Gray, Johnson, and Boyes-Braem (1976). They have shown that terms at the middle level of abstraction are the basic categories adults use because they carry the most information, possess the highest category cue validity, and are more differentiated from each other than either more abstract superordinate categories or more specific category names.

## LANGUAGE AND CONCEPTUAL DEVELOPMENT

One may well ask what relevance the adult use of terms has to the child's semantic development. Macnamara (1972) addresses the question directly. As he suggests, words are used as messages about meanings the adult speaker intends to convey. The child, in turn, must try to figure out what the meanings of those messages are. Thus, the utility criterion used by adults is probably the most helpful from the child's point of view. But, as Macnamara points out, the whole process probably begins with the child already knowing the meaning the speaker wishes to convey and then determining how the language of the speaker relates to that meaning. Thus, the child knows about things such as mommy, dogs, and milk and about such actions as kissing, barking, and spilling. The initial problem then becomes one of establishing the relationships between the objects and events in the child's cognitive conceptual system and the language that may be used to talk about those objects and events. In short, at the beginning of the language acquisition process, the child's thought has already developed substantially. Piaget (1936) has, of course, been arguing that point for some time. Thus, the child has already developed many conceptual categories and knows the relationships among events and the effects of the actions of persons (including itself) and objects on other persons and objects. The child is, therefore, ready with the concepts and some notions about their relations to each other and needs only to discover how the language relates to these concepts and relations. A similar argument was advanced by Schlesinger (1971) earlier.

As Macnamara suggests, relating language to concept is no simple matter. There is no clear reason why the child should know that when the parent identifies a dog by name, the parent is referring to the dog as an entity as opposed to the color, shape, action, head, or tail of the dog, or even the ground on which the dog is standing. Obviously, the child must have some natural constraints on what will be categorized to form a concept and some strategies for deciding what words refer to when used by others. Children do not, after all, form bizarre concepts. Macnamara suggests, for example, that the child adopts the strategy of taking a word he or she hears as the name for an object as a whole rather than some attribute of the whole. If the child uses such a strategy, then it follows that only after object names have been learned will attribute names be acquired. He argues further that the child adopts the strategy of attending to changing attributes of objects prior to permanent or invarying attributes. Thus, the opening and closing of the refrigerator will be attended to and named before the color of the refrigerator.

Macnamara's hypothesis is reasonably simple (although the mechanisms by which it is implemented may be complex) : children attend to aspects of their world and in so doing they conceptualize those aspects. Subsequently, children attempt to relate the concepts which do have meaning for them to the language which does not have meaning. The argument is most convincingly made in the case of logical connectives, such as the words *and* and *or*. There seems no possibility that children could acquire such abstract terms correctly without already knowing the logical relations expressed by those words in their own thinking and then looking for how those relations are expressed in language used by those around them.

## FEATURE THEORY

In the course of looking for the meanings in language, children might be expected to make errors in deciding the meaning-language relations. Clearly, children do not always assign the same meanings to words and sentences as adults do. The question thus becomes one of determining the nature of those errors. If we conceive of words as composed of features of which their meaning is comprised (Katz, 1972), then a reasonable hypothesis might be that a child acquires the features, and thus the meaning, piecemeal. Such a hypothesis has been advanced by E. Clark (1973a) as a natural blending of linguistic theory and some research results which seem easily interpreted within that framework.

Let's begin with the research which stimulated the theory. Some of the first researchers to begin to look at aspects of semantics were Donaldson and Wales. They undertook a large project at the University of Edinburgh in an effort to gain some insights into the relation of language acquisition and a general theory of cognitive development. The first paper they published (Donaldson & Balfour, 1968) dealt with preschool children's comprehension of the terms *more* and *less*. The study was of considerable interest because the children appeared to have no difficulty correctly comprehending the meaning of *more* but they did not comprehend *less*. They did not, however, respond randomly to *less* but rather treated *less* as if it meant *more*. When they were presented with two cardboard trees with differing numbers of apples on each tree and asked "Which tree has *less* apples?" the children unhesitatingly pointed to the tree with the larger number of apples on it. They behaved as if *less* meant *more*. This finding has been replicated with a variety of materials (Palermo, 1973; 1974). Donaldson and Wales (1970) and Wales and Campbell (1970) also reported findings related to a much broader set of relational terms in their superlative and comparative forms, e.g., *longest-shortest* and *thicker-thinner*. Their results suggest that superlatives are acquired before comparatives. Second, and most important to subsequent theorizing, the positive or linguistically unmarked end of the relational continuum is acquired before the negative or marked end, although the period of synonymous use of the two polar adjectives is not as apparent with the other relational terms as it was with *more* and *less*.

The results of this research led E. Clark (1973a) to formulate a set of hypotheses about the acquisition of the semantic system by the young child. In her semantic feature hypothesis, she assumes that the meanings of words are composed of features, or meaning components, and that children learn the meanings of words gradually by adding more and more features to their lexical entries until the entries for each word are complete by adult standards. Furthermore, the features for at least some words are hierarchically arranged in terms of the generality of the features. Children appear to acquire the most general features first and the more specific features later.

These aspects of the theory are illustrated in a study by Clark (1971) on the acquisition of the terms *before* and *after*. The meanings of these words can be represented in terms of the features [time], [simultaneous] and [prior]. Clark's analysis suggests that the word *before* is composed of the features [+ time, − simultaneous, + prior] while *after* is composed of [+ time, − simultaneous, − prior]. As in the case of the comparative adjectives, the difference between *before* and *after* rests on the difference in marking of one feature low in the hierarchy of features. Thus, according to the feature hypothesis, the child should recognize first that the two words pertain to time; second that the terms pertain to serial relations between events; and, finally, that *before* refers to prior events and *after* to following events. Only after the latter feature is acquired will the child treat the two terms as having contrasting as opposed to synonymous meanings.

Clark presented preschool children with sentences such as: (1) The boy jumped the gate before he patted the dog; (2) Before the boy patted the dog, he jumped the gate; (3) The boy patted the dog after he jumped the gate; and (4) After the boy jumped the gate, he patted the dog. The child's task was to act out the sentences with toys which were available. The prediction was that children who knew neither word would follow the order of mention of actions in acting out the commands. Once they had acquired the terms, the initial response would be to treat all the sentences as if *before* and *after* meant *before* and, finally, correct performance would be observed. In general, the results supported the hypothesis although there were few children who appeared to treat the two words as synonymous and meaning *before*.

In another study, Klatzky, Clark, and Mecken (1973) attempted to provide further support for the argument that there is an asymmetrical acquisition of bipolar adjectives such that the word for the positive end of the dimension involved is acquired prior to the negative or marked words, i.e., *long* before *short, high* before *low,* and so on. Preschool children were taught to describe objects which differed with respect to height, length, and thickness by means of a new vocabulary consisting of nonsense words. The dimensions were big-small, high-low, long-short and thick-thin. The children learned the nonsense names for the positive terms faster than for the negative terms. The results were interpreted to support the conclusion that the acquisition of polar adjectives is based on an underlying conceptual asymmetry.

With the data of these experiments at hand, Clark (1973a) looked for evidence from other sources to expand her theory of semantic acquisition. An extensive review of the studies reporting language development of children from diary records proved a rich source of information about semantic development. In particular, Clark examined the diary reports for evidence of the semantic overextension of words. In all the reports examined, covering a wide variety of languages, overextension was observed in the productive speech of all the children and this behavior occurred primarily in the age range from about one year to two-and-one-half years. The period lasts about a year for individual children, although overextension of any particular word does not last more than eight months. When vocabulary expands rapidly, generally in connection with the appearance of "What ('s) that?" questions, the period of overextension ends. The features that are used as criteria in the overextensions appear to be derived from perceptual input such as movement, shape, size, sound, taste, and texture. Clark provides a large set of examples of each type, e.g., one child used "mooi" to mean moon, round cakes, round marks on the window and in books, and other round things while another child used the word "cola" to mean things related by taste; chocolate, sugar, tarts, grapes, figs, and peaches.

Clark argues that overextensions are pervasive and the observations related to the relational terms which were discussed above are also overextensions. In addition, she interprets two other observations as examples of overextension. The first relates to the research of C. Chomsky, which we discussed in the previous chapter, concerned with the correct interpretation of the complements of the verbs *ask* and *tell*. Clark argues that the interpretation of *tell* is overextended to *ask* until the semantic features associated with *ask* are acquired so that *ask* is differentiated from *tell*. Last, she points to the research of Piaget which suggests that there are stages in the acquisition of the meaning of *brother* and *sister*. The child treats them initially as synonyms of *boy* and *girl* and then adds the sibling feature and finally the reciprocal relationship between two children in the same family.

Clark concludes from these disparate sources of evidence of overextensions in children's language that the lexical entries for the meanings of words in the child's vocabulary are incomplete by virtue of missing one or more features. It is the deficiency of features which results in the semantically-related but imprecise use of words referred to as overextensions. When the features become a part of the lexical entries, the proper differentiations in meaning are made and correct usage ensues.

Having taken the position that meaning is composed of features which are gradually acquired until complete meaning is achieved, the question of the source of, or basis for, the features arises. Clark suggests that the earliest semantic features are related to the features of perceptual development. Her hypothesis is that there is a set of universal semantic primitives, as suggested by Bierwisch (1970), and the perceptual features are a subset of the semantic primitives. Furthermore, she hypothesizes that the first components of meaning are fragmented individual perceptual features and only after a number of features are acquired is it possible for them to be integrated into a single whole meaning. In this view, acquisition of the semantic system begins with the absolute perceptual features of objects, but Clark goes on to argue that perceptual features are basic to the acquisition of relational terms as well. The hierarchical relations among dimensional polar adjectives postulated by Wales and Campbell (1970), for example, is accounted for by Clark in terms of perceptual features. The pair of adjectives *big-small* is acquired first because the perceptual features which comprise their meaning impose few constraints on the application of those adjectives while other dimensional adjectives, such as *long-short* or *wide-narrow,* are limited by their additional perceptual features to particular dimensions. For example, one can describe all tall objects as *big* but many big objects cannot be described as *tall.* Thus, Clark argues that the more general terms are acquired first because they involve features which are more widely applicable. The more specific or distinguishing features are acquired later, leading to more particular meanings.

Closely related to the hierarchical order of acquisition of perceptual features in terms of generality is the hypothesis related to perceptual salience. Clark suggests, for example, that perceptual features associated with three-dimensionality will be acquired prior to those associated with two-dimensionality because the latter are less salient or perceptually natural. Thus, *big* and *in,* referring to three-dimensional objects and spatial relations, are acquired prior to *long* and *on,* which involve only two-dimensional objects and spatial relations. As the child acquires terms for reference points, lines, planes, and terms which deal with extent, position, directionality, spatial, and temporal terms, other aspects of perceptual saliency and naturalness come into play. The meaning of each dimension, for example, is composed of features which distinguish the positive and negative ends of the dimension with respect to some zero point or primary reference point. The positive direction along the dimension serves as the name of the dimension (e.g., *long-length; high-height*) and is acquired first because the child is predisposed to orient perceptually to that end of the dimension. It is hypothesized (H. Clark, 1973) that the child has an asymmetrical orientation to relational, spatial, and temporal dimensions. As a result, the unmarked words such as *big, long,* and *wide* are acquired before their marked opposites *small, short,* and *narrow.* Similarly, *front* is acquired before *back* because it is perceptually apparent while *back* is not; *up* (above ground) is visually apparent while *down* (below ground) is not; *before* is temporally analogous to the spatial term *front* and is, therefore, acquired before *after.* In short, there is a perceptual basis for the semantics of relational terms as there is for most other early semantic distinctions. Other features related to functional and social aspects of meanings are assumed to be acquired later.

# EVIDENCE CONFLICTING WITH
# FEATURE THEORIES

While much of the early research evidence seemed to confirm the semantic feature hypothesis, there are a number of reasons for considering alternative theoretical accounts of semantic development. Before examining some of the logical arguments that mitigate against accepting any feature theory as a complete explanation of semantic development, we shall consider the variety of recently accumulated research evidence which seems to conflict with some of the premises of, and predictions from, the feature theory.

Huttenlocher (1974) has presented data which raise questions about the interpretation made by Clark (1973a) of the diary data. All the overextensions evident in the data cited by Clark are production errors. The children used one word to refer to a variety of related objects. Huttenlocher, however, observes that overextensions of the productive use of words reflect a limited vocabulary which does not necessarily imply that the meanings of the words are overgeneralized. In her own longitudinal study of three children, Huttenlocher found evidence for overgeneralization in the productive use of words as had been reported in the earlier diary studies reviewed by Clark, but Huttenlocher found no evidence of overextension in comprehension. It would appear, for example, that a child may use the word *dog* to refer to a cat when the word *cat* is missing from his or her vocabulary but would not, when faced with an array of animals, pick out a cat when asked to identify the dogs. Children use the word tools they have available when they want to convey a message and recognize that sometimes the tools are not perfect for the job. Huttenlocher's data with respect to comprehension do not fit as neatly with the feature theory as the production data alone.

The second area in which additional research has raised questions about the feature theory pertains to the acquisition of the various relational terms. Amidon and Carey (1972), for example, have presented evidence to suggest that the comprehension by five- and six-year-old children of the types of *before* and *after* sentences used in the Clark (1971) study is a function of syntactic variables rather than the number of semantic features associated with the lexical entries for *before* and *after*. Johnson (1975) replicated the Clark and the Amidon and Carey procedures and found that there is clearly an interaction between the syntactic framework within which the words *before* and *after* occur and the correct comprehension of those words, but no difference in the frequency of errors in comprehending *before* and *after*. Similarly, Harner (1976) found no difference in comprehension of *before* and *after* but both were understood more accurately when the reference was to immediate future or past rather than more remote future or past. Both the latter two studies provide no evidence that the unmarked, positive *before* is acquired prior to the marked, negative form *after*.

More important, perhaps, to the feature theory than the *before* and *after* studies are two other experiments, one of which examined comprehension of relative adjectives with respect to the dimensions of objects (Brewer & Stone, 1975) and the other the comprehension of spatial terms (Kuczaj & Maratsos, 1975). The researchers in both cases came to the conclusion that polarity of terms may be acquired before the dimension to which they pertain, reversing the hierarchical order of acquisition predicted by feature theory. Brewer and Stone's experiment was simple. They presented four-year-old children with four objects representing both ends of the continuum of two antonym pairs, such as two balls on a vertically mounted wire and two rectangular-shaped pieces of styrofoam which differed in thickness. Each child was asked to "Touch the high [low, thick, or thin] one." Other pairs of objects representing wide-narrow, long-short, tall-short, and deep-shallow were presented and the appropriate terms tested. Analysis of the errors indicated that the most common error made by the children was to point to the object with the same polarity as the word requested, i.e., pointing to the thin object when the low object was requested. In contrast to the prediction of the feature hypothesis, there were relatively few errors to antonym words of the same dimension, i.e., pointing to high when low was requested. Performance on the unmarked members of the pairs was, however, superior to that on the marked pairs. A more recent study by Bartlett (1976) also leads to the conclusion that polarity of size dimensions is acquired prior to the dimensions themselves and, in addition, no support was found to indicate that unmarked terms are acquired prior to marked terms.

Kuczaj and Maratsos looked at the child's acquisition of the words *front, back,* and *side.* They asked children between two-and-one-half and four years of age to place objects *in front of, behind,* and *on the side of* themselves, or objects with obvious fronts (e.g., telephone and truck), nonfronted objects (e.g., a glass and a wooden cube) and novel objects made for the experiment. The data suggest that children acquire the meaning of *front* and *back* at the same time but at different ages with respect to the various contexts used. Correct usage begins with reference to the self, then to objects with fronts, then objects which are novel, and finally, objects with no fronts. The word *side* is acquired after *front* and *back.* No child showed evidence of acquiring *front* before *back* or confusing the two terms as the feature hypothesis would predict. The children first recognized that *front* and *back* are opposites on an axis through objects, and when that knowledge was generalized from the context of their own bodies to other objects, both terms were simultaneously transferred. These authors argue that the probability that two antonymous words will be acquired at the same time relates to the complexity of the meaning of each term and the complexity of the dimension along which they lie as opposites. When the dimension of opposition is relatively simple compared with the meaning of the two terms, the antonymy of the two words may be formulated before complete understanding of the terms themselves as in the case of *front* and *back*. If the dimension of opposition is complex relative to the meanings of the two terms, then the positive term may be acquired prior to the negative term, as in the case of *more* and *less* where the dimension of opposition is much more complex than the simple axis through objects of *front* and *back*.

Finally, a study by Wilcox and Palermo (1975) concerned with the replication and extension of a study by Clark (1973b) dealing with the comprehension of the spatial terms *in, on,* and *under* raises other questions about a feature theory account of semantic acquisition. Clark's experiments with these spatial terms required children between the ages of one and five years to demonstrate their comprehension of the terms by placing toy animals in the appropriate juxtaposition with various objects such as a box, tunnel, truck, bridge, or table. The child was asked to "Put the *x* in [on, under] the *y*", e.g., "Put the dog in the truck." The performance of the children revealed most correct responses to the instructions using *in,* least to the instructions using *under,* and an intermediate number to *on* instructions. Furthermore, there was a developmental trend indicating that the three terms were acquired in the order indicated by the errors.

In discussing the results of these experiments, Clark (1973b, 1974) expanded the semantic feature theory of the acquisition of word meaning to include nonlinguistic strategies as well as feature acquisition to account for the children's performance. It is assumed that the acquisition of the meaning of words interacts with nonlinguistic strategies used to try to comprehend those words when they are used by others as the child is acquiring the actual adult meaning of the words. With respect to her experiment, Clark suggests that initially the child does not understand the words *in, on,* and *under* at all, then the child understands their meaning only as having the feature [+ locative] followed by the acquisition of the features which distinguish *on* from *in* and, finally, the features which distinguish *under* from *on*. At the stage when only the feature [+ locative] is used (between one and three years of age), Clark postulates that there are two rules based on the perceptual properties of objects and their normal or canonical relations to each other which the child uses to interpret utterances. When presented with instructions to put an object in a spatial relation relative to another object without knowing the full meaning of the word, the child observes the following ordered rules:

1. If the object is to be placed in relation to a container, put it in the container.
2. If the object is to be placed in relation to a horizontal surface, put it on the surface.

The child applies the first rule if it is applicable and the second if it is not. If these rules are followed, the child will always be correct when responding to *in*, correct when responding to *on* if there is no container present, and will put objects in or on other objects when instructed with *under*. Those were, of course, the results obtained by Clark.

Wilcox and Palermo (1975) argued, first, that the meaning of *in, on,* and *under* is probably not acquired feature by feature in a manner analogous to the antonymous dimensional adjectives since neither (1) the hierarchical relations among these three terms exists in the same sense as *big* and *tall* are related, nor (2) is there the antonymous relation among these terms as there is, for example, in the case of *big* and *small*. Second, they argued that the contextual support for the particular relations tested in the Clark study was such that the children had little alternative to the specific nonlinguistic strategies attributed to them by Clark. It seemed to these authors that given a small toy animal, the child would be predisposed to put it in a tunnel or a box rather than on it, in a truck or crib rather than under it, and on a bridge or table rather than under it because all of these would be contextually congruent with the most probable relations of these objects in the real world.

In addition to replicating Clark's contextually congruent conditions, Wilcox and Palermo asked children between one and three years of age to place objects in contextually incongruent relations to each other. For example, the children were given a boat and asked to place it *on* a bridge, or they were given a road and asked to place it *in* a truck. When the children were given the congruent instructions (e.g., "Put the boat under the bridge"), the developmental trends found by Clark were clearly replicated. When the contextually incongruent instructions were given, however, performance actually decreased with age. The older children were more likely to put the boat under the bridge regardless of whether they were told to put it *on* or *under,* a finding which confirms the results of Strohner and Nelson (1974) that three-year-olds are very likely to use contextually relevant probable strategies to comprehend sentences. There was no evidence that the children followed the hierarchically-ordered rules postulated by Clark when faced with the incongruent context. Rather, the children put the objects in their most normal or probable contextual relationships. The older the children were, the more likely they were to know that boats go under bridges and roads go under trucks, regardless of what some adult may say. Finally, there was no evidence that *on* was more difficult than *in,* although overall performance with *under* was poorer than with both the other terms.

In summary, the hypothesis that children acquire the meaning of a word by accumulating the features which comprise the meaning of that word seems to be weakened by the recent research which has explored semantic acquisition. The lack of evidence for overextensions in comprehension; the failure to find evidence for synonymity of antonymous pairs of adjectives other than *more* and *less;* the suggestion that the specific features of some dimensional adjectives are acquired before the more general ones; and, the effects of context on performance raise significant empirical questions about the feature theory of semantic acquisition.

## OTHER PROBLEMS WITH
## FEATURE THEORIES

More significant than the empirical evidence, however, are the logical and rational arguments that mitigate against any feature theory of semantic development which has been proposed thus far. Rosch (1973), Nelson (1974), and Palermo (1976a,b), among others, have raised a number of these arguments. The heart of the problem with feature theory is that it involves abstraction of features from a whole concept so that the meaning of that concept may be known. But in order to abstract the features, one must already know the whole concept in order to know what to abstract from it. As Nelson (1974) puts it ". . . the abstraction theory presupposes what it is meant to explain: namely, the principle by which common elements are abstracted *as* common and thereby the definition of the concept itself" (p. 271). Nelson goes on to point out a second problem: there is no principled way of putting the abstracted features together to form the organized whole which is the concept. In short, a list of features is not a concept. It is possible to list the features of a concept but only if those features are properly organized do they form the concept as we ordinarily think of it.

Rosch (1973) points out, and provides data to support the hypothesis, that there are some concepts which are not acquired feature by feature but, instead, are natural intrinsic categories because of the biological characteristics of humans. According to Rosch, many semantic categories are given by the nature of the organism and, therefore, are universal across languages. Acquisition of the names, or words which refer to those categories or concepts are acquired as a whole and not piecemeal, feature by feature. Rosch goes on to argue that categories are highly structured internally and do not have well-defined boundaries. The internal structure is defined in terms of a core meaning, prototype, or clear case of the concept, and extends outward on similarity dimensions to undefined boundaries of the concept. For example, *apple* might be considered a clear case close to the core meaning of the concept *fruit* while *tomato* or *walnut* might be considered peripheral but still within the conceptual category. Rosch (1975) has provided some normative data for a number of categories of this kind. The exemplars of the concept may be conceived as having a family resemblance (Rosch & Mervis, 1975) in the sense that peripheral members may have little in common with each other but commonality increases toward the central or core members which have most in common with all exemplars of the concept. For example, if we consider the concept of red, we can recognize that there is a red color which is central to our concept and yet there are lots of other colors that shade into pink, orange, and violet that we identify as red. The reds on the violet side and those on the orange side have little in common except that they relate to the core meaning of red.

If Rosch's hypothesis is correct, we might expect that given an array of reds everyone, regardless of culture, language, or age, would select the same red as the best exemplar of the array. They might differ with respect to the peripheral or boundary classifications but the core meaning should be the same. In fact, Rosch (1973) presents data to show that the Dani of Indonesian New Guinea, a Stone Age people who possess only two color terms in their language (comparable to bright and dark), select the same primary core colors as do those who speak other languages and have color terms for the primary colors (Berlin & Kay, 1969). It would appear that there is a set of focal colors which form natural conceptual categories for humans. Rosch's (1973) research indicates that (1) it is easier to learn categories in which the core exemplar is present; (2) it is easiest to learn the core exemplar name; and (3) the category tends to be defined in terms of the core exemplar. Rosch has shown these generalizations to hold for colors, geometric forms (e.g., circles and rectangles), and some other semantic categories which are not necessarily natural (e.g., fruit). Mervis, Catlin and Rosch (1975) have shown that the core exemplar is developmentally stable for colors although, as predicted, there is greater variability in defining the borders for younger than for older children.

Palermo (1976a,b) has attempted to bring together the arguments of Macnamara (1972), Rosch (1973), and Nelson (1974) in support of a theory of semantic development which is an expanded version of the kind of prototype theory which Rosch, in particular, emphasizes. Palermo begins by noting that those who propose feature theories tend to ignore the communicative function of language in their concern for the componential analysis of the lexicon. Second, recognition of the communicative function leads to a concern with contextual factors. As we have noted here and in Chapter 5, context gives different meanings to the same words (e.g., Bransford & Johnson, 1972) . Accounting for such changes in meaning is a particularly difficult problem for feature theories. Third, and perhaps most serious, those who propose feature theories either explicitly or implicitly rule out the metaphoric use of words.

Yet it is obvious that metaphor is a common, if not pervasive, yet contextually meaningful use of language. The elimination of phrases such as "the mouth of the river," "the configuration of ideas," "the eye of a needle," "crooked people," and so on is to rob language of its communicative purpose. Furthermore, it is not clear, even within semantic feature theory, where one is to draw the line between metaphoric and nonmetaphoric use of language. For example, when using the word "mouth," it would be difficult to determine in the appropriate context when that word is used in an idiomatic, anomalous, or meaningless way in phrases such as, "the mouth of the man," "the mouth of the amoeba," "the mouth of the river," "the mouth of the cave," "the mouth of the mountain," "the mouth of the church," "the mouth of the mind," and so on indefinitely. The first of these phrases must be meaningful on any account of semantics, but what of the others? It is obvious that in the appropriate context native speakers of the language would have no hesitancy in accepting them as semantically appropriate. Assigning metaphor to the categories of idiom, anomaly, or meaninglessness is to ignore not only the use of language but the conceptual base underlying language.

Thus, any theory of semantics, especially to have psychological appeal, must take into account communication, context, and metaphor. Feature theory seems to neglect all three or, at least, proponents of this type of theory have directed little attention to the problems inherent to these issues. There are three aspects of features which make a consideration of these problems difficult. First, an analysis within the feature framework is atomistic in nature. Each word is broken down into a set of abstract features which may or may not be hierarchically organized. The features are considered elements of the meaning but, as Nelson (1974) points out, no account is usually attempted of the source of the elements and, perhaps more importantly, no account is given of the manner in which the whole is constructed from the parts. To say that the meaning of a word consists of the features $x$, $y$, and $z$ is to give no hint of how those features are weighted or integrated in the single meaning of the idea a speaker is attempting to convey in some particular context.

Second, features imply discrete categories with specifiable boundaries. Such a system seems to have been successful in advancing our understanding of phonology but the analysis of the abstract system underlying the realization of speech sounds is a delimited problem, at least relative to the semantic system. The identification of the phonological features can be specified within the limits of the mechanical system available to realize the actualization of speech. Speech sounds are categorically perceived while words do not have the same characteristics when viewed within a semantic framework. The words "pill" and "bill" can be characterized as differing phonologically on the basis of one feature in a manner which does not seem analogous to differentiating, say, "girl" and "woman" in terms of one semantic feature. Further, the concepts of *table* and *liberty,* for example, are just that— concepts which can range over many exemplars depending on the scenario in which they occur. There are no specifiable boundaries which can be defined by a set of features.

The inadequacy of feature theory becomes most obvious in the case of metaphor. As soon as one allows metaphoric use of words, features become trivial because one would have to multiply the features indefinitely for each word to take into account every conceivable metaphoric use the mind might generate for a word in the language.

## PROTOTYPE THEORY

The task, then, becomes one of developing an alternative theory of semantics and semantic development to account for the way the language is used to signify the meanings or ideas a person has in mind such that those meanings may be conveyed to the mind of another person. Palermo assumes that the meanings or ideas consist of prototypic concepts, relations among concepts which are also prototypic in nature, and the representation of those concepts and relations in time and space. Thus, semantics is built on a cognitive base of meaning and/or knowledge. Language is a means of representing that cognitive base of meaning. Language may express some but not necessarily all of the cognitive base at all developmental levels, i.e., not all meaning may be expressed semantically in language. The latter point is most clear prior to the appearance of language when the child obviously has concepts but no language is evident. (It is not limited to children, however, since the meaning of many internal states appears to be incapable of complete expression in the language mode.) The developmental problem, therefore, is twofold in the sense that one needs a theory of the development of concepts in the cognitive base and, second, a theory that accounts for how language comes to reflect the meanings of those concepts a child may wish to express.

Prototypes are assumed to be of two types: those abstractions underlying what we usually call *nouns* and those underlying what we usually call *verbs*. Thus, there are conceptual and relational prototypes, with the latter serving the function of relating the former. The concepts of time and space are limited initially, from a developmental point of view, to the here and now and, as a result, probably play no significant role in the early construction of meaning. Of course, as space and time become a part of the conceptual system, these concepts will influence others.

Prototypes are assumed to consist of a central core meaning (or abstract-best exemplar) and extend from that core meaning to undefinable boundaries which may encompass exemplars with varying degrees of similarity to the prototypic core meaning and to each other. Thus, almost any exemplar may come under the rubric of a particular prototypic concept but the degree to which it exemplifies the instance will vary widely depending on its similarity to the core and the context. For example, there are many exemplars of *table* which, within a feature theory, might be identified as having a flat surface supported by four legs. But within a prototypic view, a cloud may fall into the domain of *table* if a bevy of angels surround it consuming their manna. In contrast to feature theory, the word *table* is conceived as having a prototypic meaning which allows it to be extended to cloud in such a context. A cloud, however, even in this context, would not be considered an exemplar close to the core meaning of the prototype for *table*. It is the emphasis on the functional similarities of the cloud which allows the meaningful extension of the concept to this instance. Similarly, legless and nonflat surfaces may serve as exemplars of *table* in other contexts and on the basis of other dimensions of similarity.

It is clear from the examples above that the investigation of metaphor may be a particularly fruitful entry to the nature of the prototypic concept underlying any particular word and research in this area is beginning to appear (e.g., Winner, Rosensteil, & Gardner, 1976). It is assumed that the metaphoric use of a word is successful in communication because some aspect of the core meaning of the concept is transferred to the metaphoric context. One would not be likely to rely on a peripheral aspect of a concept's meaning in metaphoric use. Thus, the investigation of metaphoric construction and comprehension may provide a technique for constructing the structure of prototypic concepts.

Prototypes are not conceived as being singularly perceptual in nature. Rather, they are assumed to include emotive and function components as well. Developmentally, the latter may be more important at first, as Nelson (1974) has suggested. The prototype is a configuration of relations among abstract perceptual, functional, and affective factors. There is, of course, some problem in discussing the latter factors. The perceptual aspects are the easiest to identify in quantitative terms but the lack of terminology should not obscure the definite functional and emotional aspects of meaning. Consider the strong functional component of the common word "gasoline" for those who know little about it except that it is required to make one's car operate, or the affective component of "death" for many persons. Incidentally, one cannot say that the person who knows only the above-mentioned characteristic of gasoline does not know the meaning of *gasoline.* That characteristic is that person's meaning for *gasoline* but the prototypic concept may be changed given the appropriate experiences. In this view, there is no arbitrary single meaning of a word. In any case, it should be clear that the three components of the prototype identified here are isolated only conceptually; for any particular prototype they are intimately interwoven as a single unity which is that prototype. Rosch et al. (1976) have made some progress in identifying a number of these components with adults.

It is assumed that the focal point or core of any prototype may be shifted or transformed by contextual factors. Linguistically, this function is executed in its simplest form by adjectives, in the case of nouns, and adverbs, in the case of verbs. For example, the core meaning of the concept *bird* will be different than that for *large bird, yellow bird,* or *cremated bird,* and so on. In much the same way, the relational concept *walk* will have a different core meaning when the walking is done "rapidly," "haughtily," or "drunkenly." The adjectival and adverbial modifiers referred to here are those Nelson (1976) refers to as *attributives* with the function of subdividing conceptual classes. The subcategorization or shift in the prototypic core meaning through the use of adjectives has been shown by Nelson to occur rather early in the language acquisition process although somewhat later developmentally than the use of adjectives to describe a specific referent. In any case, such examples of linguistic contextual transformations can, of course, be elaborated in most complex ways. The transformations may also be produced by nonlinguistic contexts, however, as in the case of *water* in the context of desert or flood, the transformation of *sword* in the context of war or museum, or the transformation of *automobile* in the context of the 1920s and the 1970s.

Those aspects of the prototype which are close to the core will not ordinarily be made explicit in language. Unless the speaker understands that the listener does not know the concept or feels that the listener has a different central prototype, as when an adult speaks to a child, he or she will not make explicit attributes inherent to the prototypic core meaning. For example, in discussing dogs, one would not ordinarily mention the fact that they have four legs because that is presumably a part of the core meaning of dog. On the other hand, attributes of the core are likely to be made explicit in language when they involve transformations of the core, i.e., "collie dogs," or when a differentiation of instances which are encompassed by the core is being made, i.e., "the border collie." The latter is a point emphasized by Olson (1970). Children themselves recognize this function in their own productions (Ford & Olson, 1975).

Prototypes are assumed to be both natural and acquired. As Rosch's data suggest, for example, some colors and geometric forms appear to have natural, built-in core meanings. There are less well-documented relational prototypes which are natural but certainly aspects of movement are probably naturally conceptualized relations while it would seem that static relations are less likely to prove natural. Macnamara (1972) has argued that this should be the case and Nelson (1973, 1975) has provided evidence that children's early meanings are tied closely to function and to changing aspects of referents as opposed to static attributes of those referents. One might also expect that process verbs would appear before state verbs in the acquisition process. In addition to natural concepts as such, there are certainly many natural dimensions which are used as a basis of other classifications of concepts shading from natural to acquired. Surely figure-ground relationships are natural, shape constancy, division on the basis of contour, and many more new dimensions currently being explored in research with infants (c.f. Cohen & Salapatek, 1975). Nelson (1975) suggests that size is an important dimension during the early stages of language acquisition. There must be many as yet unknown natural dimensions forming the basis of concept formation which are common to most humans. Certainly there are individual differences but, as Macnamara points out, children do not form bizarre concepts, indicating that there must be some constraints on what is grouped together. One could probably argue that many of the case relations which form the basis of Fillmore's case grammar (1968) are naturally conceptualized. Acquired concepts presumably derive from or are induced from objects and events classified in part on the basis of natural dimensions as well as acquired distinctions with which children are forced to deal in the environment. It seems likely that the prototypic meanings of the latter may well change with experience while natural prototypes are stable over time and development.

The sense of words referring to natural concepts is known as a function of the nature of the organism and therefore commonality of meaning of these words is assured by the commonality of the organisms. In the case of the sense of words referring to acquired concepts, however, the commonality of meaning is a function both of the commonality of the abstracting characteristics of the organism and of the particular experiences themselves. There is likely to be, therefore, greater variability in the sense of the latter than the former words. As we noted earlier, the child's prototype of a color is the same as that of an adult (Mervis, Catlin & Rosch, 1975) but the concept of *dog*, for example, may initially be a function of the dogs with which the child comes in contact in terms of particular dogs, pictures of dogs, and verbal input from others about dogs. Both a willingness by the child to overextend the concept beyond those exemplars which are included in the concept by adults and a failure to extend the concept to exemplars included by adults should be expected at early developmental points during acquisition. Both over- and underextensions should be anticipated because it is unlikely that the child's concept of *dog* would be the same as an adult's concept. It is not that the child's concept is necessarily less complete but it is likely to be different, at least with respect to the boundaries.

One last point with respect to natural concepts pertains to the concepts of time and space. It is assumed that *here* and *now* are natural concepts but that the child must acquire the concepts which extend time into the past and future and space into three dimensional distance. In some sense, these concepts are of especial interest because they combine aspects of both naturalness and experience in ways that differ from those of other concepts.

A prototypic concept is assumed to have meaning only insofar as it is related to other concepts, i.e., concepts related to other objects, events, actions and, at least in the developmentally early stages, the self. Thus, there cannot be a single prototype concept but only a concept in relation to at least one other concept. Simply, the concept of *tree,* for example, necessitates a concept of *not tree.* Inherent in the prototype, however, are orderings of transformations which the prototype may undergo and the relations into which it may enter. Since children already know the concepts prior to acquiring the language, they also know the relations into which those concepts may enter. It is assumed that language acquisition is a matter of determining the words and syntactic rules for representing those concepts and relations. To infer the sense which others are communicating, therefore, children must attend to the referents of the language used by others so that they may do the same in attempting to communicate their ideas. Early in development the limit on transformations and relations often appears to be quite severe. Macnamara (1972) has cited the example of children appropriately identifying instances of their own dolls and their own toys which included the dolls while at the same time denying that one of the dolls is a toy. Asch and Nerlove (1960) have demonstrated the developmental course of adjectival transformations such as "sweet" and "crooked" which are applicable to objects but only later applicable to people. It seems clear that certain transformations and relations appear much later developmentally than others and should be investigated as clues to conceptual development. Metaphoric use of words is likely to be a later developmental phenomenon.

By way of summary, Palermo argues that children acquire language through the process of determining from the language environment how the concepts they already have available may be expressed. Those concepts are prototypic in nature and thus the meanings of words used to communicate them have a prototypic base. In the case of acquired concepts, the child's prototypes may differ somewhat from those of the adult, particularly in the peripheral regions. It is assumed that with enough experience, the child abstracts the central tendency of the distribution of functional, perceptual, and affective characteristics of concepts to allow his or her meanings to overlap those of others to the extent which allows communication and the similar classification of new instances by both child and adult. Natural concepts provide a common base for communication even when acquired concepts may sometimes fail. It is conceivable, however, that most of the concepts, both natural and acquired, of the child and the adult are the same and it is only the conceptualization of the complexity of the relationships into which they enter that may differ. If that is the case, the syntax of both child and adult will only differ in terms of the complexity of expressed relations and not in the relations themselves. The metaphoric use of language may represent one of the most complex levels of such expression. Language acquisition then becomes a matter of acquiring ways to express concepts in more and more complex interrelations. Such a process would be limited only by the cognitive capacities of the developing child. It is, then, those cognitive capacities we need to know more about in order to understand the language acquisition process.

Finally, it should be pointed out that while the prototype theory is advanced as an alternative to feature theory, there is no denying that features are abstracted from conceptual classes. There are classes of four-legged things, barking things, fur-covered things, and animal things, all of which are features of the class of things called *dogs*. The point is that we cannot abstract those features from the category *dog* prior to knowing the category *dog* and we do not know the category *dog* by adding up the total list of feature categories. Analysis cannot precede synthesis but synthesis itself involves analysis at another level. We appear to be very close to Plato's doctrines of form and anamnesis in attempting to conceptualize the semantic development of the child and the cognitive base on which it rests. It is only through the continued interaction of theoretical formulation and research observation that we will make any progress in understanding the process of language acquisition and, subsequently, achieve an understanding of the broader function of the language of the human organism. It is a challenge well worth your effort.

## SUMMARY

Our discussion of semantic development brings this volume to a close. It is clear that the issues of concern in this area of the psychology of language are the most complex, least understood, least researched, and yet probably the most important to a complete account of the broader area. While sound and syntax provide a medium for the message, it is the meaning which is the message. Solving the problem of how children acquire the meaning so that they may send and receive messages would seem to be a key to the very nature of humankind. The acquisition process obviously relates to the biological givens, the broader cognitive system, and the relation of those biological and cognitive factors to the context in which the child develops.

This chapter has been heavy on theoretical discussion and light on research results because the latter are sparse and the former are needed to guide forays into empirical investigation of the child's language development. We have contrasted the theoretical accounts of the analytic feature theories and the synthetic prototype theories. The former have been basic to most of the research done in the area while the latter attempt to cope with issues not comprehensible within feature theory. The dichotomy, however, cannot be maintained in a manner which allows us to discard completely one for the other. Surely language acquisition, in general, and semantic development, in particular, involve both analysis and synthesis. While children cannot analyze the parts of the whole without knowing what the whole is, they are capable of conceptualizing components of the whole. The question of the processes which determine what wholes, what parts, and at what cognitive developmental levels remains open. The answers to such questions seem to lie in an understanding of the child's developing knowledge of the world in concert with the acquisition of the language system. The answers will not be simple, but the search for the answers will surely be fascinating.

## REFERENCES

Amidon, A., & Carey, P. Why five-year-olds cannot understand *before* and *after*. *Journal of Verbal Learning and Verbal Behavior*, 1972, *11*, 417–23.

Asch, S. E., & Nerlove, H. The development of double function terms in children: An exploratory investigation. In B. Kaplan & S. Wapner (Eds.), *Perspectives in psychological theory: Essays in honor of Heinz Werner*, New York: International Universities Press, 1960.

Bartlett, E. J. Sizing things up: The acquisition of the meaning of dimensional adjectives. *Journal of Child Language*, 1976, *3*, 205–20.

Berlin, B., & Kay, P. *Basic color terms: Their universality and evolution*. Berkeley: University of California Press, 1969.

Bierwisch, M. Semantics. In J. Lyons (Ed.), *New horizons in linguistics*. Middlesex, England: Penguin Books, 1970.

Bransford, J., & Johnson, M. K. Contextual prerequisites for understanding: Some investigations of comprehension and recall. *Journal of Verbal Learning and Verbal Behavior,* 1972, *11,* 717–26.

Brewer, W. F., & Stone, J. B. Acquisition of spatial antonym pairs. *Journal of Experimental Child Psychology,* 1975, *19,* 299–307.

Brown, R. *Words and things.* Glencoe, Ill.: The Free Press, 1958a.

Brown, R. How shall a thing be called? *Psychological Review,* 1958b, *65,* 14–21.

Clark, E. V. On the acquisition of the meaning of *before* and *after. Journal of Verbal Learning and Verbal Behavior,* 1971, *10,* 266–75.

Clark, E. V. What's in a word? On the child's acquisition of semantics in his first language. In T. E. Moore (Ed.), *Cognitive development and the acquisition of language.* New York: Academic Press, 1973a. Pp. 65–110.

Clark, E. V. Non-linguistic strategies and the acquisition of word meanings. *Cognition,* 1973b, *2,* 161–82.

Clark, E. V. Some aspects of the conceptual basis for first language acquisition. In R. L. Schiefelbusch & L. L. Lloyd (Eds.), *Language perspectives: Acquisition retardation and intervention.* Baltimore, Maryland: University Park Press, 1974. Pp. 105–28.

Clark, H. Space, time, semantics and the child. In T. E. Moore (Ed.), *Cognitive development and the acquisition of language.* New York: Academic Press, 1973. Pp. 27–63.

Cohen, L. B., & Salapatek, P. *Infant perception: From sensation to cognition* (Vols. I & II). New York: Academic Press, 1975.

Donaldson, M., & Balfour, G. Less is more: A study of language comprehension in children. *British Journal of Psychology,* 1968, *59,* 461–72.

Donaldson, M., & Wales, R. J. On the acquisition of some relational terms. In J. R. Hayes (Ed.), *Cognition and the development of language.* New York: Wiley, 1970. Pp. 235–68.

Fillmore, C. The case for case. In E. Bach & R. T. Harms (Eds.), *Universals in linguistic theory.* New York: Holt, Rinehart & Winston, 1968.

Ford, W., & Olson, D. R. The elaboration of the noun phrase in children's description of objects. *Journal of Experimental Child Psychology,* 1975, *19,* 371–82.

Harner, L. Children's understanding of linguistic reference to past and future. *Journal of Psycholinguistic Research,* 1976, *5,* 65–84.

Huttenlocher, J. The origins of language comprehension. In R. L. Solso (Ed.), *Theories in cognitive psychology.* New York: Wiley, 1974. Pp. 331–68.

Johnson, H. L. The meaning of *before* and *after* for preschool children. *Journal of Experimental Child Psychology,* 1975, *19,* 88–99.

Katz, J. J. *Semantic theory.* New York: Harper and Row, 1972.

Klatzky, R. L., Clark, E. V., & Macken, M. Asymmetries in the acquisition of polar adjectives: Linguistic or conceptual? *Journal of Experimental Child Psychology,* 1973, *16,* 32–46.

Kuczaj, S. A., & Maratsos, M. P. On the acquisition of *front, back,* and *side. Child Development,* 1975, *46,* 202–10.

Macnamara, J. Cognitive basis of language learning in infants. *Psychological Review,* 1972, *79,* 1–13.

Mervis, C. B., Catlin, J., & Rosch, E. Development of the structure of color categories. *Developmental Psychology,* 1975, *11,* 54–60.

Nelson, K. Structure and strategy in learning to talk. *Monographs of the Society for Research in Child Development,* 1973, *38,* Nos. 1–2. Pp. 1–135.

Nelson, K. Concept, word, and sentence: Interrelations in acquisition and development. *Psychological Review,* 1974, *81,* 267–85.

Nelson, K. The nominal shift in semantic-syntactic development. *Cognitive Psychology,* 1975, *7,* 461–79.

Nelson, K. Some attributes of adjectives used by young children. *Cognition,* 1976, *4,* 13–30.

Olson, D. R. Language and thought: Aspects of a cognitive theory of semantics. *Psychological Review,* 1970, *77,* 257–73.

Palermo, D. S. More about less: A study in language comprehension. *Journal of Verbal Learning and Verbal Behavior,* 1973, *12,* 211–21.

Palermo, D. S. Still more about the comprehension of "less." *Developmental Psychology,* 1974, *10,* 827–29.

Palermo, D. S. Sémantique et acquisition du langage: Quelques considerations théoriques. *Bulletin de Psychologie,* Numéro Special Annuel, 1976a. 251–58.

Palermo, D. S. Semantics and language acquisition: Some theoretical considerations. Paper presented at the Psychology of Language Conference, University of Stirling, June 1976b.

Piaget, J. *The origins of intelligence in children* (Margaret Cook, trans.). New York: International Universities Press, 1952 (original French ed., 1936).

Rosch, E. On the internal structure of perceptual and semantic categories. In T. E. Moore (Ed.), *Cognitive development and the acquisition of language.* New York: Academic Press, 1973. Pp. 111–44.

Rosch, E. Cognitive representation of semantic categories. *Journal of Experimental Psychology,* 1975, *104,* 192–233.

Rosch, E., & Mervis, C. B. Family resemblances: Studies in the internal structure of categories. *Cognitive Psychology,* 1975, *7,* 573–605.

Rosch, E., Mervis, C. B., Gray, W. D., Johnson, D. M., & Boyes-Braem, P. Basic objects in natural categories. *Cognitive Psychology,* 1976, *8,* 382–439.

Schlesinger, I. M. Production of utterances and language acquisition. In D. I. Slobin (Ed.), *The ontogenesis of grammar.* New York: Academic Press, 1971. Pp. 63–101.

Strohner, H., & Nelson, K. E. The young child's development of sentence comprehension: Influence of event probability, nonverbal context, syntactic form, and strategies. *Child Development,* 1974, *45,* 567–76.

Wales, R. J., & Campbell, R. On the development of comparison and the comparison of development. In G. B. Flores d'Arcais & W. J. M. Levelt (Eds.), *Advances in psycholinguistics.* Amsterdam: North-Holland, 1970. Pp. 373–96.

Wilcox, S., & Palermo, D. S. "In," "on," and "under" revisited. *Cognition,* 1975, *3,* 245–54.

Winner, E., Rosensteil, A. K., & Gardner, H. The development of metaphoric understanding. *Developmental Psychology,* 1976, *12,* 289–97.

# Author Index

# Subject Index